Creating Knowledge Locations in Cities

Cities all over the world are developing 'knowledge hotspots': physical concentrations of knowledge-intensive or creative activity. These hotspots come in many guises: science parks, technology parks, creative districts, design quarters and so on. Well-known examples are Barcelona's @22 district and Helsinki's Arabianranta area. Increasingly, such hotspots are being developed inside the city rather than at suburban greenfield sites. This makes their development highly complex.

Based on a clear and comprehensive literature review, this book contains an analysis of five knowledge locations in Europe and one in South Korea. The case studies in the book cover several European countries (Ireland, Finland, Germany, Spain and the Netherlands). The cases are well grounded in the different contexts that these national settings provide, which allows comparisons between them.

This book addresses a number of questions: What kind of benefits do knowledge locations offer, in theory and in practice? How can we integrate knowledge hubs in the urban fabric, and make them engines for innovation? How do cities frame the co-operation between the various actors (that is, project developers, banks, local government, universities, 'end-users') at the various stages of development? Do such locations generate more innovation?

This book offers no blueprints or rules-of-thumb for developing such locations: each knowledge location has its unique spatial, economic and policy context. However, it does offer greater insight into the relationships between a knowledge location and the urban environment, and a better understanding of the innovation dynamics – and limitations – of a location, enabling policymakers to ask the right questions for their particular development.

Willem van Winden is at the Amsterdam University of Applied Sciences.

Luis de Carvalho, Erwin van Tuijl, Jeroen van Haaren and **Leo van den Berg** are at Erasmus University, Rotterdam, the Netherlands.

Regions and Cities

Series editors:
Ron Martin, *University of Cambridge, UK;*
Gernot Grabher, *University of Bonn, Germany;*
Maryann Feldman, *University of Georgia, USA;*
Gillian Bristow, *University of Cardiff, UK.*

Regions and Cities is an international, interdisciplinary series that provides authoritative analyses of the new significance of regions and cities for economic, social and cultural development, and public policy experimentation. The series seeks to combine theoretical and empirical insights with constructive policy debate and critically engages with formative processes and policies in regional and urban studies.

Creating Knowledge Locations in Cities

Innovation and integration challenges

Willem van Winden, Luis de Carvalho,
Erwin van Tuijl, Jeroen van Haaren
and Leo van den Berg

Routledge
Taylor & Francis Group

LONDON AND NEW YORK

First published 2012
by Routledge
2 Park Square, Milton Park, Abingdon, Oxon OX14 4RN

Simultaneously published in the USA and Canada
by Routledge
711 Third Avenue, New York, NY 10017

Routledge is an imprint of the Taylor & Francis Group, an informa business

British Library Cataloguing in Publication Data
A catalogue record for this book is available from the British Library.

Library of Congress Cataloging in Publication Data
A catalog record has been requested for this book.

ISBN: 978-0-415-69854-2 (hbk)
ISBN: 978-0-203-12716-2 (ebk)

Typeset in Times New Roman
by Bookcraft Ltd.

EURICUR
Department of Regional, Port and Transport Economics
Erasmus University Rotterdam
P.O. Box 1738
Room H12-27
3000 DR ROTTERDAM
Netherlands
Telephone: +31 10 4081186
Fax: +31 10 4089153

Visit the website of EURICUR: www.euricur.

Contents

Figures

Tables

Boxes

Preface

Despite wide differences, cities across Europe have one ambition in common: the desire to be successful in the knowledge economy. In this study, we focus on one increasingly popular policy instrument: the creation of *knowledge locations*, that is, specific area-based developments for knowledge-intensive activity. Despite the fact that many cities invest substantially in the development of such locations, there are hardly any international comparative studies on this topic. With this study, we hope to fill this gap and draw a number of policy lessons.

For this inquiry, we visited six cities, five in Europe and one in Asia. Thousands of air miles, and countless interviews with CEOs, policymakers and other experts later, we are proud to present an analysis of the dynamics of knowledge locations in Dublin, Eindhoven, Helsinki, Incheon, Munich and San Sebastian.

Many people have contributed to this study, and we are deeply grateful for their help. First, we are highly indebted to our contact persons in the case cities, who helped us to arrange the interviews. Without them, it would not have been possible to have in-depth discussions with key informants from companies, knowledge institutions and city administrations. We thank all of them for their support during the study.

Moreover, we are grateful for the administrative support of Ankimon Vernède, in helping to organize the meetings and to finish this book. Finally, we want to thank the City of Dublin for its trust and willingness to co-organize an international conference on this theme, together with Euricur.

The authors
Rotterdam, February 2011

Part I
Introduction and theory

1 Introduction

Cities in the knowledge economy

Many cities and regions have the ambition to promote their 'knowledge economy': it is generally recognized that knowledge has become the prime source of wealth in advanced economies.

The now widely used term 'knowledge economy' refers to the increased economic significance of knowledge production, distribution and use. The OECD defines knowledge economies as 'economies which are directly based on the production, distribution and the use of knowledge information' (OECD 2006, 1996). Moreover, knowledge and creativity are considered by many scholars as engines for long-term economic growth (for example, Romer 1986), and therefore, human capital and R&D have obtained a more central place in economic theory and policy. Powell and Snellman (2004) also stress the increased speed of technological change. They define the knowledge economy as 'production and services based on knowledge-intensive activities that contribute to an accelerated pace of technological and scientific advance as well as equally rapid obsolescence' (p. 201).

There are signs that the emerging knowledge economy has reinforced the role of cities. First, the diversity of people, firms and cultures in cities constitutes a fertile ground for new ideas and innovations (Jacobs 1969). Second, the diffusion of new knowledge and technology is faster in urban areas, thanks to the density and physical concentration of large numbers of knowledge workers and knowledge-based firms (Audretsch and Feldman 1996) and rich ecologies of face-to-face contacts (Storper and Venables 2004). Third, big cities have large and specialized labour markets. This makes them attractive for knowledge-based firms (that need specialized, skilled staff) and for knowledge workers, who can more easily find the job they want, and have better career opportunities in the longer run (Polèse 2005). Fourth, due to rising incomes, consumers spend more on luxury goods, and large cities are relatively specialized in this type of goods. The 'consumption value' of cities has gone up, especially for well-paid knowledge workers (Glaeser et al. 2001). Finally, large cities are traditionally specialized in sectors that show high rates of growth in the knowledge economy: the creative industries and knowledge-intensive services. In sum, agglomeration economies have become more significant in the knowledge economy.

The urban revival is not visible everywhere, however. Some cities (national capitals, global cities, international service hubs, academic centres) have grown very fast, acting as a magnet for talent and investments, but others (small cities in rural areas, cities with an outdated economic specialization) have lost out in relative terms: they have severe difficulties in retaining knowledge workers and knowledge-intensive companies. Van Winden *et al.* (2007) discuss the differences between city types concerning their role in the knowledge economy. 'Winning' cities have particular characteristics that make them benefit from and reinforce their position in the shift towards a knowledge economy: a strong knowledge infrastructure, dense knowledge resources, large numbers of knowledge workers, a diversified economic base, good international accessibility and attractive amenities that help to lure knowledge workers.

Policies for promoting knowledge-based development

Despite wide differences in endowments, opportunities and context, city administrations across Europe have one ambition in common: the desire to be successful in the knowledge economy. In policy documents produced by cities of any type, knowledge has obtained a central place. Knight (1995) was one of the first to apply the term 'knowledge-based development' to cities, and elaborate policy implications. Urban policy initiatives are increasingly aimed at attracting higher-educated people, promoting entrepreneurship, developing clusters of knowledge-based industries and 'creative' industries. Van Winden (2010) discusses this 'knowledge turn' in urban policy across Europe, and identifies four manifestations: (1) widespread and intense efforts to lure knowledge workers and the creative class; (2) a growing role for knowledge institutes in urban development and planning; (3) an explicit 'knowledge-based' approach to the planning and design of public space, and (4) efforts to underline the identity of the 'knowledge city' using marketing and branding techniques.

Cutting across those policy manifestations, this study focuses on one particular instrument used to promote the urban knowledge economy: the creation of knowledge locations. We use this term to include a wide variety of area-based policies aimed to agglomerate knowledge-intensive activity in a designated area or city district. Thus, there must be an element of planning or deliberate policy aimed at agglomerating knowledge-based activity.

The term knowledge locations, as we use it, includes concepts like science parks, technology parks, open innovation campuses, creative districts, media hubs and so on. It excludes wider territorial concepts like regional clusters and other 'valleys', in which activities are spread over a larger territorial area, although we recognize and explicitly address the role of the wider regional economic context in analysing knowledge locations. Some knowledge locations focus on one specific branch or technology (such as bio science parks), others are more diversified.

In general, agglomerating knowledge-intensive activity in a particular location is believed to have a number of advantages, which should be assessed from a critical stance. Knowledge hubs provide opportunities for facility sharing (for example, the joint use of expensive facilities such as clean rooms or laboratorial facilities); they enhance networking and face-to-face interaction, and promote unexpected interaction between persons or companies, with positive impacts on innovation. They are believed to offer a set of economic benefits, by fostering links between industry and the local knowledge institutes and providing a favourable environment for start-ups. Moreover, as city marketing and branding takes up an increasingly important role in urban management, knowledge parks can help to foster the identity of a city as a progressive knowledge-based city: they give the local knowledge economy a face and an 'address'. Finally, knowledge hubs are increasingly seen as a powerful tool for urban regeneration. Many cities seek to transform derelict urban areas into 'creative districts' (Evans 2009).

Research questions

In this study we want to improve our understanding on the functioning of knowledge locations in the new urban economy, and add to the existing body of scientific knowledge (reviewed in the next chapters) on the dynamics of this form of urban development. We aim to provide an updated view and complement an earlier wave of studies, such as the seminal *High-tech Fantasies* by Massey *et al.* (1992) or *Technopoles of the World* by Castells and Hall (1994). Moreover, explicitly, the study is intended to help policymakers make better-informed choices and better understand the role of a knowledge locations in the wider evolution of the regional and global economy. Developing successful locations which stimulate growth in the knowledge-based economy is a complex challenge because it involves many aspects, many actors and requires an innovative approach. As each location has its unique context and needs to distinguish itself from competing locations, no blueprints or rules-of-thumb can be provided. However, greater insight into the relationship with the environment, the dynamics on a location, and in-depth study of contextual and content criteria for success, enables policymakers to ask the right questions for their particular development.

This research addresses a number of questions:

- What kind of benefits do knowledge locations offer, in theory and in practice?
- How important are 'local' networks (between actors at the location) vis-à-vis networks at wider geographical scales (regional, national, international), and to what extent is this sensitive to different modes of knowledge creation?
- How do knowledge locations emerge and evolve over time, and which factors influence these processes?
- Relations with the city: how to integrate 'knowledge locations' in the urban fabric?
- Stakeholder involvement: how are different stakeholders involved in the development, formally and informally? What are their perspectives, ambitions, expectations? How are these different interests to be managed?
- Organization and management issues: how do we frame the co-operation between the various actors (such as project developers, banks, local government, universities, 'end users') at the various stages of development (design, implementation, maintenance and/or park management)?
- How do we measure the 'success' of such locations?

Organization of the book

This book is organized as follows. The first part (Chapters 1–5) discusses relevant literature and builds a theoretical frame. Within this first part, Chapter 2 puts the development of knowledge locations into perspective. It elaborates on the variety of concepts, and sketches a brief historic overview of their development. Also, this chapter signals a recent trend of 're-urbanization' of knowledge, manifested in the growth of inner-city knowledge hubs. In Chapter 3, we review the literature on knowledge locations, focusing on evaluation studies of science parks and creative quarters. We identify some gaps that we intend to fill with this study. Chapter 4 proposes a conceptual framework to analyse the development of knowledge locations in their context, based on a recombination of insights from various literature strands. We argue that in contrast to the traditional science park model, contemporary and hybrid types of knowledge locations have a dual strategy and potential outcomes: an industrial development and clustering dimension, and an urban integration and regeneration dimension. Chapter 5 elaborates on the methodology applied in the case studies and essays and outlines the global research design.

The Chapters 6–11, which jointly form the second part of the book, contain the case studies and essays on knowledge locations in various cities:

- Chapter 6 Dublin (Ireland): the Digital Hub, an inner-city flagship IT hub with important regeneration ambitions;
- Chapter 7 Eindhoven (the Netherlands): Strijp-S, a planned mixed-use creative district at a former Philips premises;
- Chapter 8 Helsinki (Finland): the Arabianranta area, a former industrial area transformed into a highly successful multi-functional city quarter with design as a central theme;
- Chapter 9 Incheon (South Korea): Songdo, a new knowledge district developed on sea-reclaimed land;
- Chapter 10 Munich (Germany): Maxvorstadt, an inner-city quarter with a high concentration of knowledge institutes and cultural facilities;
- Chapter 11 San Sebastian (Spain): PI@, a new nexus for the local audiovisual and multimedia industry.

Chapters 12–15 form the third part of the book. It contains a synthesis and puts knowledge location into perspective. It reflects on the different components of the framework, compares evidence and suggests success factors illustrated with examples from the various case studies. On the theoretical level, it analyses constructs, relations and mechanisms of an integrative framework to understand the development of knowledge locations. Also, it provides recommendations for policymakers, as well as suggestions for further research.

2 History and trends in knowledge locations

An urban turn?

Science parks and other types of knowledge hubs have been – and are being – developed for a number of reasons and intentions: to nurture the growth of technology firms, to facilitate knowledge transfer between universities and companies, to act as a seedbed for start-ups, to stimulate innovation, to regenerate derelict urban areas, to lift a region or city into the knowledge economy, to attract foreign investment, to sustain local political discourses or to make money on real-estate inflation.

Classic science parks are the best-known and most 'visible' locations of the knowledge economy. In recent years, new generation knowledge hubs have emerged worldwide, focusing on the so-called creative industries (Evans 2009).

Science parks

Science parks are the best-known and best-documented type of 'knowledge location' (for example, Castells and Hall 1994). They are often located outside the city, built around a university or scientific institution. They contain a mix of premises for businesses, start-ups and research institutes. Typically, there is no housing or leisure function. Often, science parks are managed by public or semi-public companies, with most shares in the hands of the (local) government or the state.

Science parks can be defined as property-based initiatives that have formal and operational links with a university or other higher educational institute (HEI) or major centres of research (Zhang 2005, referenced in Tamasy 2007). Science parks come in several guises and have different initiators and business models. Just like incubators – which they often include – science parks have 'identifiable administrative centres, focused on the mission of business acceleration through *knowledge agglomeration* and *resource sharing*' (Phan *et al.* 2005, p. 166, our emphasis). Some focus on particular technologies, economic sectors or science fields; others are more generic. Table 2.1 lists the main goals of the various stakeholders in science parks.

The first well-known initiative to develop a science park (though not in a formal way) was taken by Stanford University's Dean Frederik Terman in 1951, who developed and leased university land for start-ups. This would turn into the well known Stanford Research Park, the cornerstone of Silicon Valley. Later on in Europe, Cambridge Science Park (CSP) was formally established in 1970 and

Table 2.1 Main goals of the various stakeholders in science parks

Stakeholder	Main goals
Universities, research institutes	Science parks serve to strengthen knowledge transfer (interaction) between university research and industry, particularly to derive funding for future research. It also includes commercialization of research results, eventually through academic spin-off firms and utilization of idle land of the university. In the knowledge economy: meeting targets from government policy
National and local (regional) government and (public) business support organizations	Science parks support the restructuring of the local (regional) economy. They generate new firms, high-technology jobs, income and tax. Also, they serve to improve the image of the city (region), particularly international recognition
Real-estate and financial institutions	Science parks are seen as business opportunities. They serve as real-estate investment projects to raise profits. In addition, the firms that settle may serve as investment projects
Firms on science parks	Science parks are seen as favourable environments, in terms of supply of facilities, the positive image associated with it, and network opportunities with the university and other park tenants

Source: Van Geenhuizen and Soetanto, 2008, p. 94

can be considered as the mother of all science parks. It is the UK's oldest and most prestigious science park. Its development was led by Trinity College, which limited admission to technology and research firms. Currently, it is home to over 90 high-tech companies and 5,000 personnel, but its start was slow: two years after its official opening, it had only seven tenants, and only 20 per cent of the designated area was developed (Koh *et al.* 2005). CSP focuses on basic research, and many of the companies are led by researchers and scientists rather than typical entrepreneurs. In the 1980s, the science park concept became widespread (Monck *et al.* 1988); it is currently a fully fledged and growing reality throughout the world (see Figure 2.1).

Many universities create science parks with the intention to increase knowledge spill-overs and to improve connections with industry. Typically, science parks contain incubation facilities, where young science-based firms are helped to develop. Often, firms in science parks may use facilities like university laboratories (at a subsidized rate) or other specific equipment. Moreover, science parks often offer consulting services, advice on licensing and knowledge commercialization, reception facilities and so on.

By locating in a science park, firms can gain access to structural elements provided by the park, such as infrastructure and supporting facilities, and therefore opportunities for synergy between and among high-tech firms (Maillat 1995; Phillimore 1999). Chan and Lau (2005) make a distinction between two types of support: basic structural support (shared office services, business assistance, rental breaks, business networking, access to capital, legal and accounting aid,

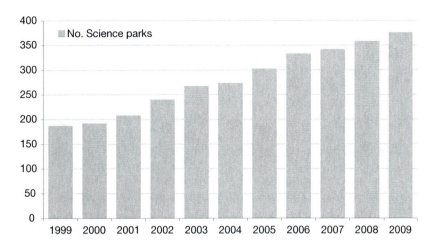

Figure 2.1 Number of science parks enrolled at the International Association of Science Parks (IASP)

Source: own elaboration, data from IASP 2010

and advice on management practices) and technology-related structural support (labs and workshop facilities, R&D activities, technology transfer programmes and advice on intellectual property).

Science parks are created to promote economic development and increase the economic impact of scientific research. Their emergence reflects the idea that science is not only valuable in its own right, but also a catalyst to economic growth: it contributes to innovation and the development of high-tech firms. In the 1980s and 1990s, this belief was fuelled by the rapid growth of high-tech sectors like ICT and biotechnology. Also, the development of science parks reflects a changing perception of the role of science in society. The view that society provides funding for science without any further claims has been increasingly challenged. Society increasingly articulated expectations of science regarding how resources are spent (Guston 2000, cited in Hansson *et al.* 2005) and became more aware of the economic potential of science and technology. At the same time, universities discovered commercialization as a new source of income, and increasingly considered science parks as effective instruments to tap.

There are several types of science park. Some focus primarily on basic research, and have strict admission criteria (the Cambridge example is illustrative). Others are oriented more towards applied research, and also allow manufacturing at the premises. Some science parks have a thematic or technology focus (like the bioscience park in Leiden, the Netherlands), others are more generic. Typical tenants of science parks are university departments, start-ups, technology companies, but also public research institutions and private research labs. Some science parks focus on production-oriented technology, and have close links with manufacturing firms. A good example is Taiwan's Hsinchu Science District. It has developed as a brain centre for the manufacturing of semiconductors and other electronic components, and top-level manufacturers are located at the site.

Over the last decade, many Asian countries invested in science parks with a view to attracting knowledge-intensive foreign investment and enhancing competitiveness. The establishment of Singapore Science Park (SSP) in the 1980s became an example for many other Asian countries. It was created to provide an infrastructure to host multinational companies (MNCs) and other businesses that need proximity to higher educational institutes. SSP was to become the R&D hub of the city state, and was meant to signal the country's ambitions to become a leader in the knowledge economy (Koh *et al.* 2005).

This signalling motive has been important in many science park developments across the world. A major example is Beijing's Zhongguancun high-tech park. This site around Tsinghua University and Peking University – known as 'China's Silicon Valley' – has attracted many Western top technology firms (like Microsoft, IBM, Google) as well as large state-owned companies such as China Mobile (see, for example, Zhou and Xin 2003; Zhou *et al.* 2009). Throughout Europe, mainly in its industrial peripheries, science parks have ambitions to signal processes of economic diversification. They develop prime conditions to attract new knowledge-intensive foreign direct investment (FDI), and often host the 'crown jewels' of regional economic diversification, the leading companies and internationalized knowledge institutes (Carvalho 2009).

The development of most science parks is initiated by the public sector, the university, or, in some cases, a property developer. But there are also science parks set up by large companies. One eye-catching example is the High Tech Campus in Eindhoven, the Netherlands (see Box 2.1). It is being developed by Philips, but open to others as well. There are also private real-estate companies that specialize in the development and exploitation of science parks. In Tampere, for instance, a specialized private company (Technopolis) manages the three parks in the city.

Beyond science and technology: the emergence of new types of knowledge hubs

Science parks typically focus on 'beta' sciences and technology, ranging from basic science to applied science to product development and sometimes even manufacturing, in a rather linear fashion. Moreover, most science parks are actually a specialized, knowledge-intensive type of business park, typically mono-functional, located at a suburban location.

In the last decade, new types of 'knowledge hub' have been developed around new thematic fields, beyond science and technology, reflecting the growing recognition that the knowledge economy is not restricted to the technological realm. Notably during the last decade and a half, the 'creative industries' emerged as a promising growth sector with a strong urban orientation and highly symbolic content (Scott 2000); consequently, many cities have developed a wide variety of territorial concepts to facilitate these industries, such as through creative city plans

---

Box 2.1 High Tech Campus Eindhoven

The High Tech Campus in Eindhoven is a private development, initiated by Royal Philips Electronics as the owner of the property. The Philips Research division is one of the major tenants (1,800 employees and 125,000m^2 floorspace) and the 'launching customer'. Philips Research has much influence on the development and plays an active role as 'enabler' for open innovation. Other anchor tenants are welcome, as long as they are a relevant partner for Philips in its innovation process. An important goal of the High Tech Campus is creating an environment for open innovation. Facilities on the campus connect to the quest for boundaries of knowledge, within the framework of commercial use. Collaboration, seen as formal innovation networks and informal value chains, is integrally connected to these goals, as well as healthy competition and mutual trust. In open innovation, stimulating knowledge transfer is essential. Seeking synergy between people involved in research and development is an important asset to shorten the 'time to market'. The concept of the High Tech Campus can be characterized as an area-based campus development where a network of meeting places on different levels is created. Open, transparent buildings as well as centralized amenities are organized as pavilions in a continuous landscape with many opportunities for social activities, sports and recreation.

(see, for example, Landry 2000). In the 1990s, Manchester was a pioneer in the development of a 'creative quarter' (van den Berg *et al.* 2001), but there are many other examples, particularly in Europe. A prominent frontrunner, elaborated in this book, is the Art & Design city in Helsinki, Finland (see also, for example, Ilmonen and Kunzmann 2007). This is a former industrial area being redeveloped with a strong thematic focus on design. Another well-known case is Barcelona's @22 district, in which 200 hectares of industrial land in Poblenou were transformed into an 'innovative district' involving a public investment of €180m in infrastructure. Contrarily to the typical science park model, these new hubs have usually a strong aesthetic and visual drive encompassing cultural facilities, museums, architecture quality, heritage preservation, public art and trendy streetscapes, with housing and living possibilities, consumption and tourism development (Evans 2009). However, the multi-functional character of creative districts may also result in conflicts between traditional and new functions (see, for example, Vicari Haddock 2010). For instance, traditional jewellery firms in Birmingham's Jewellery Quarter have difficulties in making the transition from a historical urban Marshallian industrial district into a creative district to live, eat and drink (De Propis and Wei 2007). In another case in Birmingham, new housing schemes in Birmingham's Eastside project conflict with a traditional music scene threatened with closure, while they are considered as 'the kind of cultural seed that might be expected to form the basis of a cultural quarter' (Porter and Barber 2007, p. 1339).

A number of cities have developed comparable concepts for creative industries in general or for more specific branches such as media, audiovisual, music, design and fashion. This tendency is also visible in Asia, especially in China, where creative industries were officially put on the agenda in the Fifth Five-Year Plan in 2005 (Rossiter 2008); the number of 'creative clusters' has grown rapidly in major cities. For instance, Shanghai started with fourteen 'creative sites' in 2005 which had already increased to about seventy in 2007. In Beijing, some major examples include Zhongguancun Creative Industries Pioneer Base, the Songzhuang Art and Cartoon Zone, the Huairou Film and TV Base, and the Beijing Cyber-recreation District in Shijingshan (Keane 2009). Another important example is the famous Beijing 798 district, a former state-owned electronics plant. This large site has transformed quickly from an uncontrolled 'artist based creative district' (which houses an art community that produces and trades art) towards a planned 'commercial creative district', a site consisting of galleries and exhibitions showing cheap art for tourists (van Tuijl and Van der Borg 2011).

Although the thematic focus is different, there are similarities between these new knowledge hubs and the more 'traditional' science parks described above. The economic development motives for investing in creative quarters are similar: local governments invest in this type of concept hoping to create new jobs, to gain a reputation as a 'creative city' and to attract the 'creative class', a notion popularized by Richard Florida (2002). Typically, universities and other knowledge institutes are also involved in the development, and hope to commercialize their research; in addition, many have incubation facilities and start-up support, and seek to develop local networking to promote innovation.

However, from an urban development perspective, differences are many. Unlike science parks, the creative hubs do not look like mono-functional business parks. Many can be found in city centres and/or regenerated industrial areas, and have a more urban and lively ambience that fits the needs of the type of people who work there (or are expected to be lured to the area). The tenants – design firms, architect agencies, media companies and so on – are assumed to prefer environments with a distinct and urban identity (Florida 2008). People working in the creative industries share a culture of work that is far away from the nine-to-five mentality. Work and life are mixed up in time and space. People in these industries think more in terms of projects rather than employers (Grabher 2002); there are many freelancers working temporarily together, and they use public facilities as meeting places. They are often deeply involved in cultural production and consumption, and thrive in a lively and diverse urban environment, often associated with inner-city atmospheres (Pratt 2000; Hutton 2004). 'Buzzing' cities and places are important places for knowledge transmission and innovation in these industries, favouring easier access to strategic rumours, gossip and know-who (Asheim *et al.* 2007).

Given this distinctly 'urban' orientation (see also Asheim and Hansen 2009), policymakers have come to embrace the creative industries not only as a growth sector, but also as a catalyst for the regeneration of urban areas (Evans 2009). All over Europe and the US, many worn-out industrial sites have been transformed into lively creative factories, often with substantial public sector support targeting the regeneration of many cities and districts. Some authors even speak about a 'new orthodoxy' of urban planning and regeneration based on the creative district (Miles and Paddison 2005). It is not only about physical regeneration: in some cases, urban knowledge hubs were developed with explicit social regeneration objectives in mind. An example elaborated in this book is Dublin's Digital Hub, where a derelict brewery area is being transformed into a hub for digital media firms. One element of the scheme is a training programme for local residents, and there are strategic links with primary schools in the neighbourhood.

An urban turn?

Thus, in recent years, mono-functional knowledge concepts – like the traditional science parks – are giving way to more mixed and integrated approaches. Knowledge hubs are increasingly being developed as part of the urban fabric rather than as isolated sites outside town, and they tend to become more mixed in terms of function. Interestingly, this is true not only for the 'new generation' knowledge hubs based on creative industries as described above, but also for recent developments of science and technology-based hubs which are becoming more 'urban'. A good example of the latter is the science park Sophia-Antipolis in France (see Box 2.2).

In this section, we describe some recent examples of knowledge-based quarters that explicitly link scientific and business development with urbanity, in housing, leisure and other urban functions. These new concepts try to combine the (assumed) advantages of science parks (as mentioned in the last section) with urban assets and a more open attitude towards the surrounding environment. Some interesting examples can be found in the cities of Dortmund and Newcastle, as described in Boxes 2.3 and 2.4.

Box 2.2 Sophia-Antipolis: a classic science park atmosphere

During the 1970s and 1980s, the desired atmosphere for a science park was seen almost in opposition to the rather polluted and congested urban centres of the time. In the early 1970s, the vision to develop Sophia-Antipolis science park (in a greenfield location close to Nice, in the French Riviera), one of the most famous European science parks, was based on developing a Quartier Latin in the countryside (Laffitte 1991). The founding father of the park, Pierre Laffitte – by that time a researcher of the École des Mines in Paris – had the vision to achieve 'the best of two worlds': a science location without the problems of the modern metropolis but with the 'convivial creativity' associated with the most vibrant Parisian districts. The park encompasses nowadays a very large estate with over 1,300 companies and 30,000 jobs in 2,300 hectares, mainly in bio-research and ICT, but never had an urban and 'convivial creativity' feeling. Office space and companies' premises have traditionally been rather independent from each other, with separated parking lots and the like. Most of the patented innovations developed by companies in the park from 1978 until 2002 have been developed in-house (Ter Wal 2008). Recent efforts from the park's management are to bring an urban atmosphere to the place and a more diverse functional mix, with more student housing, cultural facilities, expositions and other amenities.

Box 2.3 Knowledge locations in Dortmund

Dortmund (Germany) is a city with a rich industrial heritage, but it has faced massive decline since the 1970s. Since then, knowledge-based development has been the cornerstone of local economic policy. In the 1980s and 1990s, the city developed its science park (though in Dortmund it is called 'technology park'), around the Technical University. Its development has been considered a success: currently, it counts 225 high-tech firms and employs 8,500 people. It is now one of the largest of its kind in Germany. It is a 'traditional' technology park, in the sense that it is physically separated from the city, and business-only (no residential function).

Currently, the city is developing a second, 'new generation' hotspot on the Phoenix site, a former industrial site where one of the largest steel plants in Europe was located. In 2001, the factory was demolished and shipped to China. Now, the area (just 5km from the city centre) is being redeveloped into an integrated area for knowledge-based development. One part of the area is destined for high-tech business related to micro-systems and nano-technology. Young firms find excellent conditions in the 'MST factory', a building with a number of technical facilities that those firms need. Other sites are available for other types of firms. The area contains some industrial heritage, as a link to the past, and these old structures will be reused. To the east of this business site a lake is being created, with a harbour and promenades. The area is planned as a classy residential area. In between the business park and the lake district, there is still a 'blue collar' town quarter where steelworkers lived. This quarter is planned to be gentrified due to the development of the Phoenix site. The Phoenix project is strongly supported by the State of Nordrhein Westfalen, the city of Dortmund, the federal government and the EU.

Box 2.4 Newcastle: a science quarter at a former brewery site

Over the last few years, the city of Newcastle-upon-Tyne has successfully transformed its industrial image, through heavy investments in culture and flagship architecture. The city's next ambition is to become a significant 'city of knowledge' in the UK. Among other things, Newcastle intends developing a large 'science quarter' at a former brewery site in the city centre. To realize this ambition, the City Council works together with the University of Newcastle and ONE Northeast, the regional development company for the northeast of England. The partners intend to transform the brewery site into a new mixed-use central district, focused on attracting and developing world-class knowledge and business in science and technology.

The shift from the isolated campus model to integrated approaches has brought knowledge-based development to the heart of Europe's cities. How can we interpret this 'urban turn'? Partly, it reflects the fact that policymakers, influenced by convincing and ready-to-use recipes (Peck 2005) consider knowledge hubs a means to regenerate urban districts, and are willing to invest considerably. But this is not the full story. It also reflects changed ideas on the knowledge-creation process and the conditions in which innovation and creativity can flourish (Asheim *et al.* 2007; van Winden *et al.* 2007).

In recent years, the idea that innovations emerge from unplanned encounters in vibrant places like bars has become probably one of the most famous myths of the economic geography of innovation (Martin and Moodysson 2010). However, the idea of an isolated scientist discovering new things in an ivory tower is also now far from reality. Rather, innovation, knowledge creation and learning occur in interactive, often planned processes, in which actors combine different types of complementary knowledge and competences. Technological development has become very fast, and progress is many times realized when researchers work together in (often international) teams. Also in commercial companies, the innovation process has become much more interactive. Leading firms have set up multi-disciplinary teams of engineers, designers and marketers that work together from the early development stage of a new product to speed up the innovation process, and to ensure that research efforts will ultimately lead to a 'marketable' product that will yield profits for the company.

Moreover, there is a trend towards 'open innovation', in which companies work together and combine their unique competences to create new products or services rather than developing all knowledge in-house (Chesbrough 2003). Furthermore, companies realize that the success of their innovation is higher when the end users (citizens and/or consumers) are involved in the innovation process as well: after all, they are the ones who will buy and use the products. Progressive companies create all kinds of interactions with end-users. The knowledge economy has become an international network economy. Research and development takes place in project teams of people from different nationalities. This networked way of working asks for an environment that facilitates meetings and interaction, and not only during office hours.

Notwithstanding sectoral differences in innovation modes (Asheim *et al.* 2007), the shift from the 'ivory tower' to an interactive and iterative process of knowledge creation has implications for the planning and organization of science parks and other knowledge locations. The provision of offices and laboratory space is not enough: knowledge locations more and more cater for networking and interaction, through meeting venues, restaurants, leisure facilities, network events and a wide array of other means. One feature of this project-oriented knowledge economy is the increasing number of temporary 'expat' professionals who work on a project for a couple of months, at a certain location. Generally speaking, during that time, they prefer to stay in a more lively and diverse environment rather than on a dull campus without life after 5 o'clock.

The 'urban turn' in the development of knowledge hubs is also a manifestation of a more general appreciation of lively cities among the higher-educated. Knowledge workers increasingly prefer to work in a nice and lively working environment that offers amenities and facilities beyond just office and lab space, and where consumption opportunities are more widely available (see Florida 2002; Glaeser *et al.* 2001; Asheim and Hansen 2009, for a more nuanced view). There is pressure on firms and research institutes to meet these demands: high-quality knowledge workers have become a scarce commodity, and there is severe competition to lure them. One of the ways to do it is to offer a very attractive working environment that includes facilities for leisure and shopping, although higher-level amenities can also be found in the location's catchment area and not necessarily within the location (Carvalho 2009).

A related point is the shifting of work–life balance (Florida, 2008). Especially for younger people, work and life have increasing become mingled, and social interaction with colleagues is important. This lifestyle is facilitated well in a lively environment that offers adequate amenities and facilities.

3 Empirics

What do we know about the success of knowledge locations?

What do we know about the 'success' or 'performance' of knowledge hubs? Clearly, the appraisal depends on the objectives of different stakeholders (Monck *et al.* 1988, in Lindelöf and Löfsten 2003). We have seen that there is a large variety of them. Universities may be interested in knowledge diffusion and incubation, or to generate licence income through spin-off companies; banks and real-estate developers are driven by profit and want high occupancy rates and rising property values. City administrations are interested in the number of jobs created at the site, image effects, foreign investment, or the success of regeneration efforts. Tenants may look for specific facilities, network opportunities, or image effects. The impacts of science parks as instruments of regional competitiveness are still far from consensual and there is a way to go to define more encompassing success concepts and measures (Monck and Peters 2009).

It is interesting to look at the literature focusing on the performance of knowledge locations. There is a large literature on the performance and impacts of science parks and other locations (for example, creative districts), to be reviewed in this chapter. By the end, we will have identified current gaps in the literature and made clear how our study contributes to the existing body of knowledge.

Science parks

Shared facilities

One assumed advantage of a knowledge location is the opportunity for facility sharing (such as the joint use of expensive facilities such as cleanrooms or any other equipment). This helps to cut costs, reduce risks and allows for more investment, which keeps facilities at state-of-the-art. Moreover, sharing facilities may spark serendipitous encounters between researchers which may result in spill-over effects or cross-innovation. This latter claim is not verified in the literature, but the other benefits of facility sharing are generally acknowledged and confirmed. Feldman (1994) identified that especially small firms benefit from shared use of facilities. This is the case, for example, in biotechnology, where small start-ups can hardly afford state-of-the-art equipment and rely on shared labs in universities and science parks (Vale and Carvalho 2009). Larger companies are more likely, and able, to internalize such facilities. Garnsey and Heffernan (2005) find that firms on science parks are relatively heavy users of university facilities. Van der Klundert and van Winden (2008) also find that facility sharing is considered an important benefit for firms located in the Eindhoven high-tech cluster.

Do science parks favour employment or sales growth?

Monck *et al.* (1988) made a comparison between the performance of firms within the science park and a comparable sample of firms that are located elsewhere. Remarkably, they found that the firms located on science parks generated fewer jobs than comparable firms 'off' science parks. Why? Are science parks actually hindering business development? Lindelöf and Löfsten (2003) suggest an alternative explanation: a large proportion of the science park entrepreneurs are academics and ex-academics, and they are less likely or inclined to be entrepreneurial and grow a large business. In a more recent study, Siegel *et al.* (2003) also compared the performance of firms 'on' and 'off' science parks. They found that the returns of being located on a science park are negligible. They found no significant difference between employment growth rates of firms located on science parks and those located off science parks.

A Swedish study had a different outcome. It compared the development and performance of young technology firms on parks and off parks (period 1994–6). Firms on park performed better: they had higher sales growth, employment growth and profitability (Löfsten and Lindelöf 2001), suggesting that park milieu has a positive impact on firm performance. Löfsten and Lindelöf (2002) suggest that science parks attract more 'motivated' firms. They are also more involved in co-operation with the university, and science park managers play a positive role here. Firms on parks also proved to be more internationally oriented.

Westhead and Storey (1994) suggest that many firms locate on a science park because of the image and prestige of the site, rather than to benefit from local facilities or network opportunities with other co-located firms. Wright *et al.* (2008) note that, on the contrary, locating on a science park has drawbacks for firms in terms of image. It may reduce a firm's commercial credibility, 'sending a signal to the market that its activities involve academic research rather than a commercial focus'. The university context may bring greater bureaucracy and make it less easy to identify decision makers. The university context lacks sufficient practical, business commercialization experience, and provides for relatively weaker network ties with financiers and industry partners. University science parks may also provide less access to commercially oriented expertise and contacts than a non-university affiliated park.

Huggins *et al.* (2008) note that many parks do not survive; mortality rates are high, and many survivors fail to meet their target objectives. (Luger and Goldstein 1991, cited in Huggins *et al.* 2008). In some cases, expansion ambitions undermine the thematic focus of a park. Etkovitz (2006, cited in Huggins *et al.* 2008) mentions the Penn State Innovation Park, where the real-estate potential undermined its capacity to create an innovative climate. The original idea of the science park often gets lost. Science parks can easily become 'glorified' business parks attracting firms mainly because they offer 'real estate prestige' (Massey *et al.* 1992).

Do science parks promote local networking?

The promotion of local networking and clustering dynamics (Porter 1990), namely knowledge and information exchange between organizations, have been core arguments justifying the social added value of science parks, namely fostering 'collective efficiency'. However, despite a few positive indications that firms within science parks have stronger relations with universities than other firms (see for example Detwiller *et al.* 2006; Chan and Lau 2005) there is no strong evidence that firms on science parks are more likely to collaborate or exchange information with local universities or neighbouring firms on-site.

Bakouros *et al.* (2002) study formal and informal linkages between firms and university on Greek science parks, and found very modest synergy impacts. Similar results were found in a study of university–industry linkages on science parks in the UK (Quintas and Massey 1992). Lindelöf and Löfsten (2003) found, for Sweden, that on-site firms collaborate even less with local partners. Fukugawa (2006) found a relatively high propensity of firms on science parks to engage in joint research projects with knowledge institutes, but the linkages were not local. In the high-tech cluster of Cambridge, UK, many actors claim that global links are more important than local ones (Garnsey and Heffernan 2005). The rise of global partnerships between universities and companies illustrates this tendency. Firms in science parks are not better-informed about research that is conducted in local universities (although they appear to be relatively heavy users of university facilities like computers and libraries). Among the most significant interactions with universities are the searches for new graduates (for example, Vedovello, 1997).

The links between university and firms at the science park depend on the 'absorptive capacity' of the firms, that is, their ability to identify, interpret and use knowledge (Rothaermel and Thursby (2005, cited in Tamasy 2007). Concerning inter-firm networks, Sternberg (1999) found that contact to other firms is especially important for young firms. The later in their lifetime, the more important become the networks outside the park. There might also be sectoral nuances. Knowledge networks in biotechnology seem to be particularly structured and unplanned meetings within a park are definitely not the way biotech companies search for technical knowledge and innovate (for example, Moodysson 2008). Still, this interaction might play a role in the access to market-related knowledge and 'sensing' future co-operation opportunities (for example, Vale and Carvalho 2010). Within Sophia-Antipolis, Ter Wal (2008) found that high-level knowledge networks (leading to patents) between firms were denser in ICT than in biotech, though often associated with labour mobility and spin-offs and not directly with knowledge spill-overs.

Thus, science parks are not the 'local innovation network catalysts' they often pretend to be. This is in line with a growing consensus in the economic geography literature about not overrating the importance of local knowledge networks (for example, Giuliani 2007; Malmberg and Maskell 2006). Many innovative firms do not acquire knowledge from geographically near partners, but rather source internationally (Davenport 2005, cited in Huggins *et al.* 2008). This is especially true for firms with high levels of absorptive capacity (Drejer and Lund Vinding 2007).

Do science parks favour start-ups and the commercialization of research?

Before addressing the contribution of science parks to research commercialization, it is important to note that the extent of commercialization of academic
research is structurally very low in Europe, and somewhat higher in the US.
Licence incomes are small, overall. The average US university earns a modest
$6.6m from licensing (which is 2.8 per cent of their total research budget); in the
UK, it is only $365,000 (1.1 per cent) (HEBI 2004 and NSF 2006b in Huggins
et al. 2008). The number of spin-off companies from universities is also low.
Leading US universities annually spin off 2.8 new companies per institution. Only
four US universities spin off more than ten companies annually. In the UK, the
average for all universities is a bleak 1.3 spin-offs per institution per year.

This being said, business incubation – nurturing young firms – is a key objective of science parks and knowledge hubs. What are the results of science parks
in this respect?

Sternberg (1999) investigated the success of business incubation programmes
in Germany. Success was defined as the degree to which the incubators reached
their objectives, most commonly the support of start-ups, the creation of high-
skilled jobs, and the increase of knowledge transfer. Their results play down the
significance of incubators. The study found low levels of start-up activity and
potential, and many of the start-ups were in low-level service activities rather
than high-tech, science-based businesses. Some 19 per cent of the firms were not
really start-ups, but had existed for two years when they entered the incubator,
and only 3 per cent would have not have started the firms without the existence of
incubators. A study on US incubators (Luger and Goldstein 1991, cited in Tamasy
2007) yields similar results. In addition, they found that older incubators perform
better than newer ones. Similarly, McAdam and McAdam (2008) show that older
incubators are more successful in using incubator facilities in science parks at
the stage in the firm's lifecycle when it searches for independence and autonomy.

Hansson *et al.* (2005) are not surprised about the poor record of science parks
as engines for commercialization, arguing that science parks are often based on
outdated ideas of linear innovation models. The road from basic science to marketable products is not a straight one; new academic knowledge may or may not end up
in new products, and many loops and processes occur in between. Successful product
innovation is a highly interactive process of mixing and recombining existing knowledge. Not only technological knowledge but also skills in, for example, marketing,
management logistics, are needed. It requires entrepreneurial skills.

Koh *et al.* (2005) look at the performance of knowledge hubs in a more dynamic
way. They ask the question whether a science park is able to renew itself, that is,
develop new specializations and adapt to new emerging technologies over time. They
praise Silicon Valley (not exactly a science park) for its great regenerative capacity:
the region manages to constantly re-invent itself, and is a frontrunner in subsequent
waves of new technology (Kenney and Patton 2006). Many science parks have tried
to arrive at a similar adaptive capacity by establishing incubators at the park, or invite
venture capital firms to locate in the park to promote an entrepreneurial attitude.

Creative quarters and new urban knowledge spaces

Despite the relative novelty of the concept, many studies have already looked at the performance of creative quarters. Contrarily to science parks, the success of creative quarters is usually evaluated through their impacts on urban regeneration (economic, social and physical dimensions). However, whether creative quarters improve networking among creative companies and spur joint innovations has been a rather neglected evaluation issue.

The study of Brown *et al.* (2000) suggests that when 'creative' dynamics are not in motion beforehand, the planning of creative quarters may be disappointing. They compare the organic development of Manchester's Northern Quarter with the planning of Sheffield's Creative Industries Quarter, both with a focus on the music industry. Sheffield city invested heavily in infrastructure, facilities and marketing, expecting companies to follow and turn the area into a 'buzzy' hotspot. However, no significant new cluster was developed and the creative companies in place remain heavily public subsidized. Planned anchor organizations moved into the area, like the National Centre for Popular Music, but closed within one year; the area didn't become a lively public space, contrarily to other Sheffield districts and to Manchester's 'hands-off' experience.

In a more recent study about the planning of a cultural quarter in Birmingham's Eastside, Porter and Barber (2007) review 'stylized facts' and lessons about the development of creative quarters in Western cities (for other reviews, see also Vicari Haddock 2010):

- Together with the development of creative quarters, *property prices* are likely to rise, displacing activities and inhabitants planned to be attracted in the first place. This is valid for many segments of the so-called creative class (such as young freelance professionals) that cannot cope with rising prices or benefit from the new consumptions offers). Thus, these gentrification processes might reduce the desired diversity of the area and attention should be given to the nature of local property and real-estate markets in advance;
- Policies exclusively focused on the production side of creative quarters often overlook the quality of public space and thus may not generate the desired *urban liveliness* in the area; hence, creative quarters should combine creative production, consumption and fruition of the public space in a holistic way;
- *Flagship projects* like arts centres, museums and landmark buildings tend to benefit mainly the 'aesthetic desires' and world visions of political and cultural élites. Moreover, their eventual positive impacts are hard to measure. In order to 'root' the quarter, there is a strong need to recognize and empower local talent; creative quarters must work with the existing urban fabric and be committed to lever local talent, designers, architects and capital;
- Public debate and *local participative democracy* help align the quarter with the desires of local populations, building on the distinctiveness of the place and making local communities benefit from it.

Looking beyond the Western context, urban researchers at the Massachusetts Institute of Technology (for example, Seitinger 2004) revisited the seminal study of Castells and Hall (1994) and explored the early development of new twenty-first-century urban 'spaces of innovation', with cases from Kuala Lumpur, Singapore and Seoul. First insights (these developments are still in an early stage) reveal a massive investment scale (mainly public) vis-à-vis western Europe: they focus on creating entire cities within highly planned functionally mixed districts, planned to cater for demographic, social and physical diversity. Inspired by the 'Dubai model', those cities fiercely compete with each other for international exposure, to become English-friendly spots, to attract FDI, international business, expat talent and so on. New high-quality knowledge locations are central pawns in those strategies.

However, Seitinger (2004) doubts whether all this planned diversity will ever come into existence, and, if it does, how will it relate to innovation. The visions and discourses of public officials stress the role of 'knowledge accidents': very much the 'meeting-in-a-bar' myth previously identified by Martin and Moodysson (2010). In these projects, planned order and control are somehow at odds with the urban messiness that characterized urban development and the atmospheres in the large world cities which actually inspired those planned locations. However, one common feature in these new spaces is their role as experimentation arenas and live testbeds for new technologies, and visionary ways of urban life interaction, for example, based on ICT. This trend deserves further attention and is explored in one of our case studies: the development of ubiquitous city concepts and sensor technologies in Songdo, South Korea.

Overall assessment

Overall, the empirical evidence on the success of knowledge locations like science parks and creative quarters is not very encouraging. Despite heavy investments, often financed with public resources, many of the objectives and ambitions are not met. In many respects, the performance of firms located on science parks is not better than that of off-park firms; creative quarters may also result in urban regeneration failures, and both types of location seem to provide minor stimulus for creating businesses. With this in mind, Tamasy (2007) pleas to stop pouring public money in incubators and science parks, while Porter and Barber (2007) call for more innovative, participatory and ambitious plans for cultural quarters.

Van Geenhuizen and Soetanto (2008) note that the bleak record of science parks has not stopped policymakers from being enthusiastic initiators and supporters of parks. Policymakers continue to believe that science parks are effective instruments to enhance knowledge-based growth (Van Geenhuizen *et al.* 2004); on the side of creative quarters, as previously cited, Miles and Paddison (2005) even speak about the rise of the new 'Creative Quarter Urban [planning] Orthodoxy'.

For many policymakers, enhancing the local knowledge economy is a key objective, but a very complex one. There are many interrelated factors that influence a region's innovative performance; many actors are involved, and results of policies are not immediate but take time to materialize. Moreover, the relation between cause and effect of policies is often ambiguous. In this complex situation, policymakers typically exhibit a strong preference for policy tools that produce tangible results, and science parks belong to that category (Van Geenhuizen and Soetanto 2008); science parks 'often play the role of a symbol and physical proof that unites policymakers in the city' (ibid., p. 103). Moreover, investments in creative quarters legitimize simultaneous local investments in the fields of business, education, culture and infrastructure: typical arenas of local political action. Under the 'creative city' banner, creative quarter investments are perceived as contributing to economic development and direct real-estate revenues rather than to extra costs, which are increasingly difficult to justify under tight national and municipal budgets (Hansen and Niedomysl 2009).

Added value of this book

A lot of research has been done to analyse knowledge locations like science parks and creative quarters. What is our study going to add?

For one thing, more firmly than most studies, we put the development of knowledge hubs in their spatial-economic and political-institutional context. The context in which a knowledge location is being developed is a significant factor to look at. For example, in the US, Luger and Goldstein (1991) find structural advantages for science parks located in large agglomerations with strong technology bases, high-tech activities, universities, good infrastructure, business services and forward-looking leaders in business and academia, but do not stress what are the decisive factors for success, or how correlated those factors eventually are. Even though most of the 'successful' science parks and knowledge hubs prosper in dynamic and large urban areas in developed and/or fast-growing economies (Tamasy 2007; Sternberg 1997), there are experiences of successful knowledge hubs in regions with limited urban scale and declining industries, but with good universities (for example, Vale and Carvalho 2009), calling for more in-depth research on the socio-spatial conditions for 'success'. Moreover, policy and governance structures leading to 'success' also deserve more careful attention: the planning structures and leaderships involved in the development of knowledge locations are likely to vary widely, say, between Scandinavia and North-Eastern Asia.

Unlike many studies, and in line with Bigliardi *et al.* (2006), we take an evolutionary approach in analysing knowledge hubs. There is a need to look at these knowledge hubs over time, longitudinally, in order to better reveal cause–effect relationships. Rather than end-goals, we will consider them as part of a long-term, path-dependent process of regional-economic development (Martin and Sunley 2006; Storper and Scott 2009). They (co-)evolve in a constantly changing economic and policy context, and their goals and objectives are subject to change over time (Bigliardi *et al.* 2006, Hommen *et al.* 2006). New insights and policy fashions influence the perception of the role of any knowledge hub, and have an impact on investment decisions and the formulation of goals and objectives. Unexpected events or opportunities – an economic crisis, the investment or withdrawal of a large company, the rapid development of a new technology field – all have an impact. Also, the performance and perception of individual people (a rising star professor, a very successful entrepreneur) typically play a role.

Moreover, our essays pay special attention to the specific modes of knowledge creation (Asheim *et al.* 2007) present in different knowledge locations (for example, in biomedical activities, ICT and creative industries), and their implications for the firm's networking needs, relevant geographical scales of interaction and policies. By doing this, we also answer the call of Evans (2009) towards a better understanding of how and to what extent creative industries become intertwined with other activities (ICT, manufacturing, tourism), how these processes unfold and how relevant they are for the design of knowledge locations.

In our study, we move away from the traditional 'ex-post evaluation' assessing efficiency and effectiveness of knowledge locations in reaching clear pre-set goals. The complexity of the context and the time dimension render this type of evaluation problematic (Teisman and Klijn 2008). In our essays, we adopt assessment methods that do more justice to this complexity, looking beyond simple snapshots. Rather than only evaluating whether goals have been reached, we will analyze the processes that lead (or fail to lead) to a set of goals, in line with Corvers (2001), and Landabaso and Mouton (2005) cited in Van Geenhuizen and Soetanto (2008).

Also, we will analyse the dynamic policymaking process beyond static governance approaches (Hommen *et al.* 2006). What is the involvement of the various stakeholders in the different stages of development: what are their claims, preferences, concerns, ambitions and expectations of the knowledge locations, and how are the power relations established? This is in line with the recommendation of Van Geenhuizen and Soetanto (2008) to analyse science parks coherently with a broader set of shifting networks and connected project initiatives. Although the literature in the field of urban development has continually highlighted the need for public–private arrangements, policy networks and 'N-helixes' in economic development initiatives – like the development of knowledge locations – the fact is that the functioning and dynamics of those networks and governance processes remain very much a black box (Link and Scott 2003; Phan *et al.* 2005).

Despite the recent growth of the literature on creative quarters, much of the literature on knowledge locations focuses on science parks. There is much less attention paid to the assessment of newer knowledge-oriented urban concepts like creative districts, design quarters, media hubs and so on, and especially when both concepts start to get intertwined in hybrid models (Phan 2005), including housing and leisure functions. This further increases the complexity of assessment: new stakeholders are added in the process (housing corporations, neighbourhood councils), gentrification issues emerge, and often, new 'social' objectives are added to the traditional one of economic development and new firm creation. This book hopes to contribute to fill this gap and add to a more integrated understanding of these new-generation types of knowledge hubs.

In order to tackle these challenges, in the next chapter we unfold the building blocks of a conceptual framework to study the development of knowledge locations.

4 Building blocks of an integrative framework

In order to answer our research questions and guide our case studies and essays on the development of knowledge locations, we first conceptualize in depth some theoretical building blocks and hypothesize on a few simple relations between them. More elaborated propositions will be defined later on in Chapter 14, grounded on the evidence of the analysis.

Our aim is to start by clarifying constructs often mixed up in the analysis of different types of knowledge locations. To do so, we combine otherwise disperse constructs from economic geography, urban studies and planning, political science and public management studies, conceptualizing cities and regions as ensembles of production, innovation and political, economic and spatial systems that shape (and are also dynamically shaped by) the development of knowledge locations. The proposed framework is flexible enough to cope with diverse types of knowledge location, ranging from the development of science parks and incubators to the regeneration of old quarters into creative districts.

Spatial-economic context

First of all, we expect knowledge locations to emerge and unfold within a specific spatial-economic context. We conceptualize this context as composed of two central, related yet different systems, each of them encompassing a number of co-evolving actors and/or agents and structures and/or institutions:

- production and innovation system;
- policy and local planning system.

These systems are highly localized in space, and, for now, for the sake of simplification, we analyse these systems at the urban/regional level.

Production and innovation system

This system groups a set of economic activities, industries and competences developed over time in a specific place, as well as the associated institutional infrastructure. It shows how path-dependent features such as human action (for example, entrepreneurs, academic researchers), organized structures (for example, firms and their routines, industries, universities and their curricula) and surrounding environments (for example, established social relations, industrial policies and supportive industrial organizations) interact and co-evolve with each other (Boschma and Lambooy 1999; Maskell and Malmberg 2007). Van Winden *et al.* (2007) approximated this system as resulting from the interaction of a region's economic and knowledge base: its characteristics are shown to set the degrees of freedom for the progress of different types of cities and regions in the knowledge economy, by continually producing (positive or negative) external economies of scale and scope.[1]

A consequence from the previous analysis is that the system is not likely to change dramatically, at least in the short run, but to evolve towards related activities that make use of former regionally accumulated competences (Boschma and Frenken 2009) and institutional settings (Martin 2010).

The textbook example has been the continual reinvention of Silicon Valley's activities since the 1950s from military industries to semiconductors, computers, peripherals, computer networking, software and recently Web 2.0 applications, supported by large entrenched competences and attraction of new talent, but also by the powerful institutions associated with venture capital industry and the Valley's entrepreneurial culture (Kenney and Patton 2006). Other examples are the development of industrial design and high-tech machinery in former textile and steel regions (van Winden *et al.* 2010), or the sustained evolution of audiovisual and movie technologies in the proximity of Hollywood, as well as the related development of fashion design, furniture and jewellery activities in Los Angeles (Scott 1996).

This system is thus path-dependent in the sense that its current state at a moment in time, that is, its composition of activities, industries and institutions, is explained by what it has been before (Dosi 1997; Martin and Sunley 2006). However, it is not deterministic, meaning that there is room for human action and organizational agency to make new activities emerge: changing, redirecting or diversifying the course of events, eventually leading to new paths (Martin 2010; Gertler 2010).

On the one hand, system change can happen from inside, such as when a firm or industry responds to new market needs, through new entrepreneurial activities or, for example, when influential and motivated individuals (entrepreneurs, academics) mobilize other actors and eventually shape the development of policy networks to tackle external opportunities (such as the development of a new knowledge location). On the other hand, change can also be set in motion from certain events, external to the system ('sparks'), or from the development of linkages with other systems, in other regions: in the evolutionist literature, the access to 'variety'. One pre-eminent example is the development of the semiconductor and venture capital industry in Taiwan with the support of Taiwanese transnational entrepreneurs from Silicon Valley in the 1990s (Saxenian 2007). More recently, Vale and Carvalho (2010) report the emergence of biotechnology activities in a Portuguese industrial low-tech region through the action of several PhD returnees, networks of global contacts and the role of a tenured professor who led the institutional adaptation needed for local universities to start commercializing research results.

We expect the structures and dynamics of this system to influence the development of new knowledge locations. The system's structural features limit the degrees of freedom for the emergence and development of new activities in a certain urban region, and thus the type of activities that may agglomerate in a certain knowledge location. But at the same time, organizations and individuals within the system may act as institutional entrepreneurs (Garud *et al.* 2007) and shape the direction of events by proposing, initiating or endorsing the creation of a knowledge location. They may do so, for example, by exercising different types of power (French and Raven 1959, cited in Sotarauta 2009). They can, for example, mobilize new competences and privileged information about the type of location that should be developed to cope with emerging economic and innovation challenges (expert and information power), act as charismatic supporters and attract other parties to the project (referent power) or, on the contrary, exert resistance to the project (coercive power). For example, industrial lobbies and leader firms may exert power to defend their vested interests; or a specific research group within a university may steer the development of a new location to commercialize an emergent set of new technologies. Some actors may even play dual roles in and out of the system's structures. For example, tenured professors may play within the university's rigid structures and simultaneously support the emergence of new commercialization platforms of academic results, for example, through the development take-off of science parks. More recently in Rotterdam, large lead firms like Shell have played locally in different policy arenas: one to defend 'business as usual' chemical vested interests, another to simultaneously develop new experimentation platforms and locations for exploration of new green technologies.

Policy and planning system

Knowledge locations are not solely dependent on economic dynamics or on the power and influence of economic and innovation actors. Unlike regular firms and organizations, the emergence and development of knowledge locations are highly embedded in political discourse, bargaining and influence (Clarysse *et al.* 2005; Wong and Bunnell 2006). Despite some exceptions, and due to its perceived character of 'public good' (that is, not efficiently supplied by market forces), the development of knowledge locations is usually under the responsibility of subnational government tiers, namely local governments, articulated or not with other regional and metropolitan authorities. Those actors have important resources for the development of knowledge locations: not only land and financial resources but also legitimacy and legal power to intervene in urban and regional spatial and strategic planning issues.

Like the former production and innovation system, the policy and local planning system is also composed of agents and structures, the latter being less prone to change in the short run. It encompasses (i) a set of policymakers and related agents (such as the mayor, aldermen, elected politicians, directors, advisors, consultants, local and regional development officers), as well as other players like real-estate developers and citizens; (ii) formal organizational and administration systems, or what Carlsson (2000) calls the 'formal political and administrative skeleton' (for example, local and regional parliaments, municipal departments and companies, development agencies, community associations); and (iii) specific formal and informal institutions. Examples of the latter are local administrative procedures and planning regulations; procurement methods; municipal laws, but also informal networks with other organizations within and outside the public administration system (such as other municipalities, regional and national governments, civil society organizations, developers); routines of co-operation between different municipal departments; openness to ideas from outside the formal administrative system and the capacity (or lack of it) to plan and organize large urban development projects (van den Berg *et al.* 1997).

Note that while some of the formal institutional features stem from national policy and administration systems (for example, national land and planning regulations, public enforcement power), others are specific to local policy and local planning systems, and vary within one country. For example, within the Netherlands the City of Eindhoven has developed strong networks and discussion platforms over time with local industry and is used to actively lobbying with national and supra-national governments (van Winden *et al.* 2010). The same happens in Goteborg, Sweden, where the city has close relations with industrialists who have for a long time been involved in city planning and strategic urban policy decisions (Carvalho *et al.* 2010) and also in Helsinki, Finland where knowledge institutes, different municipalities and firms jointly set up a powerful regional development agency (for example, Van der Borg and van Tuijl 2010). In Spain, some autonomous regions and cities (for example, Barcelona, Bilbao) developed rather distinctive strategic planning routines (van den Berg *et al.* 1997) over time, as a response to external threats and specific opportunities. In Brazil, where urban planning is known for being reactive and left to private initiative, over the last forty years the city of Curitiba managed to develop a highly integrated and proactive urban planning system, with strong planning departments and inter-department co-operation routines, set in motion in the 1970s by the charismatic mayor Jaime Lerner (Mingardo *et al.* 2009).

Likewise, this system is also path-dependent to the extent that past structure and history determine its present features. Structural features change slowly over time and condition policy agents' behaviour, though co-evolving with it in the medium and long run. Also in this system, individual actors and organizations have some freedom to operate and break the structures. The literature provides many examples of the typical 'entrepreneurial mayor' or the 'visionary planning director' who provoked tension in the system, established new networks, changed procedures and established new structures, in a process of de-institutionalization and re-institutionalization (Amin 2001). But more agents in the system are in the position to act in-and-out simultaneously. For example, regional development officers are part of administrative systems but simultaneously mobilize networks and informal contacts, 'seducing' policymakers towards certain policy decisions and new innovative projects (Sotarauta 2009).

A new knowledge location may thus emerge from the action of agents and organizations within the policy and local planning system. It can happen in isolation, such as when municipalities independently develop land and infrastructure to be leased to new activities, contracting it out to other parties and managing it centrally. However, the planning and development of knowledge locations is not only in the hands of such agents; actors from other systems (such as production and innovation players) are involved in shared efforts to bring a new knowledge location into existence (Phan *et al.* 2005).Therefore, more often than not, players from both systems participate in joint policy arenas, governance processes and collective action.

Collective action and governance arenas

In the previous section we suggested that new knowledge locations emerge and unfold under place-specific contexts, framed by the structures and dynamics of two systems; those systems contain most[2] of the actors and organizations responsible for envisaging and developing a knowledge location, in isolation or through collective efforts. This section is about conceptualizing the dynamics of collective action and governance arenas established out of the interplay between those actors in the process of developing a knowledge location.

In a context of rising societal complexity, the policy and local planning system lacks the resources (information, skills, money, legitimacy) to organize large development projects by itself; this is a reason why 'partnerships' and 'governance' are now part of the lexicon in public administration spheres. The development of knowledge locations is a good example of this. There are often multifaceted power relations between various actors – like government authorities, universities, business associations, developers and local communities – giving rise to complex and dynamic governance arenas: networks of interdependent actors involved in a common venture.

But how do these governance arenas come to life? We suggest two broad sets of catalysts/'sparks', which often happen in combination:

- Catalysts from within the system(s): these refer to actions and responses motivated by specific internal dynamics of the two systems described above (Martin 2010). Examples are the perception of policymakers and other players of local and regional economic decline, or, alternatively, growth pressures and opportunities to lever the development of emerging sectors and new activities. Other examples include the pressure to regenerate old districts and develop empty spots left by de-industrialization, develop new growth areas, 'green the city' or attract clean and high added-value activities.
- Catalysts from outside the system: these refer to incentives or pressures from outside the localized systems (for example, national government framework, law or funding incentives to develop a science park or creative districts, subsidies to establish university technology transfer centres, macro-economic development or the announcement of the establishment of a large leading firm or international research institute), but also, more generally, to respond to global fundamental trends in living lifestyles, working and innovating. Examples include: (i) the acknowledgment of innovation as a social process dependent on interaction and proximity; (ii) changing preferences of

workers regarding the quality of their work environment and the blending of life and work; (iii) relevance of open innovation and temporary projects, with implications for the need for fast accessibility, connectivity and new office space ergonomics (including, for example, costly video conference rooms). Moreover, influences from other successes and 'best practice' locations where 'it worked' can legitimate the process and act as a catalyst.

Actors' interests: converging, compatible or mutually adjusted?

These catalysts are often diverse and manifest themselves in several different combinations and guises, and the actors involved in the planning of the location are also likely to be multiple, with diverse interests, knowledge and resources to bring to the process. Thus, partnerships and governance processes towards the planning and development of knowledge locations – the 'focal problem' (Carlsson 2000) – represent exemplary policy arenas for collective action, where actors struggle to align a set of interests, common or divergent, into a single compatible denominator, allowing for formal and informal coordination.

The level of involvement and object of co-operation may, however, vary substantially, over time. At the two extremes, there might be situations of effective joint co-operation and resource sharing – such as in the case of 'triple helix' schemes (Etzkowitz and Leydesdorff 2000) with strongly committed partners from public administration, industry and academia[3] – or, instead, simply one-sided 'self referential organizational decisions' (Teisman and Klijn 2002). Whether one or other sides of the gradient prevail is likely to impact the physical and organizational shape of the new knowledge location.

Some examples illustrate emerging tensions in this type of policy arena: (i) while the central interest of private developers might be to develop land at the lowest possible cost and maximize the rents from new tenant firms, municipal governments may be interested in assuring a certain functional mix and diversity in the area, at the expense of the number of office space square metres; (ii) while universities might prefer to establish technology transfer centres and incubators close to their far-from-the-city campuses, city administrations might want to ensure some decentralizing of functions to the inner city; (iii) while some policymakers might want to develop broad and more 'open' entry criteria in the knowledge location, some industrialists and knowledge institutes might claim for a more specialized location to guarantee cognitive proximity between tenants and better possibilities of interaction; (iv) while mayors and cultural élites might prefer to embed the new location with trendy streetscapes, landscape architecture, cultural facilities and lofts, the local community might be interested in avoiding gentrification and social polarization, and finding suitable jobs (for example, Ponzini and Rossi 2010). Even within the municipal administration tensions might arise, for example, between the economic development and land planning department, for alternative uses for a certain plot of land, or the infrastructure it should encompass.

An important conclusion from the previous discussion is that the interests of the actors with the resources needed to effectively plan and develop the knowledge location will rarely converge, even if they appear to do so at first glance. Different actors, namely public and private, have fundamentally different interests, and nothing guarantees that an effective partnership will emerge, or that it will be once and for all. It is, however, a fact that some different interests might become compatible and mutually adjustable after a number of negotiation rounds; but, in this case, the evolution of these arenas should better be seen as a series of punctuated equilibriums rather than fixed governance schemes (Teisman and Klijn 2008). External and internal changes in context might require new governance arrangements (such as the opportunity to access a new subsidy, the entrance or exit of an actor, or change of local political agenda); moreover, the evolution of the location might require the change of involved players in its development.

Hence, for the purpose of assessing the governance arenas involved in the development of knowledge locations, we consider a broader conceptualization that accounts for the complexity and dynamics involved in this process, way beyond a linear sequence of activities and decisions (Kelly and Palumbo 1992) likely to change over time. Thus, in line with Teisman and Klijn (2008) we start by looking at governance processes and arenas from a more open lens, as 'timelines of interrelated actions developed by a variety of action systems (managers and organizations) leading to complex and dynamic changes in landscape, content and action' (p. 295).

Outcomes of a knowledge location

From the previous discussion, we suggest that the emergence of a knowledge location results from a dynamic governance process in which actors from two distinct and localized systems strategically engage. The governance dynamics are motivated by the need to anticipate or respond to changes or challenges that can be both external and internal to the localized sub-systems. The result of those dynamics will determine the physical and organizational design of a knowledge location: what it looks like, what it is targeted for, and, eventually, its 'success' in the specific spatial-economic context.

In this section, without making further propositions, we put forward and disentangle primary types of expected outcomes resulting from the development of a knowledge location. These represent the 'societal added value' of a knowledge location.

Agglomeration and clustering

This is probably the most acclaimed expected effect from the development of a knowledge location. Based on examples of successful and innovative clusters, it is often expected that the co-location of companies will generate a number of positive external economies of agglomeration to be appropriated by the tenants and to the general benefit of the local and regional economy. Driving mechanisms of these effects may be, for example, specialized resource and equipment sharing, knowledge spill-overs and a number of formal and informal co-operative and competitive links (for example, Porter 1990). It is expected that proximity will facilitate face-to-face contacts, and that the location will become a locus for the development of 'new combinations' and a cradle of innovation (such as the development of new complex equipment linking engineering and medical science, or innovations linking 'art, design and science').

This bundle of effects depends first of all on the capacity of the location to attract a number of companies and organizations from within the region and outside it, but also from the capacity of the location to make new start-ups and spin-offs grow, for example in incubation facilities. Often anchor tenants like large R&D institutes, arts centres, multinational subsidiaries and so on, are considered essential to steer clustering dynamics; however, much seems to depend on its embeddedness within the knowledge location and the region itself. Moreover, physical proximity between companies might not be enough to steer innovative dynamics and yield the benefits of face-to-face contacts – much has to do with whether there is cognitive proximity between them and whether they can understand and benefit from each other's knowledge and resource sharing (Nooteboom 2000). In other words, it depends on whether they are related enough (Boschma and Frenken 2009). When agglomeration and clustering dynamics fail to emerge, knowledge locations are sometimes dubbed a 'firms' hotel' or 'glorified business park' (Massey *et al.* 1992).

Image

Independently of whether agglomeration and clustering dynamics take off, it is expected that a new knowledge location generates images and perceptions for inside and outside the region, becoming intertwined with a city and/or with a particular sector or cluster of activities (such as the biotech park, the media quarter). Often knowledge locations become the 'face of the new economy' in the regions that host them, and this may attract tenants. However, this does not necessarily imply the emergence of clustering and agglomeration economies in the way we defined it previously.

Image impacts have may have other dimensions. The image of a location may become associated with its proximity to élite institutions like universities and lead firms. This may reduce search costs and uncertainty for companies like multinational subsidiaries, looking for a place to settle operations (such as R&D) in a certain city – the 'safe-choice' effect. Moreover, knowledge locations become unique selling points for certain activities, signalling vibrant atmospheres, buzz and places for the acquisition of the necessary knowledge resources: the 'place-to-be' effect. Also for home-grown talent and new entrepreneurs, images of knowledge location often signal a high-quality working environment with the right support and facilities. However, there might be flip-sides. We can imagine situations where image may hamper the location decisions of tenants; for example, when a knowledge location has a very low occupation rate, or when it becomes associated with an 'old friends' club', supportive of élite interests fed by public money. Moreover, many cities show copy-cat behaviour and want to produce the same 'creative locations' or 'valleys'. This makes it harder to distinguish locations from competitors and reduces the chance for success.

Urban-spatial integration

Beyond cluster and agglomeration dynamics, another lens to analyse the outcomes of a knowledge location has to do with its fit within urban regeneration and area-based development strategies. This outcome captures the integration and role of the location within its immediate spatial environment: physical, social and economic.

From a physical lens, knowledge locations may contribute to the cleaning up of former derelict areas and improvements in the environmental quality of the place; they may also steer the renaissance of deprived urban districts into more lively places. Issues to look at are, for example, the accessibility of the location and its role in fostering a more polycentric and balanced urban development in a city region, or the way in which the location is architecturally 'gated' or opened, favouring a better fruition of the public space. These projects may also contribute to making the area safer and fostering its diversity. New locations may support the inclusion of residents, for example by creating new job opportunities, services and education facilities. However, the opposite may also happen. A new location may also become a detached urban 'enclave', dominated by urban élites, a gentrified area without the human scale of a sense of identity.

From a functional perspective, knowledge locations can complement or compete with other knowledge locations. In the first case, new locations contribute to the diversity and new added-value is created. There is also potential to create new combinations between the locations. In the second case, however, it may also result in relocation of tenants between various locations, decreasing the added-value of other locations, with the risk of having various locations which do not develop in a successful way, in zero sum games.

Knowledge locations may become rather diverse and vibrant urban areas. In this sense, they become excellent testbeds and experimentation laboratories of new urban living concepts and associated technologies. Players located there can gain first-mover advantages. Examples are starting to proliferate in Europe and elsewhere. In our cases we explore in detail how and why some new knowledge locations are providing fertile ground for the development of new innovative concepts that make use of its integrated economic, social and physical fabric.

Organizational learning

The development of a knowledge location is a complex project that requires a large number of resources, skills and organizing capacity (van den Berg and Braun 1999). They involve many people within the public administration sphere, requiring new routines and organization models, eventually more flexible to cope with the project requirements. Thus, we suggest that the development of knowledge locations generates organizational learning effects in the organization(s) responsible for its development, namely within organizational structures of local governments.

These learning effects, by definition, are dynamic and may turn into new competences. Technical staff need not only to cope with complex demands, but also to work in a flexible fashion with other departments within the (bureaucratic and rigid) administration. The acquired skills and competences (such as how to develop an integrated knowledge location) can be used for the development of similar or related projects. Learning also takes place in case of failure, when the reasons are evaluated and understood by the location's promoters. Moreover, new social capital is developed between the administration and other stakeholders involved, increasing mutual understanding between different players.

Higher order institutions

Finally, we propose that the whole process of development of a knowledge location evolves within a set of higher order institutions – or 'rules of the game' (North 1990) – specific to national or supranational spaces: different varieties of capitalism (Hall and Soskice 2001) and planning systems (for example, Newman and Thornley 1996). Differences in these contexts exist across countries and larger regional spaces (such as Scandinavia, Southern Europe, Asia) and make the planning and development of knowledge locations evolve in rather different fashions in different places. We suggest that these differences make 'best-practice' transfer difficult to achieve and, again, call for careful attention to place specificities when developing knowledge locations.

Varieties of capitalism

The literature on varieties of capitalism suggests that the functioning of markets and regulatory institutions differs across capitalist economies, and that this has deep implications for the way economic agents and actors structure and organize their actions and behaviour. This literature broadly divides liberal market economies (like the USA and Canada, and to a certain extent the UK) and coordinated market economies (like continental Europe or Japan), although there are claims to produce a more nuanced picture including, for example, differences within Europe and a better assessment of the Asian context (Peck and Theodore 2007).

There might be important implications for the development of knowledge locations. First, Asheim (2009) recently recalled that liberal market economies are more competitive in industries relying on radical innovations while coordinated market economies excel in incremental innovations. Moreover, interactive learning (very much the type expected with the development of certain types of knowledge locations) dominates in coordinated market economies like Scandinavia (though not necessarily within the physical scale of a knowledge location) and tends to require stability and trust that is found often within the company and within long-established relationships.

Second, varieties of capitalism are likely to affect the mobility choices of people in choosing cities and knowledge locations in which to 'live, work and play' – the central mechanism under the US-based creative class theory of Florida (2002), underlying the ambition of many knowledge locations. Compared, for example, with Europe, the US economy has a much larger and more integrated labour market, with a single language and institutional setting. The higher education system favours mobility. Lower social security, unemployment benefits, parental supports and female labour market participation vis-à-vis Europe steer much higher mobility and inter-city migrations. It is also not surprising that entrepreneurship – another expected outcome of developing knowledge locations – in the context of easier mobility and lower unemployment benefits, is much higher in the USA than in Europe.

Planning systems

Formal and informal land planning systems and governance mechanisms vary considerably across countries (Newman and Thornley 1996). Thus, they create variety in the ways stakeholders (developers, city authorities and so on) play their roles and exercise power in different contexts and systems. It results in some places being easier than others in which to develop an integrated knowledge location, or, at least, the process is likely to evolve in a rather different way.

In some places, for example in Asia, land development and urban policy are rather top-down, while in continental Europe bottom-up and long participatory processes are usual. Even within Europe there are considerable differences across countries on on the structure of land ownership (for example, public versus private).

Some examples illustrate our point. Nordic countries, such as Sweden or Finland, have sound planning and building regulations, where local governments play a central and powerful role throughout the process. The local government has a planning monopoly and develops legally binding, comprehensive and detailed plans, with strict building permits. The city tends to be the largest landowner, and long-lease contracts are a usual mechanism to steer land development in a planned long-term fashion (for example, ensuring social and economic mixes in certain areas). In Southern Europe, for example, and despite the existence of barely the same planning instruments, private ownership is dominant in many places, making it more difficult to design and implement integrated knowledge locations in a reasonable period of time. Collaborative approaches are usually more difficult, and there are clearer distinctions between public-owned knowledge locations and private-led developments. Another manifestation of these differences concerns the technical and market knowledge within local government and public managers. While in Scandinavia this knowledge is highly concentrated within the (high-paying) public sector, in the Netherlands, private developers and high-paid consultants often have the strongest technical skills and power influencing the development, in this case, of knowledge locations.

Differences in planning systems and regulations thus have implications for the management and 'ownership' of knowledge locations. Speaking about science parks, Queré (2007) calls attention to the fact that 'while is Anglo-Saxon countries the governance is usually dominated by universities or private structures, in countries like Germany, France or Italy the ownership is often almost 100% public or managed by public–private partnerships' (p. 49).

Summing up

In this section, based on a number of literatures, we unfolded some conceptual building blocks to understand the emergence and development of knowledge locations:

- the spatial-economic context, namely the localized systems of production and innovation, and policy and local planning;
- collective action and governance arenas, including catalysts/'sparks' of these processes;
- the outcomes of a knowledge location, namely 'clustering and agglomeration', 'image', 'urban-spatial integration' and 'organizational learning';
- higher order institutions influencing the whole development of knowledge locations in different places.

Although we conceptualized these blocks in considerable detail, until now we have hypothesized rather simple relations between them. Our framework suggests that the emergence and development of knowledge locations results from dynamic governance processes in which actors from two distinct and localized systems strategically engage: (i) spatial systems of production and innovation and (ii) constellations of political and public administration systems. The governance dynamics are motivated by the need to anticipate or respond to changes or challenges that can be both external and internal to the localized sub-systems. Subsequently, the framework conceptualizes four potential impacts associated with the new knowledge location. The unfolding of these processes is strongly influenced by higher-level political economy institutions which shape the actors' behaviour in different supra-regional spatial contexts. Figure 4.1 illustrates this framework.

In the following essays, we look into these issues in detail (although sometimes under slightly different headings) in order better to understand the relations between the constructs and answer our research questions. For example:

- in order to understand the localized spatial systems or production and innovation, and policy and local planning, in every case we take a good look at the spatial-economic context of the city and the location;
- in order to assess the collective action and governance arenas, we pay attention to the processes leading to emergence of the location, the involved stakeholders and its management dimensions;
- in order to evaluate the outcomes (and the spatial scales of its manifestation), we look at the knowledge location from different angles (for example, a certain location as an 'R&D location', as a 'testbed', as a 'place to live, work and play' and so on).

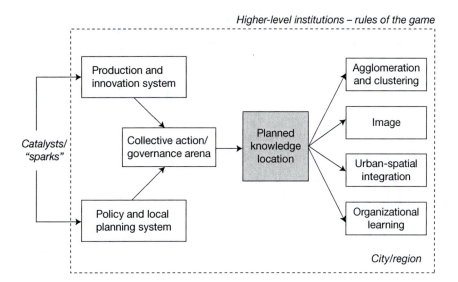

Figure 4.1 Building blocks of a theoretical framework

Source: own elaboration

5 Methodology and research design

To conduct this research we followed a multiple case study design; each of the cases – 'processes of development of a knowledge location' – was treated as a separate experiment (Yin 1984) confirming or disconfirming inferences derived from the others (George and Bennett 2005). After reviewing existing literature and combining it to make the building blocks of an integrative framework (see Chapter 4), we explored the mechanisms and processes linking those constructs through grounded theory methodologies (Glaser and Strauss 1967; Eisenhardt 1989), with recursive feedbacks and re-alignments between data collection, data analysis and theorization. By exposing the constructs of the framework to empirical assessment, our aim was to come up with grounded propositions on the processes of emergence and development of knowledge locations.

Our cases (see Table 5.1 and Figure 5.1) were selected through a theoretical sampling method, in this case with the aim of allowing a large diversity of experiences to (i) produce rich and detailed narratives of a diversified set of 'new-generation' experiences and, simultaneously, (ii) identify generalizable propositions and common features among the cases. The cases differ in stage of development, governance regimes, sectoral focus and urban integration. Most of the investigated locations focus on creative industries and are (re)developed within the urban fabric (for example, in former brownfield sites) as depicted in Figure 5.1. Remarkably, the locations under study are located in countries facing rather different political economy institutions and land planning systems (South Europe, the Nordic countries, Central Europe, North-Western Europe and Eastern Asia; see Figure 5.2), allowing us to look with particular attention at the effects of this diversity in the planning process and development of the knowledge location.

For each of the cases, a detailed case study report and/or essay was elaborated, allowing for a rich within-case analysis, looking at multiple scales of analysis, namely the knowledge location, the networks of its tenants and the urban region. In each of the cases we looked into our advanced constructs (see Chapter 4) and analysed the causal relationships between them, as well as the underlying processes. Moreover, we compared the evidence of the six cases and identified common patterns, allowing us to pursue some generalization and identify critical success factors.

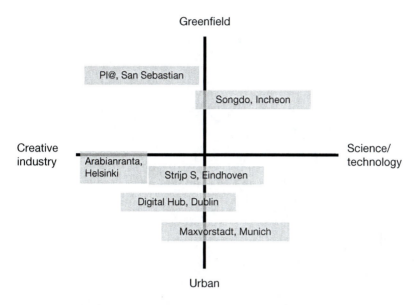

Figure 5.1 Sectoral focus and urban integration of the investigated locations

Source: own elaboration

Table 5.1 Case studies: locations, cities and location's focus

City	Knowledge location	Country	Sectoral focus
Dublin	Digital Hub	Ireland	ICT and digital media
Eindhoven	Strijp-S	The Netherlands	Creative industries
Helsinki	Arabianranta	Finland	Design
Incheon	Songdo district	South Korea	Biotech, ICT and nanotech
Munich	Maxvorstadt	Germany	Science and art
San Sebastian	PI@	Spain	Audiovisual and digital media

Source: own elaboration

The fieldwork and case studies were developed in the period from May 2008 to July 2010, in the cities and knowledge locations under analysis. In each city we focused on a particular knowledge location and its players, although taking into consideration the larger urban-spatial setting. For each case study we triangulated a diverse array of quantitative and qualitative secondary data (such as a location's associated reports, statistical sources, previous studies, press releases and so on) with primary qualitative data collected through in-depth and semi-structured interviews with key stakeholders in the development of the knowledge location under analysis.

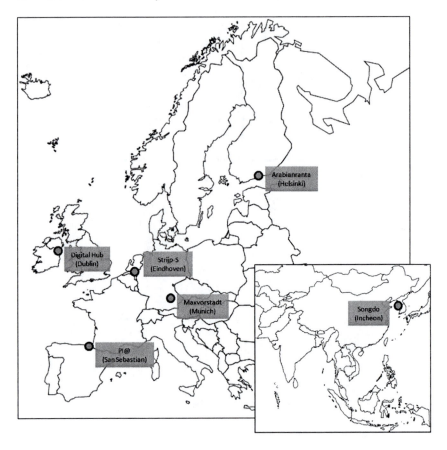

Figure 5.2 Geography of the cases

Source: own elaboration (maps from www.worldatlas.com)

The number of interviewees per location or city varied between 10 and 25 (see Table 5.2). For each of the interviews, we used a semi-structured questionnaire, focusing on the different issues under analysis in our research framework, allowing for comparability and cross-case analysis. Some interviews were rather ethnographic in nature (Spradley 1979), where we explored in depth the nature of daily life operations and routines of our interviewees. In total we held 101 interviews with several key players in the development of knowledge locations (see Table 5.2), namely science parks' and locations' managing company directors, firms, R&D institutes, cultural institutes, real-estate developers, government authorities and intermediate organizations and a diverse array of experts, community associations and event directors in each city.

Table 5.2 Interview distribution

City: location	Management	Firm	Gov.	HEI/R&D	Div.	Total
Dublin: Digital Hub	2	4	7	2	1	16
Eindhoven: Strijp-S	2	2	6	–	6	16
Helsinki: Arabianranta	1	2	4	1	2	10
Incheon: Songdo	4	6	7	3	5	25
Munich: Maxvorstadt	–	1	11	8	1	21
San Sebastian: PI@	1	7	1	1	3	13
Total	10	22	36	15	18	101

Source: own elaboration

Notes
Gov: Government institutions (local, metropolitan, regional); HEI: higher education institutes; Div: Diverse, including experts, intermediate associations, community associations, event directors, museum directors, representatives of real-estate developers and so on.

Each interview took 60–120 minutes and detailed interview reports were produced afterwards. Following the procedures of Merton and Kendall (1946) and Kincaid and Bright (1957), the interviews were conducted simultaneously by at least two of the authors, in order to reduce interpretation bias and systematically explore new emerging issues and relations. After discussion and comment by all the authors, a preliminary case study report was sent to all the interviewees in each region for comments, in order to enhance the validity of the information and relations conveyed.

Part II

Knowledge locations in practice

6   Dublin: Digital Hub

Introduction

Since 2001 the Digital Hub has been developed in Dublin, Ireland, at a special location. The premises of the former Guinness brewery are being transformed into a cluster of ICT and new media companies. The ambition of the city government is to turn the Digital Hub into a flagship of the Irish ICT industry. Currently, over 84 companies are located there. A remarkable feature of the development is the strong social component: the Digital Hub is meant not only as an economic engine, but also a catalyst for the surrounding dilapidated urban area. Since 2001, the Hub has experienced various setbacks and reorientations, and the recent economic crisis poses a new reality to which ambitions have to be adapted.

This chapter sketches the Digital Hub's dynamic development in its spatial-economic and political background. We review the current aims and ambitions of the Digital Hub – as formulated by its management – and confront them with the facts on the ground. The case illustrates how the fate of a knowledge hub sometimes depends on 'random' events and economic volatility. Also, it is a good example of an attempt to create an urban knowledge hub that is not isolated but integrated into the surrounding urban fabric.

This chapter is organized as follows: the next section describes the socio-economic and political context in which the Digital Hub is developing. The third section is the central section of this chapter. It sketches the Digital Hub's history, and its ambitions, and analyses to what extent these ambitions are being realized. The last section contains some concluding remarks on the developments at the Digital Hub and the challenges that remain.

City and economy

Economic context

With an estimated population of 1.2 million inhabitants in the city region, Dublin – the capital of Ireland – is by far Ireland's largest city. Over the last decade, its population has steadily grown (annually by 0.9 per cent). Moreover, Dublin has recently turned into a diverse city. From 1996 to 2006 diversity increased substantially: the number of non-native inhabitants living in Dublin that are not from an

English-speaking country has increased by a remarkable 500 per cent during this ten-year period. At present 19 per cent of people residing in Dublin were not born in Ireland.

Ireland was among the strongest-growing economies in Europe. The 'Celtic Tiger' was considered by many as best practice in terms of economic development, and experienced rapid growth in employment and income (Bayliss 2007). During the ICT boom of the late 1990s, Ireland was able to profit substantially from a growing world economy. Strong GDP growth led to a second boom, this time in construction in the early 2000s. Ireland was quite successful in capitalizing on a growing world market during this period, thanks to its very open economy, an attractive tax regime (very low corporate tax), and membership of the Eurozone, making it a prime receiver of FDI (especially from the USA). Moreover, the country capitalized on its business networks of Irish communities worldwide, and attracted scores of new immigrants from all over the world

The openness of the economy makes the Irish economy very vulnerable to fluctuations in world economy. After the global dot-com bust in the early 2000s economic decline set in, and Ireland needed to identify new drivers for growth (Bayliss 2007).The inflow of manufacturing FDI dried up, as Ireland has become relatively expensive *vis-à-vis* new EU member states. The government started to recognize that a more indigenous, knowledge-based intensive development was needed to provide economic growth.

The digital media industry was chosen by national government as one of the focal points for development for Ireland (NDP 2007), with the development of the Digital Hub in Dublin playing an essential part in this policy. Creating, managing and distributing digital media content was identified as an important potential growth sector which may improve Ireland's competitive advantage (Bayliss 2007).

There was discussion whether this would be a good strategy. Some challenged the ability of Ireland (and its largest commercial centre, Dublin) to compete head-on in this media industry with economic giants such as London, whereas others believed that digital media could be a very promising 'niche market'. The proponents of this strategy pointed out that for Dublin to capture only a small percentage of this multi-billion market would be a huge feat in itself. The market for digital media and technology is to a large extent a global market, fitting the openness of the Irish economy.

Digital media is not only a growth sector in its own right; it also deeply permeates and affects other sectors such as telephone services, TV broadcasting, radio and other established media. The boundaries between these different types of media are fading. Integrated devices offering telecommunications services, email, mobile television and streaming audio have emerged and are spreading rapidly, integrating the market for digital media and setting higher standards for compatibility, broadband and support services. Proponents of the Digital Hub believe that taking an early lead in digital media development would create indigenous growth based on entrepreneurship, and strengthen the knowledge sectors of the economy.

Questions remain, however. For one thing, successful Irish firms were taken over by large foreign multinationals, raising the question whether growth in these industries can be captured locally and thus contribute sustainably to Ireland's national economy. Second, the economic downturn that set in during the last quarter of 2008 affected the Irish economy substantially. Ireland was among the hardest-hit countries in Europe, with strongly falling property prices, sharp budget cuts by the government and an increasing outflow of young people to other countries. Furthermore the high value of the euro in comparison to both the pound sterling and the US dollar negatively affected export potential, further adding to the economic challenge Ireland faced. In the last three months of 2008, Ireland's economy contracted by 7.5 per cent.

Ireland's budget deficit reached a peak of 9.5 per cent in 2009, which is substantially above the EU-prescribed 3 per cent. Moreover, unemployment has more than doubled since January 2008 and is now somewhat above 10 per cent.[1] Summarizing, Ireland faces a tremendous challenge to cope with the effects of a global economic downturn. It is in this difficult context that the Digital Hub is developing.

Skill base and human resources

The ambition to develop digital media as a new growth industry can only be realized if a number of contextual conditions are met. One key condition is the availability of a diverse and skilled labour pool.

Ireland has a rich tradition in education. With free secondary schooling since 1966 (IIEA 2008), the educational level of the Irish population has developed well, and the percentage of workers with tertiary education grew fast. However, Dublin faces a structural shortage in digital media graduates, which manifests itself during times of economic growth. Irish digital media firms have trouble attracting suitable graduates for a number of reasons (indicated by our interviewees). First, there is a qualitative mismatch: there are many graduates in the fields of business and financial services but few in digital media and technology. Second, foreign companies seem to be able to pay better salaries, further diminishing the knowledge base for indigenous companies. Third, internships are limited, making it hard for graduates starting out to acquire work experience. Fresh graduates and interns are seen by some companies as too expensive in terms of training. Some Irish companies respond by attracting graduates with some experience from abroad. At present the economic crisis offers temporary relief.

Education is one of the primary policy instruments used by the government of Ireland to enable a shift towards the digital media sector. The ambition is to achieve a situation in which 'every citizen can be engaged through a laptop' (IIEA 2008).

By investing early on in education in digital media, children are expected to get a head start in digital media skills, allowing Ireland to take a leading position in the new digitally-based knowledge economy. To realize this, the IIEA (2008) suggests a number of educational reforms which have, aside from the above-mentioned advantage in the long run, three other important advantages. First, it allows for a larger skilled labour pool in the medium term, which is needed because international and Irish firms need skilled graduates. Second, it helps to close the 'digital divide', that is, the gap between rich and poor in terms of digital skills, limiting the opportunities in the labour market of the poorer parts of the population. Third, it allows for the creation of world-class universities that are considered essential for a performing knowledge economy. As Lawton Smith (2007, p. 98) states, 'universities as sources and repositories of knowledge have assumed a central role in the delivery of policies designed to drive economic development'.

Political and administrative structure

In 2003 the Irish government decided to decentralize substantial parts of policy-making to a lower spatial level. For decades, Dublin had been the centre of gravity of Ireland's economic growth.[2] It was believed that Ireland would benefit from a more balanced regional development, and new policy prioritizes economic development in other areas besides Dublin. This policy has implications for the Digital Hub; among other things, it impacts the marketing efforts of state organizations. On the website of the Industrial Development Agency, tasked with attracting FDI into Ireland, the Digital Hub is not mentioned as a strategic site or business and technology park. It is mentioned briefly as an 'emerging location' under the heading 'East Ireland', subheading 'Dublin'.

The 'Creative Dublin Alliance' was recently created to design and deliver an economic strategy for the city. It is a group of stakeholders formed by the Dublin City Council, with the aim of a 'creative/sustainable city with a rich quality of life and a vibe that is difficult to replicate elsewhere – distinctly Dublin' (Smeaton *et al.* 2009). Stakeholders include: local authorities, the higher education sector in the city, the business sector and the private sector. University development is considered essential in the framework of the Creative Dublin Alliance. According to City Management, Dublin universities have to develop themselves further to reach higher positions on international rankings, in order to attract talented students from across the globe. This will stimulate further development in the city and may contribute to a vibrant environment in the city.

Digital Hub

The Digital Hub is located in the Liberties area, on lands formerly owned by the Guinness breweries. The Liberties are located just outside the city centre and the historic core of the city (see Figure 6.2). The name Liberties derives from its location just outside the city walls during the Middle Ages. The area is one of the less well-off parts of Dublin.

This section describes the Digital Hub's development and the vision and strategy for the Digital Hub set forth by Dublin City Council (DCC) and the Digital Hub Development Agency (DHDA). Subsequently this 'grand design' is compared to what the DHDA, in co-operation with the other stakeholders, has been able to achieve.

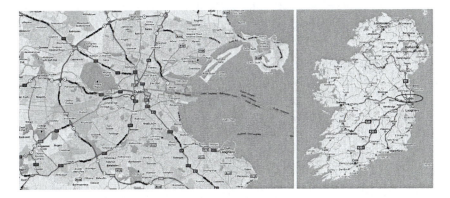

Figure 6.1   Location of the Digital Hub in Dublin, Ireland

Source: www.maps.google.com

History

Initial planning for the establishment of the Digital Hub started in 2000. One of the catalysts in the process was the establishment of MIT's Media Lab Europe (MLE) in July 2000. MLE was a research institute in digital media where staff, researchers, students and companies could collaborate on digital media innovation.[3] MLE would later serve as anchor tenant for the Digital Hub (Bayliss 2007). In April 2001 the Irish government founded Digital Media Development; this constituted the official launch of the Digital Hub project (DHDA 2003). With an act of national government in 2003 it was established that the Digital Hub would be delivered by a separate state body. This resulted in the creation of the Digital Hub Development Agency (DHDA). The DHDA was set up to deliver the Digital Hub in a commercial partnership arrangement with private project developers. The Dublin Office of Public Works (OPW) transferred the required six acres of land to the DHDA (DHDA 2007a).

In 2003 a three-and-a-half kilometre broadband ring was established (DHDA 2003); this ring should ensure high-speed internet access throughout the Digital Hub. The ring allows for speeds of up to 4Gbps, offers VoIP services throughout the Digital Hub and enables the use of state-of-the-art video-conferencing equipment, which is placed at the disposal of companies in the Digital Hub (DHDA 2004). At present, five companies are offering telecommunications services to the companies in the Digital Hub. The DHDA has relatively little influence on the offer of broadband services: due to state-aid regulation it cannot operate as a Telco or service provider. However, the DHDA does buy some broadband packages and offers them to small companies at a reduced price.

In January 2005 MLE announced its closure due to a lack of funding. Many stakeholders also mention that output was lacking as MLE's research was too 'blue-sky' to lead to practical applications. As Bayliss (2007) concludes, MLE's closure was a severe blow to the developments at the Digital Hub. However, the DHDA has managed to recover from this setback and was able to steer developments back on track.

In November 2005 a new development phase for Digital Hub was initiated, which was intended as the start of actual real-estate development. A tender was issued to identify private developers that could develop the lands owned by the DHDA. A number of developers, among which are the current contractors Manor Park Homebuilders Ltd and P. Elliot and Co. Ltd, showed significant interest in developing locations in the Digital Hub. Both filed for planning permission at the Dublin City Council in 2007 (DHDA 2007b). Their plans include a mixed-use development of over one million square feet and include enterprise, retail, residential, community and learning space (DHDA 2006).

In 2006 the National Digital Research Centre (NDRC) was founded to bridge the gap between academic research and the creation of market capital. This centre would be located in the Digital Hub, and give a new impetus to its growth. The mission and *raison d'être* of the NDRC is to create market value by developing and commercializing viable digital media technologies and content through collaborative translational research. Market capital is a value creation objective, and manifests itself in the form of partnership formation, increased follow-on investment and job creation. 'Translational research' is defined by the NDRC as a gap-bridging, innovation activity between industry and academia, which leverages the knowledge, skill sets and assets of both parties. In order to achieve this mission, the NDRC invests in and proactively facilitates value creation from applied digital technology research, effectively bridging the gap between innovative research and impact in the marketplace. This investment is made in joint venture projects between industry and academia undertaking late-stage commercially-focused research and innovation. Typically, those projects seek to leverage upwards the generation of value from previous research expenditure. The NDRC currently comprises fourteen projects, in which approximately 100 researchers are involved.

Some of our interviewees are critical about the role played by the NDRC. They state that the NDRC has not been able to fill the gap left by MLE's closure, although it should be noted that the NDRC is a very different type of research entity to MLE, and was not set up to replace MLE. Moreover, the role of the NDRC is not always clear: several interviewees were not aware of the nature and scope of its projects, or had not seen any results so far.

In 2006, a development plan for the Digital Hub was created (DHDA, 2007a). This plan was a direct result of the Community–Public–Private Partnership (CPPP) process (see below). As such it represented an agreement between the local community, public and private sector partners. The Development Plan identifies no less than 28 key principles which will have to be taken into account in the further development of the Digital Hub.

Under the contract both Manor Park Homebuilders Ltd and P. Elliot and Co. Ltd. had to have planning permission by May 2008. Their contract allowed for an extension until February 2009 (DHDA 2007b). At the time of writing, the planning permission was not yet in order. Continuation of this part of the project is therefore still uncertain; some interviewees called for national government support to ensure continuation of the project.

Digital Hub: the concept

The Digital Hub is, in theory, expected to be the spot for digital media development in Ireland and abroad. In the words of a Digital Hub executive, 'the Digital Hub is expected to be the place where the next big Digital Media development takes place'. This sub-section will consecutively cover the vision and strategy for Digital Hub and the business model employed by the DHDA.

Vision and strategy: the grand design

The Digital Hub should be much more than just an economic development project by local policymakers; it aims to combine enterprise development with urban area-based redevelopment.

According to Bayliss, 'Dublin's Digital Hub project is an attempt to link digital media enterprise and entrepreneurship with R&D and educational sectors' (2007, p. 1261). By developing a geographic cluster of strongly related companies the Digital Hub serves a number of functions: first, it is the hotspot for digital media companies in Ireland and abroad; second, it functions as an incubator space for start-ups in digital media; third, it serves as a flagship brand on digital media efforts in Dublin; fourth, it functions as a catalyst for development of a vibrant city area with high-quality amenities; fifth, it provides a basis for digital media education; and sixth, it serves as an anchor in the city, taking over the role that Guinness has fulfilled over previous centuries. These various functions can be elaborated on as follows.

As the Digital Hub is intended to be the *spot for digital media companies in Ireland and abroad*, it is intended to be 'the place to be' for digital media developments, not only in Ireland but also in a European context. The Digital Hub should, according to its management, be the location where the next big digital media development takes place. DHDA aims to reach a situation where companies view the Digital Hub as 'the right place for digital media development'.

The Digital Hub offers *incubation space for start-ups* in digital media. Based on mainstream agglomeration economies theory (for example, Rosenthal and Strange 2004; Cooke 2001; Porter 1998), the Digital Hub is expected to offer companies potential to collaborate, to share tacit and explicit knowledge and to create benefit from spill-over effects, based on a network of related firms. The digital media climate created by an agglomeration of companies creates potential for spin-outs and start-up firms, providing them with easy access to supply and demand markets, information and support systems.

The Digital Hub is also expected to *function as a catalyst for the development* of a vibrant city area with high-quality amenities. Aside from its function as an 'exciting industry of the future' (Bayliss 2007, p.1261), the Digital Hub is intended to be a 'digital district boasting ... an entire district of apartments, retail units and leisure areas'. The Digital Hub development was intended to create a vibrant city quarter, spreading 'prosperity in one of Dublin's most disadvantaged areas' (Bayliss 2007, p. 1267) through employment creation, education and economic regeneration. This has been elaborated on in this section.

Closely related to the above is the Digital Hub's role as a *basis for digital media education*. Societal remit plays an important role in the work of the DHDA as it aims to provide lifelong learning and the creation of more accessible pathways to learning and employment (DHDA 2006).

Finally, the Digital Hub is expected to serve as an *anchor in the city*. For two-and-a-half centuries the Guinness breweries have been an essential and highly recognizable part of Dublin, and formed an important part of its identity. However, the breweries have partly moved outside the city. As Guinness has been the identity of Dublin in previous centuries, digital media may be part of Dublin's identity for the twenty-first century.

Business model and stakeholder involvement

The Digital Hub project is organized in an innovative way. A separate legal entity was created which is publicly owned, but which operates like a private development corporation. This entity, the DHDA, was set up by an act of national government. Wholly owned by the Ministry of Finance, this state agency reports directly to the Irish Department of Communications, Marine and Natural Resources, allowing for and requiring a much broader policy agenda than if it answered to the Department for Economic Development. As a separate legal entity, the DHDA operates with its own assets and separate budget, and has to secure its own funding. Part of the funding is secured through rental income, another part from sponsorships and grants. The DHDA is required to develop the Digital Hub in strategic partnership with private sector developers. As such, the DHDA is acting as a private sector developer, which is uncommon for a public body.

Two developers have been awarded the contracts for actual development of the lands of the Digital Hub Development Agency. In return, these developers have to provide, first, a cash sum (€72.4 million) and second, after completion, a small amount of office space returned to the DHDA (which represents a value of €45.7 million) (DCENR 2008). All other areas can be used by the developers at their discretion, within the boundaries set by Dublin City Council. Potentially this will lead to a mix of functions around the Digital Hub, creating a vibrant area with high-quality amenities and heterogeneous residential space. This business model makes the development model of Digital Hub a risky one. Some state that the business model now manifests itself in a stalling of the project.

Community involvement is secured through a Community–Public–Private Partnership (CPPP). The CPPP includes a process of extensive consultation which started with twelve representatives of key stakeholders and slowly evolved over time to comprehensively include all relevant stakeholders (DHDA 2004; DHDA 2003). Divided over five interest areas, this process of consultation resulted in 28 principles that have guided and will continue to guide development in the Digital Hub. In consultation with the various stakeholders, developments so far have been shaped and a plan for future development has been formulated. The CPPP process involves a number of stakeholders, such as the Dublin City Council, the Department of Communications, Marine and Natural Resources, the Industrial Development Agency, Enterprise Ireland, local community representatives and local enterprise (DHDA 2007a). The CPPP resulted in the Digital Hub Development Plan (DHDA 2007a); the two private developers that were eventually chosen have the obligation to abide by the development plan and to consult with the community through a continuation of the CPPP.

Integration with the urban fabric

The establishment of the Digital Hub and its development corporation by an act of national government required a form of community involvement. Formally stated, the act requires the DHDA to 'consult with local community interests in or adjacent to the Digital Hub as part of the implementation of the development plan'.[4] The act does not specify the nature or form of such an involvement. Community involvement is expected to allow the Digital Hub to cast the net as wide as possible, not to create popular support, but to identify and retain talent, which in turn fosters more research and production. The DHDA aims to involve the community primarily through consultation and education. Through a process which they call Community–Public–Private Partnership (CPPP) the general public is involved in the developments in the Digital Hub. By promoting lifelong learning and creating accessible pathways to learning and working in digital media, economic integration is stimulated.

The Digital Hub is integrated with its environment in a number of ways.

First, the Dublin City Development Plan incorporates the Digital Hub as a Framework Development Area, which can be understood as an area that receives special attention during the time the plan covers. Such areas are considered key in the development of the city of Dublin. The development of these areas will result in spatial clusters of economic, commercial and cultural specialism which are vital to the future growth and success of the city. Each of these areas will be promoted to achieve its optimum development potential (DCC 2005).

Second, the Digital Hub Development Plan (DHDA 2007a) states a clear need for integration with the Liberties Integrated Area Plan. The other way around, the Liberties Integrated Area Plan thoroughly integrates the Digital Hub development plan in the wider context of urban development in the (deprived) Liberties area. Third, the Digital Hub's development fits the strategy for the Dublin City Development Plan on knowledge creation. The Digital Hub, together with a proposal for the creation of Grangegorman DIT campus,[5] is identified as part of a new north–south 'knowledge' axis facilitated by the release of redundant industrial and institutional lands (DCC 2008a, p. 25).

Fourth, hopes are placed on the enrichment of the Digital Hub concept with input from already existing creative industries in the area. The National College of Arts and Design is located very close to the Digital Hub development site. The DHDA and DCC expect synergies created by combining creative industries and digital media enterprises, resulting in a competitive advantage for the Digital

Hub over other digital media locations. The aim of this policy is to combine the economic benefits of agglomeration with the creative milieu associated with art and design. Creativity and digital media should prove an interesting combination. The 'creative class' is attracted by rundown areas where there is sufficient (cheap) room for creative expression and the Liberties currently fits this profile. A combination of innovation in the digital media sector and creative ideas could lead to interesting new products, and new applications for existing products. Attracting the creative class may contribute to the growth of Digital Hub, both in a qualitative and quantitative sense. On the one hand, additional, creative residents may improve the liveliness of the area, creating scope for more and higher quality amenities. On the other hand, interaction between creative minds and digital media engineers may lead to new, interesting digital media applications. Furthermore, cross-fertilization between these different kinds of knowledge may improve the skill base for digital media companies.

Digital Hub: results so far

In theory, the Digital Hub has clear potential to be a successful development. How this works out in practice is, however, currently unfolding and in some areas still unclear. This sub-section contains some preliminary results.

Vision versus reality

As mentioned in the section above, the strategy and vision for the Digital Hub contains a number of elements and goals. This section will evaluate point-for-point whether these goals are being or will be met in the near future.

Is the Digital Hub a hot-spot for digital media development?

With a total of 84 companies, the Digital Hub can be considered successful in attracting and creating a substantial agglomeration of digital media businesses (see Figure 6.2). The companies in the Digital Hub include very few large corporations and mostly (79 per cent) include SMEs or single-employee organizations (DHDA 2007c). Companies attracted to the Digital Hub need to apply to the DHDA in order to be allowed to locate in one of the offices rented out in the Digital Hub. The DHDA then decides whether the companies fit the desired characteristics of a digital media company. As such, the DHDA actively manages the concept of the Digital Hub going as far as to manage the mix of companies and their potential for interaction. This seems to work quite well; of the 84 companies, 78 can be regarded as digital media companies and the remaining six provide a local community service. Thus the concept is maintained very strictly, allowing for optimal levels of cognitive distance between the different companies.

There does not seem to be a lack of demand for office space at the Digital Hub, indicating that the area has potential. Although occupancy rates of buildings in the Digital Hub are unavailable, DHDA representatives state that the Digital Hub needs more space on a structural basis. As real-estate development is delayed,

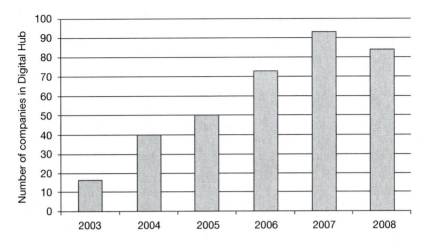

Figure 6.2 Number of companies present in Digital Hub between 2003 and 2008

Source: DHDA annual reports 2003–7; list of companies 2008

Digital Hub is investing in temporary space in the surrounding area (DHDA 2007a), implying substantial demand for office space in the Digital Hub.

Gross rent levels at the Digital Hub are comparable to those in other areas in the city, but the Digital Hub is located in one of the most deprived areas in the city (where real-estate prices are generally lower), companies locating there clearly see a benefit, as they are willing to pay normal prices for a run-down area. Moreover, real-estate prices in the rest of the city are dropping, while the Digital Hub is maintaining its price level. The fact that this does not lead to companies leaving the Digital Hub suggests that the effect mentioned above is robust. Thus, companies seem to be willing to pay a premium rent to locate in the Digital Hub. This may be explained by the number of services included. According to companies in the Digital Hub, the overall package offered by the Digital Hub is not expensive. Rents not only include the use of buildings but also an internet connection, 24-hour access and a secure facility.[6]

Based on interviews, various factors explain the success of the DHDA in creating a digital media cluster. As stated above, rent levels in the Digital Hub are competitive if the entire package of services is included. As such, price is an important attraction factor for many companies. However, some are critical about the infrastructure provided at the Digital Hub. They state: 'Digital Hub should be competitive on the entire package'.[7] At present some companies in the Digital Hub do not consider the quality of the package to be much better than that in most other places. They state that if the Digital Hub wishes to radiate an image of a location on the forefront of digital media enterprise it should offer a standard above and beyond average levels of service. Standard broadband speeds at the Digital Hub are quite low (below 5Mbps), which is lower than speeds which can be obtained in residential property. Additional bandwidth can be purchased at a surcharge, but this is not the point being stressed. According to Digital Hub companies, a cluster on the forefront of digital media should also take the lead from a technological perspective. Additionally, price is an issue. However, as stated before, the DHDA has relatively little influence here as it depends on offers from commercial parties.

The DHDA can be considered successful in distinguishing the Digital Hub as an incubation space where knowledge is shared and spill-over effects occur. The DHDA actively manages the mix of companies, increasing the potential for fruitful interaction. The DHDA offers different types of locations at different prices to accommodate the different types of organizations. Additionally, tailor-made solutions are provided to house larger digital media companies. Amazon and France Telecom are, for instance, located in individual buildings in the Digital Hub. Start-ups and spin-outs are offered space in the Digital Depot, an incubator space where flexible space and services are offered. Some companies have already been able to grow in such a way that they were able to move from the incubation space, the Digital Depot, to other locations in the Digital Hub (DHDA 2006). Collaboration is important in this respect. The ability to share experiences and general business know-how prove very valuable to some entrepreneurs.

Digital Hub and Dublin City Council aim to make Dublin and the Digital Hub more attractive for companies by offering various forms of business support. There is a wide array of support organizations: an inventory of the agencies and organizations that offer some type of business support to Irish companies resulted in a list of 23 separate, but related actors (Pinkowski 2009). These actors range from city and state agencies to business networks. Companies indicate that it is difficult for them to find the right type of support in an efficient way. The frag-mented nature of business support systems negatively affects the perception companies have of the Digital Hub and Dublin in general.

The Digital Hub is to become a *flagship brand* of the digital media industry in Ireland, but it is unclear whether this is the case in practice. Companies located in the Digital Hub feel they are in the right place, which is another attraction factor of the Digital Hub. The sense of 'being in the right place' is not, however, a hard factor which can be measured. Some interviewees suggest that this distinct iden-tity can be important to potential clients as well as to employees. Also, they note that the digital media sector is too small to support multiple locations in Ireland. The Digital Hub is at present the only digital media location that can credibly compete internationally.

The Digital Hub is envisaged as a catalyst for development of a vibrant city cluster, with high-quality amenities. As the current economic downturn has hit Dublin hard, and for most quite suddenly, the Digital Hub's prospects for the future remain uncertain. As identified by the Digital Hub Development Agency (DHDA 2007a; DHDA 2007b) the success of attracting digital media compa-nies needs to be followed up by the next phase of development, which includes the commercial redevelopment of the surrounding area. While actual real-estate development should already have started, it has not, for a number of reasons. First, the current economic downturn makes it very difficult for the private devel-opers to fulfil their obligations. Second, planning permission has not been granted for the plans proposed by the developers. These two reasons are related: because of the financial crisis, developers require a higher return, forcing them to build higher, which from a planning perspective is undesirable. According to representatives from the private and public sector and the DHDA, the above will require action from the public side (possibly on a national level) to ensure a continuation of the process. In the meantime the location of the Digital Hub in the Liberties is not considered as positive by all companies; some complaints voice insecurity (especially at night and for female workers) and a lack of amenities.

To ensure community involvement in the Digital Hub, the DHDA chose to set up a Community–Public–Private Partnership (CPPP). The CPPP was set up in 2003 to ensure a proper consultation with community, public and private stakeholders (DHDA 2003).

As part of its societal remit, education in digital media is an essential part of the work of the DHDA. In principle, the DHDA aims to fulfil this goal by creating more accessible pathways to learning. Children from kindergarten and upwards are put in contact with digital media to inspire them to learn and stay in school. Digital Hub co-operates with sixteen schools to bring new ideas into the classroom. Its learning programme seems to show some promising results. Children in the south-west inner city of Dublin are among the most proficient in Ireland in the application of digital media technology (DHDA 2006). However, skilled graduates are still hard to get: 55 per cent of companies in the Digital Hub experience problems attracting staff (DHDA 2007c).

The question of whether the Digital Hub will start to function as a new anchor in the city will have to be answered in time. For now, the potential for the Digital Hub to fulfil this function can be identified.

Interaction and networks

Inter-firm interaction in the Digital Hub is considered a key attraction factor; this shows both in the promotional material of the DHDA (for example, DHDA 2007a; DHDA 2007b) and in interviews with companies located in the Digital Hub.

Traditionally Irish firms are not known for their collaborative behaviour, according to various interview partners. However, one of the key selling points for the Digital Hub project is the potential for collaboration.

Although most companies value the possibility of positive collaboration, actual levels of collaboration between companies in the Digital Hub differ. Some co-operate on product development while others collaborate only on a very general level; 80 per cent of companies, however, state that they co-operate with other companies in one form or another (DHDA 2007c). Companies in the Digital Hub were last surveyed in 2008; this survey showed companies primarily collaborate on an *ad hoc* basis. They mainly exchange information, not only on digital media innovations, but also on general business matters, especially among the smaller entrepreneurs (see Figure 6.3.). Extensive collaboration in joint ventures and strategic partnerships (10 per cent) and collaboration on research and development (4 per cent) are still very limited. Interestingly, companies expected to co-operate more in 2008 (DHDA 2007c).

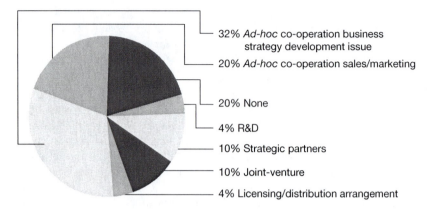

32% *Ad-hoc* co-operation business strategy development issue

20% *Ad-hoc* co-operation sales/marketing

20% None

4% R&D

10% Strategic partners

10% Joint-venture

4% Licensing/distribution arrangement

Figure 6.3 Level of collaboration with other Hub companies in 2007

Source: DHDA 2007c

At the Digital Hub, no management regime exists to manage innovation between companies. The National Digital Research Centre (NDRC) was established to stimulate collaborative research on a national basis between companies and academic researchers, in the digital and digital media technology spaces. The NDRC aims to connect different actors working on mutually beneficial innovation. NDRC projects typically involve at least one company and a research institute. If multiple companies in the Digital Hub work together and can involve a research institute, they are eligible for NDRC support (see also the next sub-section on external interaction). At present the NDRC is, however, not specifically tasked with stimulating and managing collaboration between the Digital Hub companies.

Shared space in the Digital Hub is limited. Companies mention that catering facilities are lacking in quantity as well as quality. Two on-site restaurants are available, but several tenants consider them insufficient in quality to receive customers. While company employees may meet each other in these facilities, the nature and scope of these meetings, as well as their results, are unclear. Some companies state that they do benefit from interaction between their employees and those of the other companies in the Digital Hub. Collaboration occurs not only through face-to-face interaction in the Digital Hub, but also through virtual contact online. There are some indications that geographic proximity offline may lead to virtual connections online. At the Digital Hub an intranet exists where news is shared. Furthermore, the Digital Hub sends out a newsletter. Much of the interaction at the Digital Hub may take place outside geographic space through virtual connections. Many of the companies at the Digital Hub are very open to the Web 2.0 concept. Web 2.0 can play an important role in the development of the Digital Hub and interaction among companies located there. Recently Microsoft held a large conference on the future of digital media, which was held entirely on Twitter. Additionally, groups on various online business networks such as

LinkedIn.com exist, where leads can be shared and referrals can be made. These developments represent a change in the way business is conducted. This shows the first real emergence of Web 2.0 in Dublin.

Integration in the city

The entire south-west central area of Dublin is characterized by a large percentage of social housing. According to a wellbeing survey commissioned by DCC (2008b) some of the areas in the Liberties comprise in excess of 80 per cent of local authority rented accommodation (social housing). Only one-third of the families in the Liberties own their property; compared to a national average of over three-quarters this is very low. This environment does not match with the high-end activities conducted at the Digital Hub. There is an ambition to integrate the Digital Hub further with its urban environment in a number of ways, namely socially, economically, physically and historically. While much of this integration is not realized yet, some preliminary results are promising.

Social integration of the local community is ensured by involving them in the development of the Digital Hub under the Community–Public–Private Partnership (CPPP) programme (see section 'The Digital Hub: the concept'). Furthermore, the development plan for Digital Hub is an important, integrated part of the Local Area Plan for the Liberties area (see section 'The Digital Hub: the concept') which has been displayed at the Digital Exchange (one of the buildings of the Digital Hub).

Economic integration is mainly ensured through a programme called the Diageo Liberties Learning Initiative (DLLI). The DHDA aims to play an important role in digital learning in the Liberties area, which should ensure economic spill-over effects from the Digital Hub to the surrounding area. This educational remit is delivered with a substantial sponsorship from Diageo, the current owner of the Guinness breweries. The expected benefits of this programme are twofold. On the one hand this programme enables the local community to develop the skills needed to 'survive' in the digital age, on the other hand it creates (albeit slowly) a skilled labour pool for digital media companies in the Digital Hub to source from. The DLLI consists of a communities programme, a schools programme, enterprise learning programme and a showcasing programme (DHDA 2005).

Physical integration of the Digital Hub and its environment is ensured through simultaneous real-estate development for the Digital Hub and the surrounding area. Private developers acquire the right to develop part of the area (as said, they have to provide office space in the Digital Hub and a cash sum in return, which can be used to support other aims of the development). This approach makes optimal use of the market knowledge of private parties. However, it may lead to gentrification effects, as private developers may be forced (by budget constraints) to aim at a higher market segment and attract only wealthy people to the area.

Critics mention that the redevelopment agenda of the Digital Hub may complicate matters (Bayliss 2007). Only the buildings owned by the DHDA will be managed, and therefore only tenants in these buildings will go through a selection process. Buildings that are developed commercially by the private developers will be rented out to all types of companies. In principle this may lead to a physical dilution of the Digital Hub's concept, as companies from all sectors locate very close to small clusters of digital media companies. Others stress that the primary goal of the project is to create a new city quarter, and see the digital media section as a catalyst for that.

The integration of the Digital Hub with Dublin's knowledge infrastructure leaves much to be desired. At the time of the last enterprise survey in 2007, collaboration with tertiary educational institutions (universities) was still very low at 18 per cent, although more companies recognize the potential for co-operation (DHDA 2007c).

As mentioned earlier, the NDRC, or National Digital Research Centre, aims to create value from applied digital technology research, by bridging the gap between innovative research and actual applications which can be sold in the marketplace. The establishment of the NDRC followed the closure of Media Lab Europe (MLE), the European branch of MIT's Media Lab. The NDRC is the result of a competitive tender issued by the Department of Communications, Energy and Natural Resources of the Irish Government, which was won by a consortium of Dublin City University (DCU), Trinity College Dublin (TCD), University College Dublin (UCD), Dun Laoghaire Institute of Art, Design and Technology (IADT) and the National College of Art and Design (NCAD).[8] The NDRC aims to put three actors into contact with each other to develop joint projects: academic institutions, private companies (digital media companies) and financiers (venture capitalists, bankers). In 2008 the NDRC was appointed a budget of €25 million to fund research projects over the next five years (DCENR 2008); however, at present the funds are greater than the opportunities to be funded, requiring the NDRC to refund part of the grant.

The question of whether the NDRC has been able to fulfil its mission as anchor tenant at the Digital Hub is controversial. While some stakeholders believe the NDRC is trying to perform well, they perceive actual results up to now as limited. the NDRC, on the other hand, states that it exceeded its agreed targets for 2008, and by April 2009, the NDRC had completed agreements with fourteen collaborative research projects involving sixteen different partners, representing an investment of close to €10 million. At that time (2009) just short of 100 research personnel are collaborating on NDRC research projects. Due to the innovative nature of the NDRC, a significant exercise of process development and expectation alignment between stakeholders was pursued before project engagements took off, which led to a somewhat slow start. Some of the initial supporters of the NDRC are now criticizing its functioning (though partly this may be due to conflicting business interests). Many stakeholders expected that much of their own research would be funded through the NDRC, which has not been the case.

While the NDRC's progress may not be characterized as perfect, it would be unfair to label it as unsuccessful. However, the NDRC's exposure among Digital Hub companies is limited. The NDRC potentially fits the model of the triple-helix approach, where (semi-)government, companies and educational institutions work together to reinforce innovative capacity in the region. However, there are clear misconceptions about the NDRC's mission, its programme and capabilities.

Conclusions and recommendations

The Digital Hub has come a long way in its development. The ambitions are twofold: the DHDA and the city of Dublin not only aim to realize a vibrant and world-class digital media-based cluster in the inner city of Dublin, but also to regenerate the deprived urban surroundings of the Hub. So far, the DHDA has been successful in attracting digital media companies to the area. Although some major setbacks had to be overcome, such as the closure of MLE, at present the Digital Hub can be considered successful in creating a digital media cluster in the former premises of the Guinness brewery. But will it become more than that? Unfortunately, the heavy economic downturn since 2007 complicates the start of a planned large-scale urban redevelopment scheme, which is part of the Digital Hub project. At present the public–private partnership between the two private developers and the DHDA is under considerable strain. The project was set up as an innovative public–private partnership, but, with falling real-estate prices and project financing which becomes difficult, the development is stalled. The current PPP agreement between the DHDA and the two project developers will have to undergo dramatic changes or a considerable risk exists that the PPP cannot be continued.

Perhaps ambitions for the area have been set too high, and perhaps, as some say, the Digital Hub's redevelopment agenda complicates its mission. However, it can also be argued that the city of Dublin (directly and through the DHDA) take their public responsibility seriously but are confronted with a case of bad luck where an economic downturn coincides with a critical turning point in the development project.

It is unclear what the current economic downturn will mean for the concept of the Digital Hub. At present the concept is quite strict, restricting the type of companies that can settle in the buildings of the Digital Hub. It remains unsure whether such a strong focus can be maintained. A relaxation of requirements for prospective companies may offer some relief, but it may undermine one of the strong points (also according to the tenants) of the Digital Hub: its well-defined and focused concept. Alternatively, there may be some room to lift planning restrictions for the area to enable alternative, commercially more attractive use of the other spaces, leading to an even more substantial cross-financing of the project. This may enable private actors to come up with creative solutions. Of course an obvious option would be a government-initiated development of the area, involving substantial contributions by local and national government. This, however, is more complicated than it seems because of EU regulations for state support and the already substantial budget deficit of the Irish government.

The Digital Hub, although already a successful cluster of digital media activity, has some weaknesses and faces some challenges. First, the infrastructure is not up to standard. Broadband speeds are too low; nearly all interview partners recognized that the speed of the standard package was not much better, or even worse, than elsewhere. Although maybe not strictly necessary from a technical point of view at present, the available standard broadband speed also determines the image of the Digital Hub. Companies at the Digital Hub require a technical standard that is above and beyond what is offered elsewhere, simply because they are located in the Digital Hub. State-aid regulation is a complicating factor and the influence of the DHDA on Telcos is limited. Thus, the DHDA can only play a stimulating and facilitating role. The issue is a city-wide, or perhaps even nationwide, problem where national government may play a role. There is a need to future proof the broadband offer in the Digital Hub to remain competitive as new technologies and usage patterns emerge. City-government can take the lead here to mobilize national resources.

A second challenge is to reduce the skills shortage. The shortage of digital media graduates in Ireland (and Dublin in particular) proves a long-term risk for the success of the digital media sector in Dublin, and thus also for the Digital Hub project. Many companies at the Digital Hub complain that they are not able to attract a sufficient number of new employees with enough work experience during times of economic success. At the same time, however, very few companies hire recent graduates, and therefore these graduates do not gain any work experience. Clearly this creates a circular issue, which needs to be broken to benefit graduates as well as companies. A sufficiently large internship grant may cover the costs of employers when they hire an intern. This will benefit the company, which gains productive capacity, and also the graduate, who gains work experience. Such a grant can, for example, be an extension of the Dublin City Enterprise Board's employment grant. In general, increasing the number of internships would require more formal links in the form of strategic partnerships with universities where internships are included as a supplement to or integral part of current (master's) degrees. A more formal co-operation with the national training provider may be even more effective, but this is only possible in the long term as it takes significant time to set up a new programme.

Third, the co-operation between tertiary institutions and companies at the Digital Hub is weak. The NDRC has succeeded in stimulating the process of knowledge exchange between companies and university researchers through its activities to date, but further endeavours in this area are certainly necessary. While the NDRC approximates the idea of a triple-helix approach, the Digital Hub is by its nature (linking economic development with regeneration) especially suited for a quadruple-helix approach. By involving the public and linking up residential property in the surrounding area to the fibre-optics network that has been established, residents can be involved in testing new digital media products. However, additional investments at national level may be needed to secure digital accessibility in the surrounding Liberties area. Wireless broadband technology may provide a solution here.

Fourth, the Digital Hub makes extensive use of marketing and branding techniques, ensuring its visibility both nationally as well as for international companies locating in Dublin. There is, however, one important shortcoming in the marketing efforts for Digital Hub. Due to Ireland's regional 'balancing' strategy, organizations like the Industrial Development Agency do not specifically promote Dublin, or the Digital Hub. From a marketing perspective, it is inefficient not to promote a star product.

Finally, it should be stressed that at present many of the goals of the DHDA will not be reached until the real-estate developments take off. The current economic downturn will not allow private developers to start developments on their own and maintain a desired spatial quality at the same time. Clearly this requires an increased role for government, be it local or national. If this does not occur the Digital Hub may be able to maintain its current success, but it will not be likely that more ambitious goals, such as a regeneration of the Liberties and Coombe areas, will be reached.

7 Eindhoven: Strijp-S

Introduction

Eindhoven, the 'city of light', has transformed quickly from an industrial city towards being one of the leading high-tech hubs of Europe. A key role in the development of the city has been played by the leader firm Philips that was, and still is, a major employer of the region which invested in housing and other social and cultural facilities. However, the mutual dependency of the city and the electronic giant has declined strongly, as the company reduced the importance of its birthplace in its global network (it transferred its headquarters from Eindhoven to Amsterdam), while the city has diversified its economic structure with high-tech systems and materials, food, automotive, 'lifetec' and design as key sectors. Many former Philips buildings and places have become available for other functions, like the Witte Dame – a former production plant which nowadays houses the Design Academy, the public library, Philips Design, a bar, shops and other functions – and the Admirant (the former headquarters, which is now available for commercial functions).

More recently, and on a much larger scale, has been the redevelopment of the Strijp-S complex. This 27-hectare area was labelled the 'Forbidden City' because it was a closed Philips community with key facilities, including the NatLab, the physics laboratory where major inventions were done. As Philips has restructured its assets and will move out of Strijp-S, the site has become available for other functions. The city, in co-operation with a private developer, wants to transform the area into a multifunctional area labelled as 'Creative City'. The plan is to make Strijp-S 'the best practice of an historical important industrial complex into a dynamic post-industrial city district, in which culture and technology play a key role' (KuiperCompagnons, 2007, p. 85). The idea is to create an urban sub-centre which combines living, working, cultural and recreational facilities. Moreover, there are plans to use the area as testbed for new light technologies and during the transformation process an innovative new technology has been used to clean the soil. The transformation process is complex, partly because of the size of the area, the overlap between old and new users, strict (and sometimes conflicting) regulations and involvement of various stakeholders with their own interests. In this complex redevelopment process, cultural events and SMEs that temporarily rent office space have been used to promote the area, increase vibrancy and stimulate business.

This chapter analyses the redevelopment process of Strijp-S in more detail. More specifically, we shed light on the following questions, which are also relevant in the general study:

- How has Strijp-S been managed?
- What are the drivers and barriers in the redevelopment process?
- To what extent is Strijp-S integrated in the region?

The remainder of this chapter is structured as follows. The next section introduces Strijp-S in more detail by describing its urban-economic and historical context. We also analyse the concept and the management of the area, as well as strategies to promote the area and to connect it with other areas in the region. The following section analyses the following functions of the former Philips site: as a cultural site; as a business and R&D location; and as a testbed for innovation. Specific themes in this chapter include the role of events and other cultural initiatives; the role of pioneers – SMEs that rent temporary business space with the aim to increase vibrancy – the position of Strijp-S in knowledge networks and as a testbed for new lighting projects and the synergy project (that deals with a new soil-cleaning technique). The last section concludes and provides policy recommendations that may help to redevelop Strijp-S further.

Strijp-S: context, history, planning and management

Locations, planned or unplanned, cannot be seen as separate islands and should be analysed in their regional, economic and historical contexts. Therefore, in this section we briefly describe the urban-economic context of the Eindhoven region and the history of Strijp-S. The section also describes the plan and the management of the area and the tools to promote the area and to connect it with other parts of the city.

Urban-economic context

Since the 1990s, Eindhoven has transformed from an industrial town to a leading technological hub with a strong interaction between the knowledge infrastructure and high-tech production. Or as expressed by Lagendijk and Boekema (2008, p. 925), 'it has become a "cradle of innovation" with a key position in the wider "knowledge-based" economy.' The concept of open innovation (Chesborough 2003) was put into practice at an early stage after Philips initiated the High Tech Campus Eindhoven (HTC/e) in 1999 and invited other companies to open research centres at the campus. Other important locations in the region's knowledge infrastructure include the campus of Technical University Eindhoven (TU/e), the automotive campus in Helmond, the Dutch Polymer Institute (DPI), the Intelligent Lighting Institute (ILI) and the Embedded Systems Institute (ESI) (see Figure 7.1). In later sections, we will analyse how and to what extent Strijp-S can complement these other knowledge nodes in Eindhoven's knowledge network.

Eindhoven scores high on several knowledge indicators,[1] and there is strong co-operation between TU/e and the regional industry. In a study dealing with research co-operation between universities and firms among 350 universities worldwide, TU/e has the strongest co-operation with the industry: 10.5 per cent of its scientific publications are based on industrial co-operation (Tijssen *et al.* 2009, cited in Maldonado and Romein 2009). The success also becomes clear from the fact that the city has been named the best Micro European City of the Future 2010/11. It ranks first in this league, before cities such as Cambridge and Grenoble (FDI 2010).

Various studies provide explanations for Eindhoven's success story: (i) strong triple-helix co-operation with short and informal lines between the actors; (ii) a clear vision and strategy by the regional development organization Brainport;[2] (iii) key strategies of policymakers on regional as well as higher spatial scales; (iv) presence of several large industrial firms,[3] and a strategic position in firms' global production networks; (v) facilities to support incubators; (vi) a strong (technological) knowledge infrastructure that is well connected with the industry (van Winden *et al.* 2007, 2010; Lagendijk and Boekema 2008; Maldonado and Romein 2009).

Despite its relatively peripheral location in the Netherlands, accessibility has improved considerably during recent years. The ring road system has been upgraded and congestion is expected to reduce. The regional airport has grown rapidly from 288,055 passengers in 1998 to 1.7 million in 2009 (Eindhoven Airport 2009). More growth can be expected as a study has advised the national state to increase the number of flights to and from the airport with a maximum of 25,000 in 2020 (Brainport 2010).

In spite of the success, there are also some points of attention which may hinder healthy economic development. One is sensitivity towards international dynamics and economic cycles (Lagendijk and Boekema 2008; van Winden *et al.* 2010). Another one is that design is still strongly focused on technology, while service design – design as a tool to improve the living conditions of consumers and citizens – is limited, despite strong ambitions of policymakers (Van der Borg and van Tuijl 2010). Finally, due to its small scale, Eindhoven lacks a real urban surrounding which is supposed to be crucial to attracting certain knowledge workers and artists (van Winden *et al.* 2007). The city is aware of the latter, and therefore it has targeted Strijp-S as an urban sub-centre. As it is explicitly put forward in the spatial plan of the area:

> The area Strijp-S has been considered as the location in which Eindhoven can fulfil its needs to create its missing metropolitan environment. Therefore, it is a key element in the Brainport strategy to make the city attractive for international oriented knowledge workers and artists. Strijp-S has to create the living, work and stay conditions to tie this target group to Eindhoven.
>
> (KuiperCompagnons, 2008, p. 25)

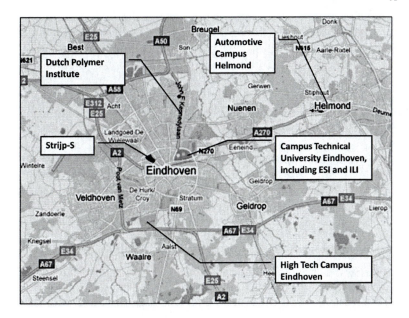

Figure 7.1 Key locations in Eindhoven's knowledge base

Source: own elaboration; map from www.map.google.com

History of the 'forbidden city'

Strijp-S is one of the largest redevelopment projects in the Netherlands. Before discussing the concept and vision in detail, it is worth understanding the history of the area. Strijp-S was developed by Philips in the early twentieth century as it needed extra space for its fast growth. Strijp-S was part of the Philips Strijp complex which used to be on a large industrial area, comprising also the 'T' and 'R' sites. Strijp-S was considered as an industrial city of Philips with its own complete infrastructure. At its peak it provided work for 15,000 to 20,000 workers. It was known as the 'forbidden city' because of the strict accessibility policy in place to protect technological development and inventions. Many inventions came from the famous NatLab, the physics laboratory that was opened in 1914. To stimulate innovation, NatLab combined technology with creativity and it worked with artists, including Le Corbusier. Another best practice might be the famous employee Dick Raaijmakers, who made music under the artist name 'Kid BalTan' (BalTan is NatLab in reverse). BalTan was an engineer and an artist and he produced the first electronic disk. The lab was visited by Einstein and in 1927 the Dutch Queen Wilhelmina spoke to the Dutch in Indonesia via an experimental radio connection of Philips.

A turning point occurred in the early 1990s, when Philips lost ground to new competitors from Asia as well as traditional competitors from the West. This forced Philips to start a large-scale restructuring programme in which it cut costs and returned to its core business. Many production units were either closed or relocated to low-cost countries (van den Berg *et al*. 1997). Within the Eindhoven region, the company has focused on a few strategic locations such as the HTC/e, Philips Business Park Eindhoven (Vredenoord), and Philips Lighting in the city centre, while other locations have been closed. Strijp-S is a part of the Philips network which will be closed. Therefore, in 2002 the company, the city and real-estate company Volker Wessels signed a contract that transferred the site to the city. The city invested €140m in the site, of which €20m has been reserved to clean the soil and to reconstruct the buildings. Philips leaves the site in stages (as many activities have been transferred to the HTC/e), with the final stage in 2012 (City of Eindhoven 2002a; Harms 2007). The city and Volker Wessels can use the site to transform the 'forbidden city' into the Creative City.

The plan and management

Large-scale urban redevelopment projects require a clear vision, strategy, political and societal support as well as strategic partnerships between public and private actors (van den Berg *et al*. 1997). For the development of Strijp-S a clear vision has been set up. The idea is to make Strijp-S 'the best practice of an historical important industrial complex into a dynamic post-industrial city district, in which culture and technology play a key role' (KuiperCompagnons 2007, p. 85). The idea is to create a multi-functional urban sub-centre which combines living, working, cultural and recreational facilities (see Table 7.1). These urban surroundings should attract international knowledge workers and artists to the city. The plan gives room for flexibility as there is the possibility to shift the ground space between functions as long as it fits the regulations. The site will be developed in four development stages as depicted in Table 7.2 and Figure 7.2. The site comprises a mixture of new buildings and monuments that will be adapted for other functions (see Table 7.3).

The concept is to keep the historical identity of the area. As put forward in the interviews:

Table 7.1 Goals for Strijp-S

	Minimum (in m²)	Maximum (in m²)	Planned (in m²)
Housing	220,000	350,000	284,500
Offices	62,000	122,000	91,500
Commercial	10,000	40,000	20,800
Cultural facilities	10,000	40,000	10,000
Optional	0	60,000	31,500
Total			438,300

Source: own elaboration, data from KuiperCompagnons (2007)

Table 7.2 Development stages of Strijp-S

Stage	Planning	Current status
1	2006–2010	Housing construction started in July 2010 Reconstruction NatLab in progress
2	2008–2010/2013	N/A
3	2011–2015	N/A
4	2014–2020	N/A

Source: own elaboration

> We want to keep the historical DNA of the area. Philips did major inventions in the area and Einstein was a visitor of the NatLab. ... This DNA is covered in the buildings, but also in the inhabitants of Eindhoven as many inhabitants worked at Strijp-S.

Therefore, the master plan includes three central themes – technology, design and culture (including urban sports) – of which especially the first aims to give the area its historical identity. Moreover, many buildings are monuments that allow only slight adaptations, which contributes to the historical identity as well. Note that there are doubts about the extent that this is possible, as natural decay and also the decay of memories generate an architectural conflict (Curilli 2007). In addition, the three chosen themes are not exactly defined as we observed differences among interview partners. One spoke about 'technology, design and sport', a second about 'technology, design and culture' and a third about 'technology, design and innovation'.

For the development of Strijp-S a special management company, Park Strijp Beheer ('Park Strijp Management') was set up in 2002, with the municipality of Eindhoven and the real-estate company Volker Wessels as the two shareholders. The City of Eindhoven selected Volker Wessels as partner via a tender. A master plan for the area was developed in 2001 by Riek Bakker and her architecture firm BVR, while Adriaan Geuze and his architecture firm West 8 devised the development plan of the area in 2002. Implementation of the plan has been by Park Strijp Management and two housing corporations – Trudo and Woonbedrijf – which act as subcontractors for Volker Wessels. Volker Wessels subcontracted its task in order to reduce risk. This was perceived positively by Park Strijp Beheer, as housing corporations are in general more focused on the long run than commercial real-estate companies (Harms 2007). Moreover, the housing corporations have a better knowledge and understanding of the regional context as they are regionally oriented, in contrast to Volker Wessels which acts mainly at a national level. Woonbedrijf and Trudo differ, as the first focuses mainly on the housing function (its 'traditional' function), while the other is more innovative and is interested in commercial and cultural functions. The key actors meet each other regularly (every six to eight weeks) to discuss what everybody is doing and to make

Table 7.3 Buildings in Strijp-S

Building (year of opening)	Development stage	Past function	Current status	Future function
Portiersloge (na)	N/A	Gatekeeper's office	Information centre (opened in June 2010)	N/A
Klokgebouw (1928)	3	Philite[1] plant	Office space of mainly the creative sector Completely rented out (about 100 tenants) Event space Cultural facilities	Mixed use
Machinekamer (1929)	2	Steam energy plant	Closed	Mixed use, with focus on catering facilities
Ketelhuis (1929)	2	Electricity plant	N/A	Special functions like bars and restaurants
Veemgebouw (1942)	2	Logistics for radio plant	N/A	Commercial functions: 'fresh market', design hotel, restaurants, shops
SWA/ Glasgebouw (1948)	4	Light bulb plant	Temporary rent for SMEs Nearly 70 tenants Top floor rented out to five cultural organizations	Office space
SFJ (na)	4	Machinery plant	Let to to companies involved in technology, design or innovation	To be demolished
NatLab (1922)	1	Physics laboratory	Reconstruction started	Work and living space for companies in the field of design Design incubator centre Art institute Catering services
Hoge Rug consists of SAN, SBP and SK buildings (1927)	2	Radio plant	Temporary office space Design Store (shows products of local artists and organizes meetings) 5 Minutes Museum Ontdekfabriek (museum for kids to get in touch with technology and innovation)	Various functions: housing, offices, commercial space and cultural facilities
SEU (N/A)	N/A	N/A	Skate hall The Building (stage for hiphop and street culture)	To be demolished
SBX (N/A)	N/A	N/A	Broet (movie platform: cinema, work space and supporting facilities for starting film makers Monck Buldergym (climbing facilities)	To be demolished

Source: own elaboration

Note
[1] Philite is the Philips brand name of the first type of synthetic plastic that was developed by the Belgian engineer Leo Baekeland. He introduced the product under the protected trade name Bakelite. The product was used in several electronic products

concrete action points. West 8 (Adriaan Geuze) is the supervisor of the area and safeguards the quality and announces major messages to the public.

The redevelopment process of Strijp-S is complex for a number of reasons. First, there are many strict and sometimes conflicting regulations. One example is the monument status of many buildings, which allows only limited physical adaptation to buildings. This hinders transformation of the buildings for other functions, which requires other facilities such as windows, lighting and heating systems. Another example is the area directly next to the train track. Due to safety regulations this space is not suited as a location for houses or apartments due to the risk of accidents with trains that transport dangerous goods. Many functions are in a grey area and there is debate about whether or not functions are allowed. Recently, there was discussion whether a school was allowed next to the track. Furthermore, buildings need to have a good accessibility for fire appliances. The strict safety and heritage regulations lead to additional costs; they increase complexity and may delay the development process.

Second, as in many development projects, there are many actors involved who have different interests which do not always marry. This leads to additional discussion and adaptations of plans. For instance, the development plan has a higher building density than the master plan as this was a major wish of Volker Wessels. Also new in the development plan is a large boulevard, the Torenallee. This boulevard – inspired by those in large cities, like the Champs-Elysées in Paris – is added to the plan to give the area a more urban character. There are also differences between the development plan and detailed plans. For example, the Driehoek area was adapted in such a way that original pipelines have been conserved and a number of separate building blocks have been selected at the cost of a closed living community. The difference in interests has also led to conflicts between the actors. For instance, the City of Eindhoven and Volker Wessels did not agree about the pricing method, as the city wanted fixed prices, while the real-estate company opted for flexible prices. As a consequence of this conflict, the board of Park Beheer changed in 2006.[4] Another example is the status of the NatLab. Originally, the City and Volker Wessels wanted to tear it down, but after protests from inhabitants and the municipal monument commission stressing the large symbolic value of the lab, it was decided to reconstruct it and to use it for other functions (Harms 2007). Finally, in our interviews it was argued that Volker Wessels has too much power in relation to that of the City of Eindhoven and the two housing agencies. It was mentioned that various contracts are too strict, leading to financial problems for the city and the housing agencies, while the financial risk for Volker Wessels is only limited.

A third complexity is the size of the area and the long time period of redevelopment. There is overlap between past, present and future functions. For instance, Philips leaves the area in stages. As it was expressed by the project manager in an earlier interview:

> Philips still has business here, so we need to make good arrangements about when they leave. Only when that has happened, we can redevelop the site. …
> After that, we can really start with the construction work. This is needed. Up

to now, we have hardly concretely shown to the city what we mean with the transformation of Strijp-S.

(Harms 2007, p. 43)

In 2010 Philips is still the largest tenant of the area as it waits to leave when it has more financial resources. It is also unknown to what extent contemporary functions (such as events) match with future functions (such as housing). In addition, in the long development process there are many external factors that cannot be controlled. In this sense, the process is seriously hit by the financial crisis and many investors have limited resources and postpone investment decisions. In order to control for such dynamics, flexibility in the planning has been used. For instance, the redevelopment of the Driehoek area started earlier than planned, while other parts start later. Another example is that the focus in housing is now on rental properties and the promotion of houses for sale will be done at a later stage. Another tool used to fight the crisis is the use of temporary tenants in the buildings. Many buildings are rented out completely and generate some income for the owners. Despite this flexibility, the process is delayed. For instance, the first stage of housing construction, planned to start in 2006 and to finish in 2010, only started in June 2010. These first houses are expected to be finished in 2012. The total plan was scheduled to be ready in 2020. This deadline has been postponed to 2024.

A fourth, and related, complexity is the integration of the area with other areas in the region. On the one hand, the area is part of the vision for the key project[5] Westcorridor. This key project concerns a large spatial development strategy for the area between the airport and the Central Station Eindhoven. This area consists of various 'hotspots' each with its own identity and function. The idea is to distinguish Strijp-S from other areas via the three core themes. Moreover, regarding the leisure function, the ambition for Strijp-S is to create an urban surrounding, with bars and restaurants, that adds extra value to the city centre. In addition, for the total Strijp complex, the three individual parts are planned to have their own functions: Strijp-S will be a multi-functional urban area, Strijp-R will be transformed to a housing area, while Strijp-T remains an industrial zone (see Figure 7.2) (KuiperCompagnons 2007). On the other hand, due to the long time period and differences in ownership of individual locations, there is overlap in function and competition between different locations. As expressed in an interview: 'Despite that the plan of Strijp-S fit with the plan for the redevelopment of the stadium quarter, I am happy this plan is delayed … This is at the favour of Strijp-S.' A major concern in this respect is an oversupply of office space in the Eindhoven region. Despite flexibility in the plan of Strijp-S, a part of the area is only suited as office space due to safety and other regulations.

In spite of the management structure (a public–private partnership), and short lines between the key actors, and due to the complexity of the redevelopment process, interviews indicate that the management can be improved. Despite its equal position in Park Strijp Management, the role of the City seems to be less than might be expected due to financial constraints (for example, due to the crisis large cuts in the municipal budget are required) and political instability. In the interviews, it was mentioned that there is a gap between the interests of the city council and civil officials; also, civil officials and municipal workers do not always share the same ideas. In addition, decision-making by the key actors in Strijp-S takes a lot of time and implementation power is sometimes low. Moreover, despite the co-operation and regular meetings between the key actors, the actors do not always share the same vision. Especially at the points of marketing and acquisition there is room for improvement. In the interviews it was expressed that there is a lack of a joint marketing strategy and the marketing of the area is too much focused on renting out office space instead of selling a concept of a creative city. All actors agree about the need for an internal leader who can reduce discussion time and take decisions fast. The supervision of an external actor would help to control the master plan, but not to implement it, and to guide the redevelopment process. Finally, in the interviews it was expressed that communication with tenants and other stakeholders of the area can be improved, especially regarding issues such as safety, rental contracts, parking and signposting during construction works. In some cases, there are also tensions between tenants and the management. For instance, currently, there are complaints among tenants about the amount of the monthly parking fee (€50). In order to raise the voice of tenants in discussions with the management, various tenants have joined forces. It is crucial to involve these and other stakeholders in decision-making in order to obtain and keep societal support.

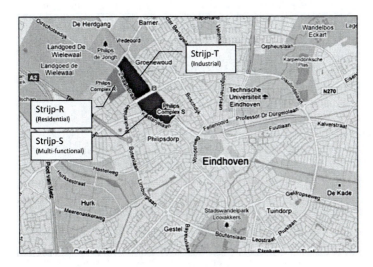

Figure 7.2 Plan for entire Strijp complex (R, S and T)

Source: own elaboration; map from www.map.google.com

Opening the 'forbidden city'

There are various strategies to develop and to promote the area. First, physical transport links are used to connect Strijp-S with other parts of the region. Therefore, it was decided to connect Strijp-S with other parts via a Phileas line (a high-grade public transport system that combines the advantages of a bus and a tram) that runs from the airport and the central station. This transport connection makes the area better accessible for visitors, tenants and their customers. In addition, as the area is on the route from the central station to suburbs and the airport, many inhabitants and visitors pass the area and can see the development. This increases the awareness of the redevelopment of the former closed city. As put forward in an interview: 'It is a sightseeing tour by accident'. Another idea to improve accessibility of the area is to upgrade the train station Beukelaan that is located next to Strijp-S. In this idea, the station will be upgraded to a major station that is linked with other major cities via inter-city trains[6] and public space between the station and Strijp-S will be improved as well. This plan is still in the concept stage. Regarding car transport, and in contrast to many other projects that aim to reduce car traffic, the area will be car-friendly and the plan contains various parking facilities. Strijp-S does not have traffic and space problems that many other (inner) cities face nowadays. Finally, in order to connect Strijp-S with the city centre, the Mathildelaan will act as a major boulevard. This road runs from the city centre via the stadium quarter to Strijp-S (City of Eindhoven 2002b). It should be noted that for the stadium quarter large redevelopment plans have also been made. Although Strijp-S and the redevelopment of the stadium quarter are both part of a larger city vision, as mentioned before, we have indications that the areas compete with each other instead of having a complementing role. This could delay the individual projects.

Another way to promote the area is via the organization of excursions, which happens in formal as well as informal ways. Formally, there are guided tours for visitors organized by the tourist office. Informally, tenants of the area and policymakers bring clients and friends to show them around the area. One illustrative example is the cultural organization BALTAN Laboratories that organized an excursion for artists who visited the European Capital of Cultural event in the Ruhr area in 2010. The NatLab organized a one-day bus tour from Essen to Eindhoven with the NatLab and Strijp-S as attractions.

In line with this, Park Strijp Management hopes to increase awareness of the area via word-of-mouth marketing, media coverage and via networks of tenants. As expressed by a policymaker: 'We want to use inhabitants as promotion tool via word of mouth marketing.' Similarly, a director of a cultural organization put forward: 'We hope to promote the area via mouth-to-mouth promotion and pictures which are taken by visitors.' Crucial are also the tenants' own initiatives. In one case, a small multimedia company created a Twitter account for Strijp-S. However, it is not clear to what extent this really contributes to the promotion of the area or whether it only functions as an internal discussion forum. Moreover, a drawback in the communication is the lack of a common website that informs current users and visitors about activities. As expressed by a tenant on the former

Philips site: 'People do not know what is going on. I live here, but I do not even know it by myself.' Various interview partners criticize current websites dealing with Strijp-S that there is too much focus on the programme and possibilities to rent office space, while information about what currently is going on in the area is lacking. Another point of attention raised in the interviews is safety. As the area is still remote from the rest of the city, the public lighting is still underdeveloped and there are no functions during the night yet, making the site an easy target for burglary. In the first seven months of 2010, the police reported seven cases of burglary in Strijp-S. Therefore, Trudo considers introducing gatekeepers in the building who also work during the night (ED 2010a, 2010b).

Other ways to develop and to promote the locations include the use of temporary tenants (so-called pioneers) and several cultural initiatives. We discuss these two tools in more detail in the next section.

Strijp-S as location for culture, business and innovation

In contrast to other mono-functional parts of the Strijp-complex, Strijp-S will be redeveloped into a multi-functional urban area. In this section we analyse the potential of various functions in more detail, with a focus on how the functions have been implemented and to what extent they fit the concept of the area. We successively investigate the role of culture and events, business, R&D and innovation functions in Strijp-S. We do not analyse the housing function as in its current development stage, there are no houses on the site.

The creative city: the role of culture and events

Inspired by key authors like Charles Landry (for example, Landry 2000), Allan Scott (for example, Scott 2000) and Florida (for example, Florida 2003), many cities invest in creativity and culture. As noted by Landry (2006, p. 1): 'Creativity is like a rash. Everybody is now in the creativity game'. Or as expressed by Waitt (2008, p. 517) 'urban festivals, along with "festival market-places", "cultural industries", "creative quarters", "creative clusters" and the "creative class" have since become buzzwords in planning- and policy-related reports.' Advantages of investments in creativity and culture include the attraction of knowledge workers (Florida 2003), development of consumer cities (Gleaser *et al.* 2001), development of tourism (for example, Judd and Fainstein 1999), revitalization of old neighbourhoods via mega-events ('the Barcelona effect') or flagship projects ('the Bilbao effect'), development of creative industries – which are often linked with other industries – and potential for knowledge spill-overs and innovation. However, there are also downsides including homogenization, or 'Disneyfication' of city centres, gentrification (for example, Zukin 1989; Evans 2003), low wages in cultural industries (Kloosterman 2010) and are there several critics of the creative class (for example, Peck 2005).

Also Strijp-S has been labelled as the 'Creative City' with the aim to attract knowledge workers. Culture, one of the central themes of the project, and creativity play key roles in the development of the area. This happens in two major ways: (i) by stimulation of several cultural initiatives and (ii) the use of SMEs of the creative industries ('pioneers').

In order to support cultural initiatives, in 2008 a special cultural fund was set up by the City of Eindhoven, Volker Wessels, Trudo, Woonbedrijf, Spoorzone BV and SRE. [7] This cultural fund has an annual budget of €600,000. A culture project leader, a seconded municipal worker, coordinates the budget. Already many cultural initiatives have been taken and there are many ideas as shown in Table 7.4. Here a number of observations can be made. First, nearly all events fit in the central themes of the area and aim to bring back the historical DNA. The latter is especially true for BALTAN laboratories, that directly aim to bring the NatLab alive in the theme and function. Another example is the music studio Room 306 that focuses on electronic music; as expressed by one of the initiative takers:

> In the nineteen fifties, for the first time in the world history, music different from acoustic was played. And that happened here, in the NatLab! Produced by Dick Raaijmakers, the man who later named Kid 'Baltan', which is an anagram of 'Natlab'. He carried out his ground-breaking work in Room 306.
> (cited in Van Gool 2010, p. 30)

However, it should be noted that the section of the NatLab which contained Room 306 has recently been demolished to make space for a new part of the building.

Second, the initiatives differ in aim and in the degree they are linked to Strijp-S. Various initiatives focus on Strijp-S and aim to promote the area (such as Flux-S), and to increase vibrancy ('construction of a consumer city'). Other initiatives are wider than Strijp-S and are targeted to stimulate innovation, create networks among different actors or to promote and strengthen business networks. Related to this is that the spatial scale of the functions differ, from local (for example, Room 306) to international. The best example of the latter is the Dutch Design Week (DDW) which attracts several international visitors. Various parts of this event are organized in co-operation with partners in Helsinki.

Third, a large number of art festivals are organized on the former Philips site. Literature has shown that events, just like other cultural initiatives, may have advantages – like attraction of investment capital, development of tourism, revitalization of old neighbourhoods, creation of jobs and skills – as well as drawbacks, like too much focus on certain target groups, and there are questions about the added value for cities (for example, Getz 2008; Waitt 2008; Paiola 2008; Gibson *et al.* 2010). Many events are organized at Strijp-S, some of which are especially organized to promote the area, such as Flux-S, and others which are attracted to the area for the characteristics of the site itself. The old buildings offer large spaces which are suited to housing large exhibitions; this is especially the case with the ground floors of the Klokgebouw and the buildings of De Hoge Rug. Festivals are also attracted to the site because of its history: 'Strijp-S was the only logical choice [for festival X]; it shows history and the future of technology' (interview). In addition, the rough style of the buildings and the unfinished character of the area give a special atmosphere which makes it attractive for the organization of art events. Besides, as there are no inhabitants at the site yet, there is less risk of complaints (for instance, about noise).

Further development may make the area less attractive for events, and there is a risk that events will disappear. As an event director said: 'Strijp-S offers roughness. There is also a possibility to party. Further development kills the unique atmosphere which makes it less attractive for our event'. There are also doubts about the success of events which differ case by case. The DDW attracted 115,000 visitors in 2009, and many of them visited the activities organized on Strijp-S. So, it is very likely that this contributed to increasing awareness of the area. For other festivals, like Flux-S, which attracted 9,000 visitors to the area in 2009, the future is uncertain for financial reasons. It should be noted that the success of events should be measured by other than only economic goals and that the success of events for urban regeneration depends on the management model used. Events can be seen as successful if a bottom-up model has been used as it fits the need for creating the event as a shared product (Paiola 2008). In the case of Strijp-S, many events are locally organized with support of private as well as public actors. The existence of the cultural fund indicates the ambition to make culture (including events) as a shared product and all key actors agree about the importance of culture for redevelopment.

Fourth, as a common characteristic of many cultural activities, many initiatives on Strijp-S depend on subsidies and sponsoring, and continuity is far from guaranteed. This is especially the case in times of economic downturn, where policymakers often cut cultural budgets and firms reduce sponsoring. As mentioned by a director of a cultural initiative: 'Cultural initiatives are always sensitive for economic cycles. We want to stay, but it depends on policy makers whether we can continue.' It was also mentioned in many interviews that there is a need for investment in a flagship facility to really give an image to the area as a cultural site. Such a facility should act as a magnet for visitors who may also visit other facilities on the site. In addition, such an investment may attract further investments. The idea of the establishment of the Instituut van Beeld en Geluid (Dutch Institute of Image and Sound) is the most realistic example of this. This institute has signed an intention agreement, but further studies are needed before the decision will be taken to open such an institute at Strijp-S. Another, more idealistic, idea is to build a landmark designed by a famous architect and to create a Bilbao effect. However, this is less realistic as there is a shortage of financial incentives for such mega-project. In addition, a landmark by a 'starchitect' is not always a guarantee for a successful revitalization.

From Philips village to Bosch and pioneers: Strijp-S as a business location

Although the explicit use of art in urban development strategies is only recent, the use of artists as agents for urban regeneration is not new (Currid 2009). Following Jacobs (1961) and Zukin (1989), many studies have shown the 'Soho effect' in which artists transform old industrial areas into vibrant bohemian centres, attracting investors which drive up real-estate prices and push out the

Table 7.4 Cultural initiatives[1]

Intitiative	Type	Function	Funding	Link with Strijp-S	Status
BALTAN	Art science lab	Research, network, educational, exhibition and promotional function	Subsidies	Strong focus to contribute to the concept of Strijp-S by linking technology with art[2] Located on Strijp-S, in SWA building; idea is to move to renewed Natlab at a later stage	In operation as a pilot (started in 2008)
STRP	Art and technology festival	Educational and promotional function Promotion of city and local business	Subsidies and sponsorships	Management office in Strijp-S Strijp-S is the location for the event Fit in themes art and technology	Organized since 2006: growth from a three-day to an eleven-day event
Dutch Design Week DDW	Design festival	Network function Tourist attraction Promotion of business and city	Subsidies and sponsoring	Strijp-S is one of the locations of this festival Fit in theme design	Organized since 2002: 115,000 visitors (2009)
Flux-S	Art festival	Promotion of Strijp-S: create awareness among general public	Subsidies from municipality and private sector	Organized to promote the location Event organized on location	Organized in 2009: 9,000 visitors
Glazen depot	Museum for contemporary art	Leisure/tourist attraction[3] Research and educational function	N/A	Plan to open at Strijp-S Fit in theme culture	Fund-raising stage: plan to start pilot in 2010
Instituut van Beeld en Geluid	Museum for broadcasting	Leisure/tourist attraction Educational function	N/A	Plan to locate on Strijp-S Fit in themes technology/history[4]	Concept stage: intention contract has been signed
Ontdekfabriek	Technology museum	Leisure; focus on children Educational function	Subsidies, sponsoring, ticket revenue	Located on Strijp-S Fit in theme technology	Opened in 2009
Vijf Minuten Museum (5MM)	Museum for modern art	Leisure	N/A	Located on Strijp-S Fit in themes art and technology	Opened in 2009

Intitiative	Type	Function	Funding	Link with Strijp-S	Status
Broet	Platform for film production	Support independent film makers: networking; cinema	Revenue from tickets and sponsoring	Located on Strijp-S	Started in 2008
Area 51	Indoor skate park	Leisure	Sponsors and ticket revenue	Located on Strijp-S Fit in theme urban sports	Opened in Strijp-S in 2006[5] On average over 70 visitors per day
Monk Bouldergym	Indoor climbing wall	Leisure	N/A	Located on Strijp-S Fit in theme urban sports	Opened in Strijp-S in 2007
The Building	Podium for hiphop and street culture	Leisure	N/A	Located on Strijp-S Fit in theme (urban) culture	In operation
Opus 28	Theatre, between professionals and amateurs	Leisure Platform for new talent	Subsidies, sponsoring and ticket revenue	Located on Strijp-S Fit in theme culture	Started at Strijp-S in 2007
Room 306	Music studio	Leisure	Subsidies from cultural fund	Located on Strijp-S Fit in theme culture/history[6]	Opened in 2009

Source: own elaboration

Notes
1 This table is not comprehensive
2 Note that BALTAN is an anagram of NatLab
3 By tourist attraction we mean attraction for tourists as well as for inhabitants
4 In the 1930s Philips planned to start TV production in Strijp-S, but it changed its focus and as a consequence it was decided to set up a broadcasting facilities in Hilversum. Hilversum is now also the location of an already existing Institute Beeld en Geluid
5 Area 51 started in an old hangar in Meerhoven in 2002
6 Room 306 used to be the room number where Dick Raaijmaakers used to work

artists. Eindhoven uses this idea explicitly for the transformation of the former Philips site. Therefore, some of the (monumental) buildings have been rented out to SMEs, so-called 'pioneers', who can use low-cost working spaces. The rental contracts of these buildings differ from building to building. For instance, the SWA building (or 'Glasgebouw') offers relatively small spaces of minimum 100m^2 at a price of €65 per m^2. The rental period is maximum five years with flexible monthly contracts which can be cancelled by the tenant or the agency. The SFJ building has been rented out for periods of five to seven years against a price of €95 per m^2. This building is only rented out to tenants who are active in design, technology or innovation, and thus fit the concept of the project.

Also many tenants of other buildings fit the desired profile of the management and many pioneer companies are from the creative sector. These companies are seen as the agents who can increase the vibrancy of the area and fit in the theme of the project. Of all 191 tenant companies, 37.2 per cent are active in the creative industries.[8] As depicted in Figure 7.3, in two buildings (SK and Klokgebouw) this share is even higher than 40 per cent. The figure also shows large shares in the categories art and culture (16.8 per cent), consultancy (13.6 per cent) and other business services (16.2 per cent). Remarkable might be the low share of the category R&D and technology (2.6 per cent), but these concern often larger companies (for example, a remaining part of Philips falls in this category, just like Bosch Security Systems), whereas the other categories are dominated by SMEs. If employment data were used, the share of the R&D and technology category would be much higher.[9] Concerning the category 'art and culture', it should be noted that there are concentrations in some of the buildings in the area which are completely filled with tenants of this category: SBX (including a climbing hall and a film platform); SBU (a skate hall) and SBP (two art and antiques designers and two museums) (not expressed in Figure 7.3). Focusing on the creative industries, we see a high concentration of architectural firms and graphic designers, counting for nearly half of all creative industries (see Figure 7.4). All other categories within the creative industries are smaller, ranging from three to eleven tenants per category. Thus, many tenants fit in the broad themes of the area (culture, design and technology), which jointly count for 56.6 per cent of all tenants. This share might be even higher if we take into account the niches of firms categorized in other industries. For instance, the firm Keukenconfessies – categorized in 'other industries' – provides catering services using food designers to offer meals and concepts in an alternative way by 'playing' with colours, kitchen utilities and themes.

There are various reasons why the tenants have opted for Strijp-S as a business location. A first reason is the combination of relatively low rent prices with suited working spaces for start-ups and SMEs, especially in the creative industries. As expressed by a craft designer at Strijp-S: 'A workspace like this was our objective from the very outset. First of all, to control the costs, but also to carry out all sort of things, as much as we want to' (Van Gool 2010, p. 60). Similarly, the founder of an ICT firm told us: 'I went to Strijp-S as it is possible to rent this small office space for a low price'. The possibility of renting space on a temporary basis is not perceived as a problem, as expressed by a designer:

'We can stay here until 2013. Five years is a nice length of time to plan ahead for. What we will do then, we will see when we get there. For time being, we are fine here' (Van Gool 2010, p. 60). Another location factor, especially important for companies in the creative sector, is the roughness of the area: 'We aren't architects for nothing! This is such an inspiring location ... who knows, perhaps there will be a nice project for us as well' (interview with architect, from Van Gool 2008, p. 8). The latter also indicates a third location factor, the presence of other firms as (business) partners. This argument was also put forward by an interior designer:

> The great thing about a space such as this is that you regard each other as potential co-operative partners. You stimulate each other ... The *architectuurcentrum* is next to us. All we have to do is join them for drinks and we immediately meet ten architects. It is fun and convenient that we can boost our networks enormously, from inside our own building.
>
> (Van Gool 2010, p. 66)

Physical clustering is also used to increase co-operation between various cultural initiatives. Therefore, one floor in the SWA building is let to five cultural initiatives. This is perceived positively, according to a director of a cultural initiative: 'It is very convenient to drop in the office of my neighbours and to meet each other. It is important that we can speak the same language with our neighbours.'

In some cases, companies benefit from business provided by the management of Striijp-S or the housing corporations. One example is a multimedia company that is developing a website for Park Strijp Management. Moreover, the management organization leases an interactive information desk from this multimedia company and uses it in the information centre of the area. Another example is

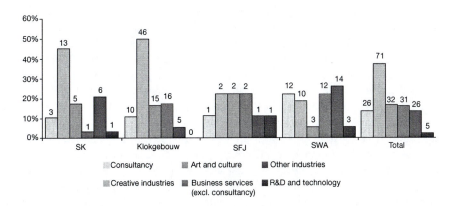

Figure 7.3 Share of tenants per industries in the buildings, with absolute numbers above the bars

Source: own elaboration

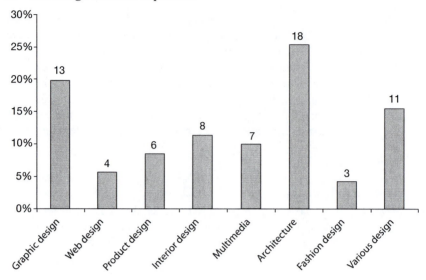

Figure 7.4   Share of industries within the creative sector (based on number of firms; absolute numbers above bars)

Source: own elaboration

a food design company that is running various projects for a housing agency.
For instance, it provides catering services in a canteen in the Klokgebouw that is
provided by the housing agency.

Hence, the location factors for the tenants include: low rents, the presence of
suited workspace, the roughness of the area and physical proximity of (potential)
business partners.

The strategy of the supply of temporary office space seems to be successful
at first glance. Many of the buildings are completely or largely rented out. This
prevents decay of the buildings, generates income – especially important during
the financial crisis – and it may increase vibrancy and stimulate local business
networks. Moreover, an advantage for Strijp-S is the presence of Strijp-T and
Strijp-R as new spaces for the temporary tenants as soon as Strijp-S develops
further, loses it 'roughness' and real-estate prices rise. Although the complementary function of the two parts of the entire Strijp complex is not documented,
several interview partners raised awareness of this benefit. For instance, it was
expressed that 'the presence of Strijp-T is ideal … Now the pioneers can move.
Pioneers are mobile.' However, in the interviews some interview partners also
raised their concerns that Strijp-T will be developed too early, before finalization
of Strijp-S, as already some studies have dealt with the development potential
of the area. If Strijp-T is partly developed at the same time as the 'S' part of the
complex, the opportunity to use Strijp-T as an alternative location for the pioneers
– including office space for firms and a festival site – will be limited because of
higher prices and a lack of attractive working spaces.

Another issue raised in the interviews is a limited supply of meeting places, such as hotels, bars and restaurants. According to a fashion designer: 'It is a shame that we do not know many people beyond our own building. ... A central meeting place in the building would be great' (Van Gool 2010, p. 66). Another tenant stresses in a regional newspaper: 'Strijp-S is and remains a dull and impersonal working environment. In order to create a creative community, there is a need for a "hangout"' (Le Blanc 2010). Various meeting facilities are planned, but because of the financial crisis and the early development stage of the area, investments in facilities such as restaurants and bars are low, or plans fail due to financial problems. One illustrative example is the Veemgebouw, which is planned to be transferred to 'one large design attraction', including a design hotel, a large market for fresh food, an exclusive department store and restaurants. The developer's plan was to get licences for the construction work in 2009 and to build it in 2010 and 2011 (ED 2009). However, more recently it was announced that the plan to transform the Veemgebouw will be postponed for an uncertain period.[10] In July 2010 the area counted only one restaurant, PopEi. This restaurant belongs to a cultural stage that offers practice rooms to music bands and theatres. This restaurant has recently made a restart and in the interviews there were some doubts whether it will be a success because of the small target group. Another bar which is likely to be opened in the short run is a 'seats2meet' bar, for which an intention contract was signed in April 2010. Another example includes the Machinekamer, a restaurant in the former steam energy plant of the complex. This restaurant closed in the winter of 2009 as there were not sufficient heating facilities in this building. It is uncertain whether or when this facility will be reopened.

The ideas expressed about the limited supply of meeting places are mixed. Many agree about the importance of such facilities to meet other people and to create vibrancy in the area. On the other hand, in the interviews it was also mentioned that there are enough meeting places in other parts of Eindhoven which can be reached easily. This limits the need for facilities at Strijp-S. As expressed in an interview: 'It is nice to have meeting facilities at Strijp-S, but we do not need them *per se*, as we can simply receive business partners at other places'. It should also be mentioned that there are informal initiatives to meet each other on a small scale. For instance, in some cases, drinks are organized by tenants who invite other tenants who rent a workspace on the same floor of a certain building.

Besides SMEs, and still some parts of Philips, Strijp-S is also home to a subsidiary of the large multinational Bosch. It 'arrived at' Strijp-S via a takeover of a former Philips division. Currently, Bosch is even extending its activities on the former Philips site, as a consequence of the closure of a subsidiary in Breda for cost reasons. Production facilities will be transferred to China and the remaining activities in Holland will be transferred to Eindhoven. Bosch has evaluated various locations in the Eindhoven region for these remaining activities. Ultimately, Strijp-S was selected for a number of reasons. First, and from a practical view, Bosch is already located at the former Philips site. This makes internal communication more efficient. A second advantage of the Strijp-S location is the presence of space for extension. Due to the movement of Philips, space and offices have become available for other companies. Currently, Bosch is in negotiation with Park Strijp Management whether to rent an old Philips building or to build a new one. It should be noted that the credit crunch favours Bosch in this negotiation process as it is more difficult for Park Strijp Management to rent out space. A third reason is relatively low rental cost as Strijp-S, which is lower than other good locations such as the HTC/e. A final advantage of Strijp-S is good accessibility by train and car.[11] This is important for the commuters who live in the Breda region.

Strijp-S as an R&D location

Strijp-S, especially the NatLab, formed the heart of Philips' research network. It is a major aim to keep this tradition alive via the central themes of technology, design and culture. But what is its current role as a knowledge location? This section discusses the relations of Strijp-S with other knowledge locations in the Eindhoven area and its position in knowledge networks. In addition, we discuss the potency of the area as a testbed and the role of innovation.

Knowledge and educational facilities are crucial assets for the competitive position of cities. As mentioned earlier, the Eindhoven region has various locations with concentrations of research facilities (see Figure 7.1) with a different focus. The HTC/e is an open campus with research centres of companies; the automotive campus in Helmond includes various public and private research institutes focusing on automotive technologies; while the TU/e campus includes a technical university, the Intelligent Lighting Institute, and the Embedded Systems Institute.

In contrast to the other locations, Strijp-S has hardly any educational or knowledge facilities. The major exception is BALTAN Laboratories, which started in the SWA building as a pilot study for a future art and science lab that will be established in the reconstructed NatLab building at a later stage. BALTAN's main goal is to keep the historical tradition of the NatLab alive by linking art with technology. Its functions include the creation of networks, stimulation of research projects, organization of workshops, lectures and school projects. For (research) projects, and to function as a 'real lab', BALTAN has a working space where artists and researchers can perform experiments. Artists can express creativity by using modern (ICT) technology – available in the lab – and their own inspiration. Crucial is its network function as it aims to link various disciplines (art and technology) and the local with the global dimension. The latter happens via the invitation of international artists who work temporarily in the working space of the lab. The artists stay in Eindhoven for some months. Somewhat remarkable might be that the 'visiting artists' do not live at Strijp-S, despite the ambitions to create a Creative City and the possibly attractive character of the area (the low rents and the roughness of the site). It was argued that other areas in the city provide sufficient suitable accommodation for the international artists. To stimulate networks, the lab has established relations with various actors. It co-operates with different educational institutes, including the Design Academy, TU/e and Fontys University of Applied Sciences. For instance, the lab is involved in an educational programme of Fontys' in which ICT students are asked to work on art projects in which they combine their ICT skills with creativity. The project has been developed with support of the four artistic advisors of the lab. These artistic advisors are artists who played a major role in the establishment of the lab. Moreover, internships are available to students at the lab. The lab has also relations with the private sector. For instance, from a management perspective, a representative of Philips Research has a seat on the board of BALTAN.

The role of Strijp-S in the region's educational infrastructure might increase because of the attraction of educational facilities. Currently, there are plans to attract parts of the Eindhoven School and Sint Lucas College (both vocational level). The idea is to establish creative parts of these schools on Strijp-S (such as a design school) in order to give more content to the site's design theme. It should be noted that it is not the location's role to house students.

Next to public research and educational facilities, private actors can also invest in R&D facilities. Strijp-S has some small high-tech companies, a remaining part of Philips Applied Technologies, and Bosch has its research centre in the area. The R&D centre of Philips on Strijp-S focuses on new product introduction services and packaging solutions. This centre will move to HTC/e in the near future. The research centre of Bosch, as part of Bosch Security Systems, focuses on the research and development of new security systems. Just like many other Western technology firms, Bosch has changed its focus from hardware to software and IP technology. In Eindhoven, R&D concentrates mainly on the software of cameras. In the past, Bosch was involved in developing hardware (microchips, etc.), but this has increasingly been standardized and can be done by a rising number of competitors. Through its focus on software, Bosch hopes to stay ahead of competitors.

It is the regional scale, complemented with global relations, that is especially important for the research activities of Bosch, while the local scale (Strijp-S) plays a minor role. The company is based in Eindhoven as Bosch wants to benefit from the advantages of the technology cluster of the region, along with its specialized labour pool, the presence of suppliers and research partners and the presence of competitors that keeps the firm alert. It makes use of some specific niches that belong to the specialization of the technology cluster, including design, ICT and embedded systems.

Due to focuses on security systems, it is logical that the R&D activities are strongly internal in order to reduce the risk of knowledge leakage. Nevertheless, there are also relations with external parties. From a historical perspective, there are relations with Philips. Many employees still have personal contacts with their former colleagues. In addition, and in a formal way, Bosch works on joint projects with the Dutch multinational. The company also co-operates with other regional research partners since it outsources parts of the development process; 30 per cent of its R&D activities has been done by external parties; design, especially, has been outsourced. The majority of the R&D partners come from the Eindhoven region. Bosch mainly uses R&D partners from their own R&D network as Bosch knows these partners and they can guarantee the quality required. R&D partners are mainly involved in development (and not in basic research), which can be done entirely by the R&D partners or in co-operation with Bosch. Besides regional partners, Bosch uses its global company network for research and research projects have been done with other Bosch subsidiaries abroad.[12] In these projects, the actors involved and the geographical scale of co-operation differs case by case. Especially in the initial stages of new projects, face-to-face contact is crucial. Therefore, 'temporary proximity' is created in which researchers stay at other Bosch locations. Besides this, and in later project stages, there is communication via video conferencing.

Bosch also tries to get in touch with regional knowledge institutes, like TU/e and Fontys. The major aim in establishing linkages with these institutes is to promote the company among students. This happens via open days and internships: the company provides ten to twenty internships annually.

The example of Bosch illustrates that the local dimension is less relevant, and that Strijp-S is complementary to other knowledge locations in the region (and the world). Currently, discussions are taking place to strengthen the linkages between Strijp-S and HTC/e and TU/e. A major topic of discussion is to find out the specific function of Strijp-S and how it can precisely complement these other locations. One possible way in which the former Philips site can complement the other locations is via its role of testbed of new technologies, as we discuss in more detail in the remainder of this section.

Strijp-S as a testbed

Due to improved IC technologies, firms are able to communicate directly with consumers and consumers are increasingly involved in innovation in order to adapt and develop products according to their desires. This has led to an increasing use of new concepts such as 'user-driven innovation' (Von Hippel 2005) and 'co-creation' (Prahalad and Ramaswamy 2004). More recently, and due to various trends in society such as an ageing population and increasing privatization of public services, cities have also become interested in the implementation of such concepts. Therefore, cities increasingly provide physical city quarters as playground, testbed or living lab to test new concepts. New city quarters or major transformation areas are especially suited to such experiments, as the infrastructure development is still in an early stage and it is possible to involve users in innovation from the beginning.

Strijp-S is also planned as a major testbed in two respects. First, the Sanergy concept, which combines groundwater remediation with groundwater energy, is being used to clean the soil of Strijp-S. The area is heavily polluted as a consequence of decades of industrial activity. Philips, which takes the responsibility for cleaning the soil, took the initiative of Sanergy in 2004. In 2009, the concept was implemented – for the first time in Holland – with support of Park Strijp Management, Philips and the consultant firms Arcadis and DEC. The sustainable idea of the concept is to combine the soil-cleaning process with a groundwater energy system. This is done by using groundwater circulation and bacteria, nutrients and contaminants, working like a giant 'biowashing machine'. Strijp-S is a key location to implement the new concept, not only for the pollution, but also because of high requirements for a sustainable redevelopment and the presence of monuments which make alternative cleaning solutions difficult and expensive. As the project is still at an early stage, results are as yet unknown. Arcadis is involved in a second project where the concept is used in the inner city of Utrecht which started in 2010 (Slenders *et al.* 2010). It is not clear to what extent experiences from Strijp-S have been used in Utrecht or vice versa.

Second, the area has been selected as a test area for new public lighting concepts. To this end, Park Strijp Management asked Philips Design, in 2008, to develop a lighting vision for the area. Although Philips is leaving the area, it is aware of its potential as a testbed for revolutionary lighting, as expressed by the director of Philips Design:

> Strijp-S is going to be a dynamic and vibrant area. Different types of activities will take place in the area during the day, in the evening and at night – and lighting can help change the identity of the area to reflect these changes. It can also be used to emphasize seasonal changes and special occasions. ... Lighting is the perfect tool for this because it offers more flexibility than physical structures.
>
> (Philips 2009, p. 1)

Based on the vision, a flexible lighting plan has been set up. As Strijp-S will be developed in stages, various prototypes will be introduced during different stages of the transformation process. Currently, two projects have been implemented. One concerns an animated pedestrian crossing of the Phileas line, in which lights change from green to red when the Phileas passes and it is not safe to cross the street. The second project, also related to Phileas lines, is an animated line along the route of the area by integration of LED points in lamp-posts and in the pavements. Depending on the location of the bus, the colour and intensity of the LEDs change. This increases the visibility of the vehicle and reduces light pollution when the vehicle has passed (Philips 2009).

Besides these projects, the area has been used as a showroom for new technologies via various festivals in the area. One example includes the STRP festival which organized a pilot of a Licht Café ('light café'), an exhibition that shows new light technologies to the public. Philips aims to set up such a facility permanently at a later stage, but used the festival to test the concept in a 10-day pilot. It is worth noting that the festival organization is also involved in the lighting plan, just like TU/e, Philips, Park Strijp Management and some smaller local companies.

In addition to lighting, the area might be a testbed for other technologies as well, including electronic vehicles and safety systems. As posited in an interview: 'Strijp-S has the potency to be one large testbed'.

Nevertheless, there are also limitations in the testbed function. A major barrier includes regulations. Therefore, there is an idea to create an area with fewer restrictions, and to make contracts with users (for example, inhabitants) whereby as they are in a test lab they cannot complain when trials produce drawbacks, such as electricity stoppages. However, this plan is still in a concept stage, and further implementation is highly uncertain. In addition, despite the initiative of Park Strijp Management and willingness of Philips Design and other local organizations to participate, there is no permanent organization to initiate, promote and stimulate concrete projects and to create networks. Finally, Strijp-S the testbed and show-room function does not lead to permanent investments in the area: most actors involved in tests are not based at Strijp-S. In this sense, it is worth mentioning that the Intelligent Lighting Institute (ILI) opened in July 2010 at the campus of TU/e and not at Strijp-S. The ILI is an open innovation network dealing with new lighting technologies. The network includes six faculties of TU/e, and is initiated by various firms including NXP, Philips and Luxlab. Of these actors, only the latter, Luxlab, a company focusing on light design, is based at Strijp-S. However, various tests of the research programmes of the new institutes – including intel-ligent street lighting; natural light sources in urban areas; effects of light on well-being and health; new ways of interaction between people and light; and other new light concepts – might be implemented at the former Philips site.

Conclusions and recommendations

Many cities face the challenge of the transformation of brownfield sites into new city quarters. Old industrial sites have been transformed into new knowledge loca-tions with various fancy themes such as creativity, culture, technology, design and R&D. A major challenge is to change locations in various dimensions, not only in a functional and physical way, but it also requires a change in perception taking into account the future as well as the history of the area. In this chapter, we have dealt with the transformation process of Strijp-S, a closed Philips community close to the city centre of Eindhoven. The site, including the NatLab, the former physics laboratory of the Dutch electronic giant, had a glorious past in terms of technology, innovation and creativity, since many inventions were made on this site. A major vision of the redevelopment of the location – after Philips decided to restructure its business and to leave Strijp-S – is to keep this glorious history alive by creating the 'Creative City'. The aim is to develop a multi-functional urban surrounding, which is lacking in the region, in order to attract international knowledge workers to the city.

In the remainder of this section, following the two pillars from our theoretical frame, we first draw conclusions on how the transformation process has been managed and success factors and barriers in this process. Second, we conclude about clustering, networks and the integration of the site in the larger urban region. We end the chapter with policy recommendations that may help to redevelop the area further.

Management, success factors and barriers

The vision to 'keep the history alive' has been translated into three core themes: technology, design and culture. There are various strategies to give content to these themes and to keep the historical DNA of the area. First, the site has a number of monuments, which allow only small adaptations, so the historical image remains concrete.

A second strategy is the use of culture. There are many cultural initiatives in the area (see Table 7.4). The success of this large number of cultural initiatives can partly be explained by the existence of a joint cultural fund. All key players contribute to this fund and agree about the importance of culture for the redevelopment process and as a future theme in the area. Festivals are seen especially as a success formula to promote the area. Nevertheless, there are also some points of attention regarding the cultural initiatives. One is the sensitivity of culture to economic cycles, as both public and private actors can easily cut cultural budgets, with the consequence that the future of many initiatives is far from guaranteed. A second, and related point of attention, is that many initiatives are still in the concept stage and their realization is uncertain. Especially important is the need for a permanent 'flagship attraction' that gives a face to the area as a cultural site. This attraction should attract visitors to the site daily, promote the site on higher spatial scales (national and international scales) and stimulate further investments. Realized current initiatives are either small-scale attractions, or temporary attractions in the form of events. These initiatives help to (temporarily) increase vibrancy and increase awareness of the site on a regional scale, but may not attract visitors and workers from higher spatial scales, hence national and international scales. So, it might be questionable whether the current initiatives help to attract international knowledge workers which is one of the main objectives of the plan.

A third strategy, regarding the theme of technology, is the use of the site as a (potential) testbed for the synergy project, new public lighting concepts and maybe for other technologies. Despite the potential of the area for this function (for example, the early stage of development), the willingness of key actors to join, many ideas and some first tests, there are various barriers to develop this function, including regulations and the lack of permanent organization to stimulate, organize and guide projects.

A fourth strategy is the use of the pioneers. This seems to be a success, witnessing the large number of tenants in general, and the large share of them which fit the key themes of the area. It should be noted that chosen themes are relatively broad, so it might be easy to fit into these themes. The tenants are attracted to the area because of low rents, the presence of suited workspace, the roughness of the area, and physical proximity of (potential) business partners. However, long-term success is uncertain because pioneers may not remain in the area when prices rise, the site loses its roughness and there is a risk of possible conflicts with other functions. The same is true for festivals in the area. So, a major point of attention is how and to what extent can the themes be fulfilled in the long run?

The transformation process is complex for a number of reasons: the presence of many, sometimes conflicting, regulations and requirements (for example, monument requirements of buildings versus the need to adapt them for other functions); the size and long development time of the site; the integration of the area in the region; sensitivity to external factors that cannot be controlled, despite flexibility in the concepts (for example, the transformation process is seriously delayed due to the financial crisis); and the presence of many stakeholders with different interests. The area seems to be managed well via a public–private partnership with regular meetings, willingness to co-operate, a shared concept, successful joint ideas and products (such as the cultural fund), and an external supervisor which guarantees the architectural quality. However, the management of the area has not always been without conflict, and there is room for improvement in the management, especially regarding the marketing strategy and the speed of decision-making and the implementation time of concepts.

Clustering, networks and integration with other areas

As mentioned, Strijp-S has attracted several SMEs from the creative sector. Many of these firms benefit from the direct proximity of the other firms as potential business and project partners. The companies find each other through informal networks and via 'corridor meetings' as many similar firms rent space in the same building. A drawback, however, is a limited supply of meeting places, which can be explained by the early development stage of the area, the financial crisis and a small market with high risks. The involvement of the SMEs in knowledge networks and the spatial scales of these networks are unclear from our data and this topic deserves further research. In general, knowledge networks on the site seem to be limited, because of a low number of public R&D and educational facilities (a major exception is BALTAN as a platform organization and a major experimental lab) on the site. More educational facilities are planned, but these are mainly lower level educational facilities. A key private R&D institute is a research lab of Bosch Security systems. This lab is relatively closed because of the characteristics of the business; concerning external relations, much co-operation takes place on the regional and global level, while the local scale (on Strijp-S) is limited. The example of Bosch is illustrative for Strijp-S as a potential complementary location to other knowledge locations such as HTC/e (focus private R&D), TU/e (including ILI and ESI), automotive Campus Helmond and DPI. The best chances for Strijp-S in this line seem to be its role as a showroom for innovation (expressed in museums and during events), and as a testbed for innovation.

Besides the functional connection of Strijp-S with other knowledge locations, the site also needs to be connected with the rest of the region. The 'opening of the Forbidden City' happens in various ways: opening of a physical public transport link by a Phileas connection with the city centre; promotion of the area via events; word-of-mouth promotion; and via own initiatives of tenants. Points of attention include the lack of a common marketing strategy and we have indications that promotion is too much focused on renting out space rather than selling the concept of a creative city. Promising for the transformation process of Strijp-S is the planned complementary functions of Strijp-R (residential) and Strijp-T (industrial). Especially important is the role of Strijp-T as potential location to house the pioneers and events as soon as Strijp-S is in a further development stage. Therefore, and to prevent competition between the sites, it is crucial that the transformation of Strijp-R takes place after the realization of Strijp-S. In this sense it is also worth mentioning the oversupply of office space in the region and competition between several sites to attract business.

In conclusion, it is difficult to judge whether the redevelopment of Strijp-S is a success and whether the aim of the development of a Creative City that attracts (international) knowledge workers can be realized in the long term. On the one hand, the area successfully attracts pioneers and is suitable as an event location and has the potential to complement other locations in Eindhoven's knowledge infrastructure. Moreover, several attempts have been made to connect the site with the rest of the city. On the other hand, there are also development barriers, such as management problems, the financial crisis, competition with other sites, difficulties in increasing vibrancy (the development of meeting places, burglaries, delay in housing construction) and to attract (cultural) flagships. These development barriers have caused a delay in the process and there is a risk of losing political and societal support which are crucial for a successful redevelopment.

Challenges and recommendations

In the previous sections we have described the drivers and barriers for the redevelopment of Strijp-S. In this final part, we end with some concrete recommendations that may help to develop Strijp-S further.

First, 'ships cannot be steered from the shore; there is a need for a captain on the boat': the supervision of an external architect may help to guarantee the architectural quality of the concept, but it is not sufficient to guide the process, to speed up decision-making and implementation of projects and develop joint strategies. A major challenge includes the development of a joint marketing strategy, in which internal communication should not be forgotten. There is a lot information available dealing with the future plans of the area, as well as possibilities to rent space, but we have indications that information on current events in the location is limited. A good marketing strategy is also crucial to maintain political and societal support, because delays in the project lead people to lose trust.

Second, and related to the first, other improvements in the management can be made. For instance, in order to create a better balance in power between the different actors, the city and the two housing agencies can co-operate more intensely in order to have a louder voice against the most powerful player, Volker Wessels. In addition, the city could increase its effort in the project and integrate it with more projects and other policies. In the interviews it was suggested that only a few persons from the city are dealing with the project. If more persons are involved, political support may increase along with the speed of decision-making and implementation. This is especially true if more persons with decision-making power support the project. Therefore, one interview partner even suggested getting more support and involvement from the mayor. Another suggestion regarding improving the management is to set up a specific centre to communicate with tenants. This special 'one-shop' centre should deal with practical questions of tenants, advise them and increase their role in discussions regarding the development of the area. This centre should be complementary to the current information centre ('Portiersloge') which mainly serves general visitors and tourists.

Third, in order to prevent unnecessary competition between different sites (such as the stadium quarter, and other parts of the Strijp complex), the city should not work on too many projects at the same time. Instead, major projects should be done one after the other, so overlap between the functions of the different sites can be reduced and the sites do not compete for the same resources at the same time.

Fourth, 'make use of the testbed potential: do not sleep on it, but organize it in a proper way and play on it'. The site has potential to complement other knowledge locations in the region as a testbed. As mentioned before, the area is still in an early development stage. In addition, key actors are aware of the potential of the testbed function and are willing to join initiatives. Nevertheless, a permanent organization that initiates, promotes and stimulates projects, and creates networks may help to develop the testbed function further. A suited actor to initiate such an organization might be Strijp-S management as it has relations with all other actors. Besides, it has access, directly or indirectly, to tenants and future inhabitants, required to create a database of potential participants of various experiments. In this sense, much can be learned from the Living Lab in Arabianranta, as described in Chapter 8 on Helsinki.

Finally, 'do not wait until the wind changes direction to attract flagships, but use tugboats to get them'. Both a cultural flagship as well as a flagship firm is needed to give a face to the site as a cultural location and as a business location, respectively. This requires more (joint) acquisition work; especially the role of governments might increase in this respect as was indicated in the interviews. A suggestion given in the interviews is to develop a joint acquisition plan that can be implemented by a special, and independent, acquisition manager with a budget to travel and meet potential tenants of the area. It might also help if a powerful organization such as Brainport helps to attract business to Strijp-S. It should be noted, that despite Philips leaving the area, Bosch is still there. Although this flagship is relatively closed due to its business, it might be used to promote the area and to strengthen (knowledge) networks with the area.

8   Helsinki: Arabianranta

Introduction

The Arabianranta area in Helsinki has captured the attention of many urban planners worldwide as a success story of creative urban regeneration (Ilmonen and Kunzmann 2007). In a nutshell, Arabianranta is a regenerated former wasteland area in the north-eastern part of Helsinki which combines, in an open urban district, living, working, studying and leisure functions in an exemplary fashion, centred on a holistic theme – 'design, art and creativity'. As one of the first large-scale public–private partnerships for area-based redevelopment in Finland, it is known as an example of best practice, combining knowledge and innovation activity with urban regeneration projects.

Development of Arabianranta started in the early 1990s and was planned to take place until about 2010. Construction is at an advanced stage. According to the plan, the area hosts many national and international design, media and ICT-oriented firms in diversified types of premises, a set of renowned higher educational institutes (HEI), for example, the University of Applied Sciences and the University of Art and Design Helsinki, quality residential areas for diverse social groups, as well as leisure and cultural facilities such as shops, restaurants and museums. Arabianranta is to become the leading centre of art and design in the Baltic area (City of Helsinki 2007), as envisioned by the venture partners – City, HEIs, key companies and residents' association – in a quadruple-helix fashion (Carayannis and Campbell 2009).

Aside from the success of the physical integration of the district in Helsinki's urban fabric and its ability to capture a concentration of knowledge-intensive activities, distinctive organizational and technological novelties lie at the core of the interest in Arabianranta as a 'knowledge location'. The area pioneered in 'last-mile' broadband optical fibre infrastructure across the entire district, making online connectivity a commodity not unlike water, electricity or gas. The last part of the network connecting the different houses to each other and to the internet is owned by the (collective of) residents, enabling broadband connection at much lower and more stable prices. Moreover, it pioneered in promoting the development of a number of integrated virtual platforms organized around a network of so-called 'e-moderators', building a strong sense of community in a rather open and diverse area. This 'social infrastructure' supported the first successful application of user-driven innovation processes through 'Living Labs' methodologies

(Eriksson *et al.* 2005). These achievements led some commentators to dub Arabianranta a 'Social Silicon Valley'.

In this chapter, we try to inductively make sense of the causal relations and underlying factors behind the success of Arabianranta as a 'planned knowledge location'. We are interested in shedding light on the following questions, which are also at the core of our general study on knowledge locations:

- What are the necessary conditions behind the development of Arabianranta as a knowledge location?
- What factors facilitated and accelerated (or moderated) the development and success of Arabianranta?
- What effects is Arabianranta generating at relevant spatial levels (metropolitan, urban and local)?

We base the analysis of these relations informed on literature in urban studies and economic geographies of innovation. Combined, these research strands enable an integrative understanding of the emergence and functioning of 'urban knowledge locations'.

On the one hand, recent studies on the geography and spatial foundations of innovation have been providing more nuanced insights on the role of proximity, face-to-face contacts and buzz in innovation (for example, Boschma 2005; Asheim *et al.* 2007) which are not yet incorporated in the 'taken for granted' notions of: Jacobian urban diversity (Jacobs 1969); localized innovation networks (Camagni 1991); and buzz and the creative class (Florida 2002; Landry 2000). These notions implicitly lie at the root of the development of many culture- and knowledge-led 'agglomeration promotion' large-scale urban developments. On the other hand, by taking an integrative approach, urban (governance) studies provide often ignored insights on the role and functioning of urban-based policies and area developments in the sustainability and dynamics of cities as complex ecosystems of activities in need of urban management (for example, van Winden *et al.* 2007; van den Berg and Braun 1999; Malecki 2002; Scott 2006).

Integrating these literature strands, we argue, is important for the purpose of allowing an integrative understanding of what 'knowledge locations' are and how they work. On the one hand, it is unlikely that agglomeration externalities and knowledge spill-overs will take place by concentrating firms and organizations into a single planned and bonded location, as suggested by many commentators. On the other hand, the development of knowledge locations cannot be seen only as the most effective and efficient solution for 'bringing people together to innovate and learn', but also as an instrument to pursue other urban development objectives such as image building, mobility management, environmental and energy efficiency, and institutional and organizing capacity. Bringing the two literature branches together (and illuminating the constructs and mechanisms involved) allows a clearer assessment of the causal relations steering the systemic development and evolution of a planned knowledge location.

Cross-fertilization among these different insights is of particular relevance to policymaking. Potentially, every city government in the world would like to have an 'Arabianranta' or other form of knowledge district, 'brain parks' or 'intelligent hubs' depicted in earlier studies (for example, Da Cunha and Selada 2009). These kinds of flagship project are more and more seen as part of the 'holy grail' of local economic development because they combine the knowledge 'hype' with other more traditional local policies centred on education, culture, land development and planning. The success stories are increasingly well documented; yet, an understanding of the causes and mechanisms behind these successes is often lacking. This is partly due to a weak incorporation of the time dimension in the analysis of clusters development, where stories tend to sketch a static picture. In these descriptions, cluster success often coincides with well developed infrastructure such as knowledge parks, making it difficult to identify the causal relationship (what led to what? X to Y or the other way around, or maybe both?). More than often this analysis provides misleading insights for policymaking, or what Wolfe and Gertler call 'the perils of reading off causal relations from spatial associations in ex-post analysis of successful clusters' (2006, p. 257). By introducing a time dimension in the analysis, the genesis of locations and clusters (for example, Braunerhjelm and Feldman 2006) becomes clear, shedding light on the question: 'what leads to what, and through which mechanisms?' Moreover, a better understanding of the system of interaction, and an analysis not solely based on isolated parcels, may help policymakers to deploy what Malecki (2007) calls 'intelligent benchmarking' to support more informed investment plans with potentially higher returns for local and regional economies.

The remainder of this chapter is structured as follows. The following section describes the urban-economic context of Finland and Helsinki, the historical development of Arabianranta and the management of the area. Next, we analyse Arabianranta as a business and knowledge location, and in the section that follows, as a place to live. The final section concludes and provides policy recommendations that may contribute to further development of Arabianranta.

Arabianranta: context, history and management

The Arabianranta area plays a key role in Helsinki's history. It is the location where Helsinki was originally founded in the sixteenth century and it is the 'birthplace' of the factory of Arabia, once one of the biggest porcelain companies in Europe. After the plant was restructured in the 1980s, space and buildings became available for other functions. This has led to one of the largest urban redevelopment projects in the Helsinki region. In order to understand the drivers of development in Arabianranta, this section describes the urban-economic context of Helsinki, the history of the area, as well as the goals set, the development realized so far, and the management of the area.

Urban-economic context

Locations, planned or unplanned, do not develop in isolation. Therefore, we proceed briefly to describe the urban-economic context of the Helsinki region. Helsinki is referred to as a strong knowledge city (van Winden *et al.* 2007), with a highly educated workforce and with ICT as the major growth sector. It scores well on various wealth, knowledge and innovation indicators. For instance, it ranks second on the European Innovation Scoreboard in 2003 (the first position is held by Stockholm), and with over 100 patents per active worker, it ranks fifth after Eindhoven, Oberbayern, Karlsruhe and Stockholm (Commissie Sistermans 2006).

The Finnish economy was dependent on sectors like wood, pulp and mechanical engineering – for instance, associated with machinery and shipbuilding – in the early twentieth century. The country's economy was from the mid-1940s until the late 1980s closely intertwined with that of the Soviet Union (Roper and Grimes 2005). After the fall of the Soviet regime and a painful economic recession that followed during the 1990s,[1] Finland became a well-known case of a successful transition from a production-based economy towards a knowledge economy, namely through an economic diversification process led by ICTs, spearheaded by firms like Nokia and many others in associated fields.

Previous research provides advanced explanations for the Finnish success story: (i) high educational levels compared with any international benchmarks:[2] Helsinki and Finland as a whole host high standard universities and R&D centres, and, thus, a large supply of highly-skilled workers in the fields of technology and engineering, but also in arts, humanities and sciences; (ii) a very proactive technological and innovation policy, linked with innovative and 'spatial sensitive' policies like the establishment of competitiveness poles and innovation platforms across sectors, supported by bridging governmental agencies like TEKES; (iii) contingent factors like a specific regulation system in the telecommunications sector which led to the need to jointly innovate towards new technologies, reinforcing the partnership behaviour and institutionalized co-operation culture rooted in Finnish society; and (iv) internationalization of capital markets and an open attitude of local policymakers towards all forms of mobile communications (Boschma and Sotarauta 2007; Sotarauta and Kautonen 2007; Roper and Grimes 2005).

Aside from more technologically-oriented sectors like ICT, Finland has a long tradition in furniture and appliances, an industry intensive in art and design. Although the production and manufacturing plants of Finnish companies are scattered over Finland and elsewhere, headquarters and design operations (the 'brains') tend to be located in Helsinki. Metropolitan Helsinki (economic, population and political centre of Finland)[3] is composed of the city of Helsinki and the surrounding cities of Vantaa, Espoo and Kauniainen. These surrounding cities are more than just commuter residences. Vantaa is an important logistical hub and Espoo, hosting the campus of Helsinki University of Technology and many headquarters, an important R&D location. Despite co-operation and joint planning for strategic objectives,[4] cities in Finland are strongly decentralized, giving them substantial (fiscal) power, leading to competition for the attraction of public and private investments.

In spite of the strength of the Finnish economy, there are also some drawbacks in its economic structure. One is the (too) strong dependency on the ICT sector (for example, van den Berg *et al.* 2005). Within the ICT sector, there is a strong dominance of (and potential dependence on) key player Nokia (Roper and Grimes 2005). This may be a drawback, as Nokia increasingly sources its knowledge (R&D and design) from various strategic hotspots in the world, potentially weakening the ties in the home region (Van der Borg and van Tuijl 2008). In order to increase the competitive position and to reduce the dependency on hardware (technology), which can be replicated more easily by new entrants from upcoming countries such as India and China, the focus has been shifting to software (for example, design) and increasingly to the combination of hardware and software. This has occurred naturally, through the market (for example, Nokia has shifted from technology to software and design) and through changes in the institutional structure. A good example of the latter is national legislation giving rise to a merger of the universities of technology, design and economics. This merger is conducted in order to facilitate multidisciplinary research and to train students in various crossed disciplines.

Accessibility and 'quality of life' indicators in Helsinki are considered moderate compared with international benchmarks.[5] Possible explanations include the cold climate and the geographic distance from the European core. However, Helsinki is part of the dynamic corridor Stockholm–Helsinki– St Petersburg and has an international airport with a hub character. The Finnish capital has all the relevant and high level 'amenities' of every European capital, although it might miss a real 'underground culture' of other cities such as New York and Berlin. The population of the city of Helsinki has grown from 490,872 in 1990 to 568,531 in 2008 (City of Helsinki 2008). Qualified workers, skilled immigrants and the 'global hub' character tend to be associated with the Helsinki 'excellence' in particular economic and knowledge fields, like ICT, but also, and increasingly, design. Finnish design has (still) a strong international brand and the University of Art and Design Helsinki attracts a very large number of international students. Despite these trends, the nationalities of Helsinki's residents are not particularly diverse. Cultural features are still relatively homogeneous.

Story and background of Arabianranta

Arabianranta is one of the major large-scale urban development projects in Helsinki. Before detailing its concept and vision, it is worth understanding the context and history of the area. The location was considered in industrial times, at the peak of the porcelain production in the Arabia factory, as rather far from Helsinki's city centre. During the second half of the twentieth century up until the 1980s, the area became physically and socially degraded. Industry closure led to high unemployment. By that time, the surrounding area consisted of wastelands and abandoned premises of sewage plants: polluted and hosting socially disadvantaged groups. The city had no specific plans for the area.

A turning point occurred in the mid-1980s, when the old buildings of the Arabia factory were rented by the University of Art and Design Helsinki (TaiK), formerly located in the city centre and looking for space to accommodate its growth. The former factory fitted TaiK's requirements: it provided a space physically suited for classrooms and larger studios and workshops, and it had the tradition and character of an old 'design intensive' factory linked with the history of the university itself; moreover, due to improved transport connections, it was relatively close to the city centre. It should be noted that initially TaiK was looking for temporary space, but it remains in the area in 2009 and forms one of the major anchors in the area (see below).

During the years 1986–88, TaiK initiated talks and meetings with the City to assess whether their new premises would be temporary or an option for more stable growth. By that time, the City of Helsinki and its Planning Department were considering converting Arabianranta into an urban green park, making use of its quality as a waterfront location. Before the end of the decade, the decision was made to transform the area and create a functional mix, making use of its advantages: the presence of TaiK, a waterfront location and a strong identity. In 1992 the City started to detail the area's new master plan; soil remediation was necessary and earth cleaning took place until the late 1990s, when housing construction began.

A key driver for the redevelopment of Arabianranta, its spatial plan and management, is the context of the period when the redevelopment started. In the late 1980s and early 1990s, Finland was hit hard by an economic recession with an unemployment rate around 20 per cent. The aim for Arabianranta was closely tied with job and (tax) income creation by attracting companies. The creative industries were seen as a solution to change the tide and realize growth. The city, National Ministry of Trade and Industry, and landowners, aimed to create 7,000 jobs in the area. A concrete agreement was made by various partners: Iittala Group (the owner of the Arabia factory), Varma (pension funds), the City of Helsinki and the State. Nowadays, it is common in Finland that various stakeholders work together, but the Arabianranta development starting over twenty years ago might be seen as one of the first large-scale public–private partnerships.

In order to guarantee success in the long run, a central and differentiating theme for the area was needed. Design was chosen as this central theme, transversal to various functions: housing, education, industry, research and innovation. The functions of the area evolved accordingly. First, the area attracted more 'artistic' educational institutes following TaiK. Nowadays, Arabianranta includes five higher educational institutes. Second, next to Iittala Group, other companies from the 'creative industries' (mainly art, design and media) located in the area. Companies refer to the creative atmosphere, contact with TaiK and (potential) relations with other companies as important attraction features of the area. Third, design is reflected in housing and architecture. The city is the biggest landowner of the area and via contracts, to be obtained via tenders, companies can lease the land. The selection of the companies is to a large degree based on architectural design and the use of art in public space. This tendering process can be seen as the biggest public art project ever done in Finland as developers were required to invest 1–2 per cent of the total construction costs of all real estate in art projects. In addition, gardens are communal (collectively owned) and are used to implement design and build identity.

Management, features and goals of Arabianranta

Arabianranta was planned as an extension to the city centre combining 'an urban feeling with a natural surrounding of the lakes and forests', and not as the suburb it later became. In 1995 a letter of intention was signed by the City of Helsinki and TaiK in order to found ADC – Art and Design City Helsinki. ADC, a public–private company, was (and still is) responsible for the coordination of development in Arabianranta. It is tasked with involving the relevant stakeholders, namely landowners, private parties, universities and HEIs and inhabitants. Other players also have shares in ADC, including the Ministry of Trade and Industry, companies that moved to the area in the meantime (for example, Strawberry Group) and other HEIs in Arabianranta, including the foundation for the Pop and Jazz Conservatory and the University of Applied Sciences. Under the umbrella of ADC, different players were involved to share and jointly develop ideas for the area. This proved especially important to overcome the rigidity and physically oriented philosophy dominant in the City Planning Department,[6] bringing innovative ideas, communicating openly between partners and overcoming the lengthy, closed and bureaucratic decision-making processes. It was indeed the first time that the City of Helsinki planned a fully integrated urban-area development around a holistic theme, going beyond traditional developments based on general physical infrastructure, industrial premises or isolated housing. The area was planned to host a coherent and diversified mix of functions around the topic of 'art', associated with distinctive quality of life, tapping into its distinctive resources.

The construction of Arabianranta started in 2000 and is to continue until 2010. Arabianranta's shareholders have put forward the following vision: to 'make Arabianranta the leading centre of art and design in the Baltic Area' (City of Helsinki 2007), a centre organized around design and art, with education, production and consumption. ADC is responsible for daily and strategic management of the area, acting as a 'spider in the web' linking the different parties and reconciling the players' interests.

In order to realize growth, the vision was translated into a number of concrete goals for the end of 2010. The goals have already been reached or are expected to be reached in the near future (see Table 8.1). Hence, the project has been running according to schedule and the initial concept and thematic orientation for Arabianranta have been successfully kept until today.

Arabianranta is located approximately 5km away from Helsinki's city centre and has good accessibility by car and tram. It mixes an urban feeling with nature and water. Just as planned, it is already a very diverse area: a mix of age groups, social statuses, nationalities and urban functions – education, living, working and leisure. The area has attracted many firms, students and residents and there is still demand both for residential space and office space (for example, a Finnish multinational working with industrial design-related activities expressed interest investing in the area). New constructions and developments are taking place to fill in the last plots of land and cope with the demand. In terms of types of companies, the 'selection criterion' has been broad from the beginning, focusing on firms in the 'new economy', namely media, digital content, ICT and design.

Table 8.1 Goals for Arabianranta and progress

Goal	Status (September 2009)
1,300 students	Realized
7,000 jobs in creative industries	5,000 to 6,000
10,000 inhabitants	Expected to be realized in 2012

Source: own elaboration, based on data obtained through interviews

The global economic downturn of 2009 did not seem to have hurt Arabianranta's prospects, apart from the construction of two office buildings that has been delayed until the market recovered. The crisis did not influence prices in the area. On the contrary, as a distinctive 'premium' location, the prices have been stable or even slightly on the rise, especially for privately-owned real estate (according to Varma, a pension insurance company investor, confirmed by the ADC's CEO). The global crisis did not lead to a change in the strategy, and it is unlikely that it will be the case in the future. Overall, rent levels for residential property in Arabianranta are still lower than Helsinki's city centre and higher than in other suburbs. For example, according to ADC, in controlled-rent houses the price is around €8 per m^2 while it rises to €25 per m^2 in the city centre. For total private housing the acquisition price is around €5.5 per m^2 and close to €20 per m^2 for rent.

So far, ADC and its partners have accomplished what many other area management companies can only hope for: attraction of several companies and knowledge institutes, a socially diverse mix of inhabitants and stable prices in times of global crisis. The clear focus on art and design, managed in a triple-helix partnership, steered the development of a distinctive and economically vibrant planned knowledge location where people can live, work and play. The leaflet story stops here. However, in order to better understand the causes and mechanisms that led to these achievements, and, more importantly, derive insights that can be meaningfully used in other contexts, in the next sections we dig deeper into the evolution of Arabianranta as a business and knowledge location and as an urban experimentation arena.

Arabianranta as a business and knowledge location

To realize Arabianranta's goal – to become the leading centre for art and design in the Baltic and job creation in these new industries – a strong knowledge base and the presence of key actors with strong networks are required. This section analyses the development of Arabianranta as a business and knowledge location. After an analysis of the production ecosystem of art and design in Helsinki and its relation with Arabianranta, we briefly analyse the positioning of some firms and HEIs in Arabianranta, their reasons for 'being in Arabianranta' and the geography of business and knowledge networks. In this latter part, we also pay attention to the relations of Arabianranta with other locations in the larger Helsinki region.

The production ecosystem of art and design in Helsinki: a co-evolutionary account

In the last decades a global trend emerged where the aesthetic and symbolic components of products more and more determine their perceived value by customers, giving rise to what Allen Scott (2006) calls a Chamberlin–Robinson competition model: not based on price but increasingly on symbolism and differentiation. This global trend clearly brings design functions (such as industrial design) to the centre of many firm's innovation and marketing strategies, and benefits the (long-established) productive structures of cities like Helsinki, with a strong tradition in industrial design activities and related knowledge and expertise.

Helsinki has for a long time been a very relevant job market of industrial and craft design jobs, and 'produces' a relatively large number of élite designers and craftsmen. Helsinki hosts large, Finnish, design-based, multinational companies (in industries such as furniture, pottery, decoration and fashion) as well as many small-scale design offices and freelance entrepreneurs. Moreover, other industries absorb design as a key component of their branding and differentiation strategies (although with room for improvement – see Van der Borg and van Tuijl 2008). The city has been a long-time host of international design networks, and is an important global design centre when it comes to industrial and product design, mixing tradition and innovation in an intelligent fashion.

Long before the first plans were made to develop Arabianranta as a knowledge location the seeds for this development were sown. In the late nineteenth century Helsinki became a relevant centre for design. The first documented developments date from 1875, when the Finnish Society of Crafts and Design was founded by a group of leading cultural personages and industrialists who aimed to bring design into educational programmes and improve the quality of Finnish products. The Arts and Crafts School had been founded four years before, and passed through different organizational mutations until 1973 when it was dubbed the University of Art and Design Helsinki (TaiK).

In the early 1900s, Finnish design gained international recognition. For instance, it was shown during the World Exhibition in Paris. In the 1950s and 1960s, Finland had become a reference in design and applied art – applied, for example, in furniture, decoration, ceramics, pottery, glass or fashion – and Finnish brands such as Arabia (founded in 1873), Artek (1935), Iittala (1881) and Marimekko (1951) played a major role in the country's exports (Design Forum 2004). Renowned designers from the early 1900s like Alvar Aalto or Kaj Franck inspired and trained many other Finnish designers, giving rise to a genealogy of design talent throughout the century, localized in Helsinki. Apprentices of design masters, the former employees of large design companies, launched new spin-off ventures. New generations of graduates trained in TaiK fed the design capabilities and innovation in the region, anchoring knowledge and skills while attracting new talent from outside. Finnish 'design intensive' artefacts are sold at high prices in the top markets and increasingly penetrate new ones. Moreover, other sectors of Finnish industry also procure and integrate design functions, such as machinery,[7] ICT,[8] furniture and medical devices. Design played a major role in the country's exports and Helsinki has built reputation as a 'showroom of design'.

The Finnish capital benefits nowadays from the most developed supportive infrastructure and institutional setting in Finland. It hosts the Finnish Society for Crafts and Design, specific promotional organizations (like the Design Forum Finland, which organizes prizes, exhibitions, festivals and promotes Finnish design national and internationally), renowned institutes and excellent universities, like TaiK. The Finnish Innovation Agency – TEKES – recently considered design as an important innovation field to foster, after a previous focus on 'hard' technology. The BSc, MSc and PhD programmes provided by TaiK seem to provide a great fit for the direct needs of more directly design-based industry, focusing on (i) applied art and design; (ii) ceramic and glass design; (iii) industrial design; (iv) spatial and furniture design; and (v) fashion and clothing design, textile art and design.

In sum, a productive art and design system has been deeply rooted in Helsinki's economy, and this legacy enabled the development of art and design functions presently operating in Arabianranta (and also the feasibility of this topic as a central theme in the location). In other words, it was not Arabianranta as a new planned knowledge location that steered the development of new art and design economic activities in Helsinki, but it was the long productive and knowledge legacy rooted in Helsinki (firms, universities, genealogy of designers, institutional supportive institutions and so on) that made Arabianranta possible and as successful as it is nowadays.

Firm and HEIs

The success of Arabianranta is partly due to the firms and organizations that located in the area. Arabianranta has become home to a significant number of Finnish and international companies. Unlike many other business parks, there are no strict admission criteria: firms should fit the broad category of 'creative business' or 'knowledge economy'. As a result, the area is populated by firms with different sector profiles and sizes. It is home to many small companies with connections to design and media.

A considerable number of firms are located in a number of iconic buildings:

- The Arabia building (see Figure 8.1), developed and exploited (let) by Varma, hosts showrooms and offices of some of the most important furniture and interior design firms in the area (for example, EFC, PENTIK). It also hosts the Arabia museum, expositions, a library and shops as well as the TaiK.
- The six office buildings of Portaali Business Park concentrate a total of 4,000 jobs, spread among many companies, restaurants and joint facilities, in rented premises. Besides temporary work, HR and other general consultancy services, the space is dominated by firms in media and technology, ICT, the entertainment industry and other types of design. These are usually firms who relocated or opened new offices (selling and research

Figure 8.1   Arabia factory in Arabianranta, Helsinki, Finland

Source: own elaboration

points of a larger network). The large majority are mature and well implemented corporations.
- Other buildings in the area also host firms, usually smaller ones. The office
space for this type of initiatives is considered rather expensive by some of
our interview partners. As a result, sub-renting models tend to emerge, for
example, many micro firms sharing one large privately-owned open space.

There is an incubator managed by the HEIs in the area (namely TaiK and the
Institute of Applied Sciences). New firms can stay there for up to two years, at
reduced prices, and can make use of joint meeting rooms and other services such
as accountancy or legal support. The incubators usually house firms in new media,
ICT and design (broad focus, but aligned with the area). An incubator has capacity
for roughly 20 new firms per year and provides services, such as training for
entrepreneurship and mentoring.

There are various HEIs that followed TaiK to Arabianranta: the Helsinki Pop
and Jazz Conservatory (since 1995), the Faculty of Culture and Services of the
Helsinki Polytechnic Stadia (1996), an audiovisual educational institution (2003),
Arcada, the Finland-Swedish University of Applied Science (2004), and the
Prakticum Vocational Institute (2005). TaiK stands out because of its excellence
and tradition, and it is a magnet for design talent.

Location factors and networks

Major location factors for the companies, according to a recent survey and our interviews, are: the 'image' of the area as a location, the presence of TaiK, the creative atmosphere and accessibility. It is important to note that many of these firms have mainly showrooms here, not really production or even design, but they tend to launch antennas to 'see what is going on'. As a director of a firm said 'this is the spot to see what is around'.

Arabianranta may be a new pole for firms with knowledge-based strategies to tap and mobilize new sources of knowledge. This is important from a strategic perspective, but it does not generate *per se* the large number of jobs or revenues that might be expected. It potentially makes search costs to firms smaller and makes it possible to get inspiration and to find suitable labour. Thus, Arabianranta can be seen as a 'big inspirational bazaar' (there is a mixture of firms, students, designers, business customers and inhabitants) or as a 'business showroom'. The mixture of various actors and the easy access of the location are important to see what is going on and to spot the latest trends. Hence, tapping into the area's 'buzz' – here especially referring to market trends – played a major role for local business when first considering their location in Arabianranta.

The question is whether this really had a significant impact on firms' business or innovation, and whether this 'buzz' really materialized. This is much more open to debate. Some firms have well-established innovation processes and search mechanisms which do not rely on buzz at this micro scale. Other firms came to Arabianranta with expectations of high 'buzz', but were disappointed in this respect. Many of the firms in the area have few contracts and partnerships inside, although the contrary was expected by some of our interview partners before moving to Arabianranta. Occasional meetings resulting in new networks proved to be limited. Some firms even tried to create meeting platforms (such as 'Fountain Fridays') to meet people working in the same building, but that did not work out in the long run. Lunch facilities were not available in the beginning. There are buildings without a single internal business relationship in Arabianranta. For many firms, the key sources of innovation are the clients, which locate in other places (for instance Nokia in Espoo). Although firms do not directly benefit from local contacts, their business is not hampered as face-to-face contact is also possible with firms in other locations. For many of the firms in Arabianranta, innovation takes place through stable relationships and social networks, and not on pure 'buzz' and 'rubbing shoulders'.

Thus, the role of buzz and proximity for a firm's innovativeness might have been overestimated in Arabianranta at its conception. We know nowadays that physical proximity in one location does not seem to be a sufficient or necessary condition for innovation (Boschma 2005). Firms in Arabianranta source from design firms in the area, but also from other locations. One example is Iittala Group (the largest company in Arabianranta with about 400 employees) that buys the majority of the designs from specialized design firms (it employs only 30 to 40 designers). Of these, only three to seven small design firms that work for Iittala are based in Arabianranta. It also works the other way around: companies outside

Arabianranta source from design firms in the location, and there is no need to open facilities next to their clients or suppliers. For instance, Nokia sources from firms in Arabianranta, for instance the Strawberry Group that produces hinges for mobile phones. Thus, regarding design, there is no need to be directly located next to clients or suppliers. This is especially true for multinationals, such as Nokia, that source design from specialized firms all over the world and have their own design centres in global hotspots (in the case of Nokia, among others in California and London).

As mentioned, TaiK plays a key role for Arabianranta. First, it boosts the image of art and design in the area and it attracts firms. It is also definitely important for the innovation efforts of firms as it produces qualified and creative designers. However, with regard to the recruitment function, there does not seem to be a need for geographical proximity. As one interview partner noted: 'It doesn't matter where good designers are; companies can find them anyway'.

Firms that locate in Arabianranta tend to look to TaiK for graduates, but there is no systematic co-operation. There is some joint co-operation in lecturing and 'opening the doors for students', but again, 'buzz' does not seem to be a central issue. Firms see the location here as (i) a nice place to show their brand and get reputation, and (ii) as a place to put out antennas to check market trends. For foreign firms, there is one extra blockage in fostering innovation: their main design centres are located abroad close to the company's international headquarters, so it is not easy to match directly local designers and the firm's design departments – there are many 'filters'. Moreover, these firms are not systematically looking for designers; it is not their aim, as they have partners in which they trust and with whom they work regularly. These firms do not 'pick the first student', but rely on their own network partners. Many companies have antennas and selling points in Arabianranta, but produce elsewhere in Finland and abroad.

Linkages with other urban locations

Locations do not evolve in isolation and interact with other locations in the city; actors have networks on different geographical scales. The major locations in Helsinki that concentrate on art and design are summarized in Table 8.2. Arabianranta is part of the 'science axis' that stretches from the University of Helsinki in the city centre (social sciences) to Viikki, where the University of Helsinki focuses on biological sciences. The city centre, which forms the cultural heart of the city – with urban amenities comparable with those of other capitals – also includes the Design District Helsinki, a major showroom which exhibits and sells art, aimed at tourists and inhabitants.

Another major node in Helsinki's knowledge system is the city of Espoo, which hosts the Helsinki University of Technology as well as the headquarters of large multinationals such as Kone and Nokia. Espoo is also home to the recently established Design Factory, a facility that brings together engineers and designers in the newly formed Aalto University (after a merger between TaiK, Helsinki University of Technology and Helsinki School of Economics) to share ideas and to design and develop new products.[9] It is important to note that there are plans to create a

Table 8.2 Major (complementary) 'art and design' locations in Helsinki

Location	Major facilities	Function
Espoo	University of Technology	Technology and headquarters
	Design Factory	Design and development of new products, jointly innovated by designers and engineers
City centre	University of Helsinki: Human Sciences	Culture, tourism (showroom of design product for consumers) and social sciences
	Design District Helsinki	
Arabianranta	TaiK and other HEIs	Industrial design, showroom of design for business markets
		Labour pool of designers
Ruoholahti	Cable Factory	SMEs in various creative industries (artists, music, media, museums and so on)

Source: own elaboration

physical science axis by the construction of a metro link connecting Arabianranta with the city centre and Espoo. This would connect the campuses of three universities (TaiK, Technical University Helsinki and University of Helsinki).

Arabianranta is clearly different from the other locations. Its major focus is in industrial design and marketing for business markets, whereas other locations focus on technology (Espoo), tourism and culture (city centre) and SMEs in creative industries (Ruoholahti). It functions as a showroom of design for the business market. The Cable Factory is an old Nokia plant that provides office and exhibition space for artists, gallery holders, small media designers and museums. It is owned by the municipality and offers lower-priced spaces and in that sense it might be complementary to Arabianranta, where the rents are too high for start-ups. Moreover, the Cable Factory still exhibits the original 'roughness', which is important for certain parts of creative industries such as artists, in contrast to the Arabia building which is already too neat and polished. However, not all interview partners agreed with the complementary roles of Arabianranta and the Cable Factory. There are more low-cost locations, even in the city centre and Arabianranta, as expressed by an interviewee: 'If you search low-cost locations, you can find them everywhere'.

A major development that will have an impact on the integration of Arabianranta with other locations is the merger of three universities in Helsinki in the newly formed Aalto University. In September 2009 the spatial strategy of the new university was not fully clear and there was also no decision taken which campuses of the old universities would be used. This uncertainty explains why there is no new vision for Arabianranta. A scenario of Arabianranta without TaiK (in case the board decides to focus on the Espoo campus which is much larger and closer to the major business partner) is different from the scenario in which Arabianranta keeps its design school, making immediate planning difficult. Nevertheless, all interview partners agree about the importance of TaiK for the location, even though formal networks are less strong than could be expected.

Arabianranta as a place to live, play and experiment

Cities increasingly foster mixed environments in order to prevent 'dead areas' after working hours. Arabianranta is such an area, planned to have working, studying, recreation and living going hand in hand. This section focuses on the more spatial and urban functions of Arabianranta; we pay special attention to Arabianranta as a 'Living Lab' in which citizens are directly involved in the development of new product and technologies in an urban environment – an important experimentation feature associated with the area.

Housing and leisure

In order to attract a diverse group of inhabitants to Arabianranta, there are different land ownership schemes. Before the redevelopment of the area, a large share of the land was owned by the city, but nowadays also by private owners and corporate groups. Within the public–private partnership of the various stakeholders (such as the City of Helsinki, industry and other private partners), the land development models are diverse (city-owned land, long-term lease to private investors or private property), resulting also in different exploitation models (city regulated, full and partial market pricing) but sharing common standards and regulations for the entire area. Tenders have been used to decide which companies can develop parcels that are owned by the city. The city has the legal power to set rules, but does this in co-operation with other involved stakeholders. This is a central issue in the development in the area, and has resulted in many innovative ideas. Overall, around 40 per cent of the space is price regulated (for instance, establishing maximum rents).

Another strategy to attract a variety of inhabitants has been to offer a mix of different housing (see Figure 8.2): luxury private housing (fully market-based prices, developed by private developers); private rental housing with controlled prices; city social housing; student housing (for Finnish and foreign students); other specific buildings for (i) 'problem' youths, (ii) elderly and (iii) people with multiple sclerosis, all endowed with proper amenities for the different groups. For the latter groups, innovative architecture designs help to keep residents moving, active and integrated. It is worth mentioning that these groups are involved in the design of the houses in order to adapt them to their needs. With the increasing number of residents, Arabianranta attracts a growing number of 'market-based' amenities like shops, restaurants, malls, gyms and so on.

Arabianranta is located at 'Vanhankaupunginkoski brook' (waterfront), embedded in natural scenery. Moreover, there were interesting novelties in the design of public space. Residential buildings share common backyard and garden areas, with no fences, with art pieces and sculptures, facilitating socialization (which is not as common in Finnish culture as in other European countries) (see Figure 8.2). This is designed to foster community culture, monitoring, responsibility and co-operation among the residents. Besides, developers of the area are required to invest 1–2 per cent of total construction costs in art works (such as sculptures and paintings). This is done for three reasons: (i) it improves the sense of a pleasant place to live; (ii) it consolidates the image of the area around the core theme of art and design; (iii) it fosters creativity in developing innovative housing, new techniques, experimentation and quality of architecture. Recent studies show that residents rate this as one of the most valued features of the area (Kangasoja and Schulman, 2007).

Despite the focus on art and design, Arabianranta is not targeted as a tourist destination. Apart from art in public spaces and the historical renovated Arabianranta plant, there are no other potential tourist attractions. Nevertheless, the location is attractive for 'business visitors' who are interested in the redevelopment of the area and the living labs. The CEO of ADC receives on average two international delegation visits per week to learn about the location. It should be noted that there seem to be differences among the visitors: Asian visitors are particularly interested in technologies used, while European and American visitors show their interest in the social aspects of the 'Living Labs' (see below).

The mixed housing schemes, the variety of the houses and the perceived high quality of life have attracted many inhabitants to the area, and demand for housing is still rising. Nevertheless, in the interviews we have also found some points of criticism. First, despite the mixed housing schemes, it was mentioned that Arabianranta might be too expensive, running the risk that only higher income groups are attracted. There is no subsidy system to compensate for this. Second, although the supply of (basic) services increases, the service level is still lagging behind demand. Moreover, there are some doubts about the vibrancy of the area because of restrictions in opening hours of major facilities and the limited number of events. For instance, the Arabianranta building, that hosts various central facilities, closes at 22:00 hrs and is closed during weekends. The coffee shops in the

Figure 8.2 Mixed housing development in Arabianranta with communal gardens

Source: http://www.arabianranta.fi/asuminen/

building close even earlier at 18:00 hrs. These developments are at odds with the intention to create mixed areas which remain vibrant and active through the entire day (and also outside working hours).

ICT infrastructure, Helsinki Virtual Village and Living Labs

Since the beginning, Arabianranta has been an experimentation arena for pioneering urban development. In the preparatory phase, before construction, the city decided (together with Helsinki Energy) to endow all the Arabianranta area with 10Mb optical fibre broadband infrastructure. At that time companies were not interested in the fibre, and the development was largely driven by the public sector, with support of universities. Later this was seen as a first step to create a real 'connected community' out of Arabianranta.

Supported by ADC, the city of Helsinki and the developers created a 'last mile' infrastructure (rented out by ADC) to distribute fibre optic connections to the entire area. This led to the development of a physical and virtual community linked by an internet based local network, which is called 'Helsinki Virtual Village', managed by ADC. Helsinki Virtual Village works to develop a highly connected physical and virtual community of firms, residents, workers and educational institutes. It makes it possible to get the best deals with telecom operators to serve the entire area by means of a single tender.

Later, it became clear that this broadband infrastructure and the last-mile model, supported by a diversified mix of 'users' present in Arabianranta and linked by a strong sense of community, allowed Arabianranta to be one of the world 'Living Lab' pioneers. Hence, it was acknowledged suitable as a 'testbed' for user-driven innovations involving companies, research institutes, public actors and users who directly interact with each other.

But what is a Living Lab? The concept of Living Lab was first mentioned by Prof. William Mitchell in the Massachusetts Institute of Technology (MIT).[10] A Living Lab is defined as 'a user-centric research method which can be used in a real life environment to identify and build prototypes, and to evaluate multiple solutions which are needed more and more in constantly changing living environments'.[11] It is (or seems to be) inspired by the Eric von Hippel's (2005) user-driven innovation and is also in line with the concept of open innovation (Chesbrough 2003). A major difference is that Living Labs are based on public–private partnerships and often public actors are the major investors (Almirall 2008). This explains why Living Labs in the USA are less successful than in Europe. The concept is less interesting for companies as many tests fail. Also in the case of Arabianranta, the contribution of companies, such as Nokia, is relatively small, and the majority of the investments are made by national agencies such as TEKES.

The start of Living Labs in Arabianranta was to a certain extent coincidental. It had a very appropriate structure in the form of the broadband networks, although this was not the goal of the construction of this network. The concept was brought to Finland by a professor who visited MIT. Concrete projects in Arabianranta were under the leadership of ADC since 2002. The concept reached European political discussion in 2006 when the term was introduced by the Finnish prime minister during his term as EU president (Katzy and Klein 2008). Later a network of European Living Labs was established. At the end of 2009, this network included about 130 Living Lab projects and it received €60 million from the EC (interview). Arabianranta might be seen as an example of best practice in the Living Lab network, although there are many types of Living Labs which are place-dependent and therefore difficult to compare.

In Arabianranta, all residential buildings (blocks) have an intranet and a 'house ICT platform'. Each building has an e-moderator who is responsible to set discussions, filter info, organize topics and so on, and can be seen as an administrator of the building. These platforms have high rates of usage. Through these platforms people meet first virtually and at a later stage personally, to discuss house-related topics. Through these platforms it is also easy for researchers and/or firms to find people to test within Living Lab projects. There are also meetings between all the e-moderators, to launch new topics, discuss participation, common needs of the residents and practical problems. The platforms are very interactive, not only to access house documents but mainly to interact in forums with each other.

The e-moderator and the ICT platforms play a key role in Arabianranta's success as a Living Lab. Residents have diverse needs, and this increases the chance for user-driven innovation. There are also new mixed models and two-way modes of innovation arise, including both firm–user and user–user. A simple example is that an elder used a taxi to get one bottle of milk. Elders communicate with others to go shopping together; the occupancy rate of the taxi increases and the elder meets other people (and social exclusion declines). Arabianranta is well placed to realize such initiatives, since networks (ICT platforms) already exist in the area. Trust is crucial in these networks, which can be created by the moderator. He or she is required to be a resident of the building.

Another success factor for Living Labs in Arabianranta is the mixed population (residents, students, entrepreneurs, firms and so on). Usability is a central element in Living Labs, and Arabianranta's mixed population is suited to test new prototypes or gadgets in various target groups or to test it in a diverse population. The group represents a 'true living life experience'. The first trials in MIT were not so successful or interesting, since they were done in a very homogeneous group of only 20,000 students and academics. Arabianranta, in contrast, provides different ecosystems, such as small business ecosystems, real-life ecosystems and so on. Moreover, users are known by 'membership' of the ICT platforms, making it possible to select the right population for individual projects.

In sum, the broadband infrastructure and the last mile model, the ICT platforms, networks, e-moderators, presence of public–private funding and a heterogeneous test group, make Arabianranta one of the world Living Lab pioneers, stressing in Arabianranta what has been recently dubbed a 'Social Silicon Valley'.

However, there are also some drawbacks and limitations to the Living Lab concept in Arabianranta. First, many projects are location-specific, making it difficult to export successful projects to other places. Second, as noted before, Living Labs are largely dependent on public funding, and the involvement of private actors is limited. Third, and in relation to this, there are some doubts about the value of the tests for the community. It was argued that the rewards for inhabitants are limited, and in some cases they have the feeling that they are monitored all the time at the cost of privacy. Or as one interview partner argued: 'They feel like a rabbit in a cage ... and have a Big Brother feeling'. Fourth, due to the excellent broadband connection, investments in new ICT technologies are limited. For instance, Arabianranta has a limited number of Wi-Fi hotspots.

Conclusions and perspectives

Many cities promote themselves as 'creative and vibrant', willing to attract and retain investments and skills. The so-called creative industries – such as 'art and design' – are often pivotal in these efforts. Therefore many cities have explicit policies to foster creative or cultural clusters. In this chapter we dealt with the case of Arabianranta, a recent large-scale urban area-based (re)development focused precisely on the transversal theme of art and design, with a formulated vision to become 'the leading centre for art and design in the Baltic area'.

This new 'knowledge location' has a long tradition in industrial design. It was the cradle of Arabia, one of Europe's first and largest porcelain plants. However, Arabia restructured its business during recent decades, leaving land and buildings empty and potentially available for other functions. One of the first 'new entrants' was TaiK (during the mid-1980s), the renowned Helsinki University of Art and Design, becoming anchor and engine of a steady redevelopment process since the early 1990s. During the last decade, the site has turned into a mixed-use urban district, combining studying, working, learning, leisure and living (as actually highlighted in the area's promotion material). Moreover, Arabianranta was one of the world's 'Living Lab' pioneers: it is particularly suited as 'testbed' for user-driven innovation, involving a large number of different stakeholders, directly interacting with each other towards the development of innovative solutions in the diverse fields.

So far, Arabianranta has accomplished most of its objectives, namely concerning the area's number of students, residents and workers. It is home to many 'art and design related' knowledge institutes and many students and residents have chosen Arabianranta as their place to live. There is a large variety of housing, renting and buying schemes in surroundings that combine an urban feeling with nature. Moreover, Arabianranta is known as a best practice model in the origins of the European Living Lab network. An indication for this success is the large number of research visits (about two per week) hosted by the area's public–private management company. In this case study we attempted to obtain a deep analytical understanding of the preconditions and processes behind this 'success story'.

Some insights result clearly from our analysis. First of all, it was not Arabianranta that steered the development of a strong art and design productive and innovation system in Helsinki. The causality seems to be precisely the opposite. It is the rooted system of (design) activities, accumulated skills and supportive institutions co-evolving in Helsinki that explains why Arabianranta emerged as an area dedicated to art and design activities. Arabianranta as a planned knowledge location is thus better understood as part of a longer and broader co-evolutionary process sparked a long time ago (Boschma 2004; Maskell and Malmberg 2007), when

Helsinki emerged as a national, European and international reference in design. From the start, the anchors of the project have been well established design organizations (lead firms, TaiK), the same who lobbied (through influential persons) to redevelop the area around the theme of art and design instead of other options open to the city in the early 1990s (for example, to develop the land into an urban park). Moreover, if Arabianranta attracts design students and artists to study, live and work it is because Helsinki has for a long time been an attractive 'design' spot and hosts a pole of differentiated skills for design activities – Arabianranta became one of the 'faces' of this system. It is likely that Arabianranta will play a role in supporting Helsinki further as an art and design hub (for example, though enhanced image and informal knowledge spill-overs), but the previous existence of this 'system', in its broad sense, was a central precondition for success.

Another important precondition was the long established Finnish co-operation culture, facilitating the smoother development of complex large-scale public–private partnerships around issues of joint interest. Moreover, the Finnish urban planning system and institutions (with high legitimacy for coordinating area-based developments, land ownership and public power over private parties) made possible the integration of (mixed) functions, theme establishment and diverse housing schemes. This integration would have been much more difficult to accomplish in the context of other planning systems, where the power of private actors is much stronger and the planning rules and institutions are looser.

Success factors and strategic urban management

Other factors, related to the former, facilitated and accelerated the success of the location, but were hardly sufficient conditions *per se*.

First, there was a clear shared vision and theme selection, associated with a strong urban management capacity to mobilize the right persons and networks in times of crisis (1990s). The theme 'art and design' has a historical as well as a contemporary value, and was assumed by all the parties as a long-term vision. TaiK acted as a flagship, anchor and image builder of the area (as well as the Iittala Group). Second, the development of some distinctive features of the site was steered by the close involvement of key persons acting as 'gatekeepers', linking Helsinki and other knowledge sources worldwide. For example, the first Living Lab experiences were supported by professors of TaiK who brought the concept from the USA (MIT) and subsequently diffused it Europe-wide. Third, the establishment of a dedicated agency represented the interests of the involved players while monitoring the implementation of the holistic concept for the area. Fourth, a number of contingencies and right 'timings' helped to steer the project in the right direction. TaiK was searching for temporary space; when the site was developing, Helsinki was growing and in need of new office and residential space. Another example was the set-up of the broadband infrastructure that critically facilitated the development of Living Labs – it was not planned from the beginning but was critical in the set-up of the ICT platforms and the social interaction (e-moderators) allowing for the development of Arabianranta as a 'Social Silicon Valley'.

Results of Arabianranta

We further looked at the results accomplished by Arabianranta from two complementary but different perspectives, which should not be confused: (i) the development of clustering and agglomeration economies and (ii) effects on spatial
development and urban experimentation.

Clustering and agglomeration economies

Arabianranta attracted (Finnish and international) actors in the fields of art and
design (and also multimedia), and there are some observable spatial clustering
effects. Many firms state that they located in Arabianranta for image reasons,
associated with the presence of TaiK. Arabianranta is considered an excellent
design showroom and has good accessibility to the city centre. Moreover, due
to TaiK and other firms, there is a specialized micro-labour pool making it easy
to hire new designers and spot what other firms and consumers are doing; many
firms hope to benefit from this 'buzz' in order to catch the latest market and
consumer trends.

Nevertheless, it is arguable whether this 'buzz' is really taking place and to
what extent it is really important for firms' innovation and competitiveness. We
found evidence that local networks are limited and many networks evolve at larger
spatial scales, with stable partners. We have seen that many design firms supply
and source 'knowledge' to and from other parts of Helsinki and that systematic co-operation with TaiK concerning training students is limited. Moreover,
companies are able to find good designers from various places and physical proximity to labour markets is not often required. Also, companies in Arabianranta
have different innovation models; for example, digital content producers rely
much more on stable partners and clients in Espoo (like Nokia) than from other
players in the location. Other companies do not have any design departments in
Arabianranta, and use it as a simple showroom and sales office.

Another remark that should be made is that Arabianranta focuses mainly on
the higher/professional design market (also due to relatively high prices). The
location seems to miss the vibrancy and facilities to attract other design niches.
There is no underground culture to attract the artists that form the cultural
humus of a city. On the contrary, the cultural supply lags behind the demand
of the new inhabitants. Moreover, Arabianranta is considered too expensive
for entrepreneurs and small firms. In addition, apart from an incubator centre
(Arabus), support for starters and SMEs is limited. It should be pointed out that
Arabianranta is only one of the locations in Helsinki in which art and design
play a role. For instance, the city centre can be seen as a tourist attraction
selling consumer art products, and the Cable Factory offers cheap accommodation for artists and offers space for small-scale cultural events. It is still to be
seen whether Arabianranta will develop as a distinct city district for knowledge
production as companies, HEI and residents start to create social proximity, or
whether it will be just one more office and housing space hub in a larger design-
relevant cluster in Helsinki as a whole.

Spatial development and urban experimentation

It would be highly partial to look at Arabianranta only as a place to foster knowledge production and innovation. From a more integrated urban development perspective, Arabianranta had so far enacted important spatial and organizational effects in Helsinki.

First, from a physical perspective, Arabianranta developed as a new centrality in Helsinki, enhancing the quality of the urban space and constituting itself as a relevant new urban pole, an extension to the city centre without the suburb feeling. It structures nowadays an important 'science' axis, also including the city centre and the Espoo area where the University of Technology is located. It is one of the 'thematic activity' areas of the city, promoting a clear image (others, such as Viiki, are dedicated to bio-medicine). It reinforced the position of the city of Helsinki as a quite polycentric metropolitan area.

Second, Arabianranta allowed for a number of urban-based experiments, some of them becoming or in the way of becoming mainstream. It allowed the testing of new local broadband solutions, enhancing the digital connectivity of the area. At that time (late 1990s and early 2000s), broadband optic fibre was a novelty, and few locations in the world were endowed with this infrastructure. As previously described, associated with portals and digital platforms in each building, it facilitated the development of social interactions and a sense of community in each building and in the area as a whole. The emergence of 'e-moderators' as brokers and gatekeepers of sociability allowed for the development of Living Lab experiments, enhancing the portfolio of activities of the area, as well as the development of constant social innovations for Arabianranta. Also, socially, Arabianranta is a case of success and integrated planning – it hosts a mix of social, ethnic and age groups in different housing schemes integrated in a location of growing charisma.

Third, the process of developing Arabianranta enhanced the capacity of local government to organize this type of demanding partnership, namely by helping to institutionalize regular co-operation with other parties (such as developers, universities, firms) around large-scale and integrated developments. Moreover, it required the establishment of regular co-operation between municipal departments around transversal issues (such as planning, transport and economic development departments). Arabianranta also showed the need to develop communication plans and the importance of establishing dedicated entities and public–private structures to monitor the development of large projects over time (ADC). Many of the lessons of Arabianranta are nowadays being used and considered in new thematic area-based developments in other city locations.

Challenges and recommendations

As a location is never finished, there are some challenges for future development. The first and probably biggest challenge relates to the recent merger of the three Helsinki universities – the new Aalto University. The role of the individual campuses in the new organization is still unknown. The uncertainty of the future role of TaiK is a major reason for the absence of an updated vision for the area,[12] but there is consensus that there is a need to keep TaiK in Arabianranta – at least its major functions – as it is seen as the flagship of the cluster. Without TaiK, Arabianranta may lose its 'face' and a major source of 'buzz' and attractiveness. The same goes for Iittala – besides its anchor role, it would be a huge challenge to find new tenants to take the empty space.

A second challenge is to reduce the dependency on key persons. As we have described, much knowledge and leadership are dependent on key persons who connect Arabianranta with other key places and institutes (such as MIT) and steer developments in the right direction. The challenges are: to keep these persons, attract successors and reduce the dependency on key persons by the establishment of more structural and institutionalized networks. Third, it is important to prevent Arabianranta from becoming a prisoner of its own past. Therefore, there is a need to innovate constantly and adapt to contemporary requirements. For instance, there needs to be investment in energy efficiency techniques and in Wi-Fi hotspots. At the time of construction, these issues were not on the agenda. This may steer further experimentation and keep Arabianranta at the edge of experimentation. Fourth, it is a challenge to connect Arabianranta with other locations in the region. How can Arabianranta be complementary to newer locations, such as Viiki and Ruohalahti? Furthermore, it is crucial that the science axis becomes a physical axis that connects Arabianranta with the city centre and Espoo, where other initiatives and incubators (like the design factory) are located.

Finally, it is important to pay attention to other issues, such as improving the cultural supply and making it better to live in. Moreover, tailor-made policy and support SMEs in the area should probably be paid more attention, at least ensuring good connections with areas which are more suited for SMEs (such as the Cable Factory) would be an important effort.

9   Incheon: Songdo International City

Introduction: setting the scene

> Take a man-made island, roughly twice the size of Central Park. Fill it with state-of-the-art schools, hospitals, apartments, cultural amenities, and universities. Replicate architectural features from around the world, including Venice's canals and New York's parks. Make English the *lingua franca* and – presto – you have the world's newest city: it is Korea's answer to Shanghai and Dubai … Financing it with recycled real-estate profits sounds like an act of lunacy. Yet this is what is happening in South Korea, and strangest of all, it appears to be working.
>
> (McNeill 2009)

Since the 1970s and together with Singapore, Taiwan and Hong Kong, South Korea had been part of a rather well known group of economies dubbed the 'Asian tigers' or first 'newly industrialized economies'. These are nowadays high-income countries that experienced remarkable growth and change over the last half-century. Despite the recent emergence of fast-growing global giants like China, India or Brazil, South Korea has been considered by many commentators, such as Goldman Sachs, McKinsey or *The Economist*, as one of the economies with largest growth potential for the future (Florida 2005; McKinsey and Company 2010).

Despite the country's astonishing success, the history of South Korea has been far from stable. Korea's peninsula was annexed by Japan in 1910 and later occupied by Soviet and American troops in the aftermath of the Second World War, when it was divided along the 38th parallel into North Korea (under Soviet influence) and South Korea (occupied by United States troops). A North–South civil war followed (the first armed conflict of the Cold War), ceasing fire in 1953. By this time, basic infrastructure was destroyed and South Korea faced unemployment and poverty. To change this state of affairs, the state launched an import-substitution industrial policy, with an export focus, supporting the emergence and growth of large conglomerates of industrial activities (called *chaebol*) such as the world famous Hyundai, Kia and Samsung, parallel to making sound investments in infrastructure and education. Seoul's city and region became the face of the country's rapid change, nowadays a dynamic metropolis, centre of business and trade, with highly advanced technological infrastructure. Seoul was the first Asian city after Tokyo to host the summer Olympics back in 1988. Its fast industrialization and continuous growth, particularly around Seoul (for example Incheon city, Gyeonggi Province) transformed South Korea into a $US trillion economy and world-class manufacturer. This success story has been widely described as the Miracle on the Han River.

South Korea's growth has proved resilient as well (Roach and Lam 2010). Its economy recovered fast from the 2008–9 financial crisis, just as it did after the 1997 Asian debt crisis and the International Monetary Fund intervention (IMF 2009). From this period on, market-driven and neo-liberal reforms gained strong momentum and South Korea launched policies to increase openness to foreign capital and FDI (Wang 2007), willing to support the development of new economic activities beyond manufacturing, like services and new knowledge-based industries. This was seen as a necessary step to keep the country's progress apace with that of the previous decades. In the early 2000s, under this reformist turn and tapping into the country's strategic location, the Korean Ministry of Finance and Economy (2002a) published a strategic document with the vision to make South Korea 'Northeast Asia's Business Hub'. This strategy had spatial implications. Seoul would still be the country's main economic and knowledge centre, but new growth engines would contribute to fulfil this hub character. The metropolitan cities of Busan (a large port city in the south of the country) and Incheon (only 30km away from Seoul, with a brand-new international airport) were among the natural strategic choices. In 2002, together with local governments, the Korean Government legislated for the creation of special Free Economic Zones in different Korean cities, strategic tools of the country's new knowledge and development strategy.

Incheon, the third largest metropolitan city in South Korea (after Seoul and Busan), with 2.7 million inhabitants, early became a central pawn in the 'business hub' strategy. Incheon grew significantly in the last decades as a manufacturing hub, attracting population from the countryside, even though erosion of the manufacturing base has occurred in recent years due to rising land prices. In 1995 it became administratively one of the six metropolitan cities of South Korea, yet was considered part of (Seoul's) capital region as well. Despite its economic relevance, and due to its strategic location, Ducruet (2007) comments that in the last decades, Incheon has played the role of maritime and industrial extension of the capital Seoul, which still concentrates the core of advanced services, knowledge and decision functions of the country. The creation of IFEZ – Incheon Free Economic Zone – the country's first of its kind, envisaged changing this situation, endowing Incheon with a much more strategic role as international hub for logistics, business, leisure and new high-tech clusters. Mostly based on sea-reclaimed land, IFEZ is being developed through the creation of three non-contiguous 'new cities': Songdo, Yeongjong and Cheongna.

This case study focuses on one of these new cities – the new Songdo district – planned to become a fully-fledged international business hub and knowledge location by 2020, with 250,000 new inhabitants, in an area of 50 square kilometres. Despite being a rather recent development (construction works started in 2003), Songdo has already caught the attention of many commentators and research disciplines. It has been a case study, to name a few, of international business studies (Segel 2005; Lee and Hobday 2003); real-estate finance (Kang 2004); the development of environmentally friendly and sustainable cities (Whitman *et al.* 2008; Ekblaw *et al.* 2009); comparative development of free economic zones (Kim 2007; Bang and Park 2005); politics of place promotion (Kim 2010) and knowledge-based urban development (Lee *et al.* 2008; Murray and Greenes 2007). Moreover, attention has increasingly been given by international press, for example by the *New York Times* (Cortese 2007). Furthermore, Songdo has been referred to as a highly promising development by organizations like the OECD (2005) and the Creative Class Group of Richard Florida (Florida 2005). With strong involvement from private foreign (particularly US) capital, Songdo is among the largest 'polderization' real-estate developments in the world. The master plan for Songdo's international business district won an international award from the American Institute of Architects. It proposes an integral urban development project, combining a holistic portfolio of urban functions and amenities. The project is orchestrated by the Metropolitan City of Incheon with the strong commitment of the National Government. Besides tax cuts and other incentives, large sums of money are being invested in excellent transport infrastructure as well as sound funding for science, technology and firms' innovation.

In this case study, we go beyond a snapshot description of what Songdo is nowadays and systematically analyse its emergence and development dynamics as a 'planned knowledge location'. By doing so, we move away from the more conventional place promotion discourse (Kim 2010), and try to unravel critical processes and mechanisms involved in the development of Songdo. More precisely, we try to answer the following two central questions:

• What drivers and catalysts are behind the emergence of Songdo?
• How has Songdo developed over time, both as an international business and knowledge location and as a functionally integrated urban area? And what factors have critically influenced this development?

We argue that Songdo can be seen as the urban 'face' of a number of converging national and metropolitan strategies to create distinctive competitive advantages for South Korea, the capital region and Incheon, *vis-à-vis* other Asian competitors. At the national level, Songdo is among the first testbeds of a number of ongoing political, social and economic reforms in South Korea (such as economic liberalization, social openness, deregulation, and attraction of foreign capital), a protected arena to overcome vested interests, facilitate looser and more flexible regulations and the development of new knowledge-intensive clusters. Moreover, it reflects the wish to overcome the neutral or unfavourable image of Korea for external investors and expatriates (Graves 2010; Kim and Lee 2007) towards a more open, global business and knowledge location. At the metropolitan and city level, by creating a new high-stature business and knowledge hub, a visionary, functionally integrated 'tomorrow city', Incheon targets the activation of new and distinct growth engines within the capital region and Seoul.

This study has two central aims: one is analytical, and we assess the state-of-the-art of Songdo's development, the antecedents and catalysts behind its emergence and early growth. A second one is prescriptive: here we bring forward challenges and policy recommendations. The chapter is organized as follows: after this introduction, in the second section, we start with a broad contextualization and narrow down progressively, by (i) sketching the socio-economic and institutional structures and dynamics under which Songdo emerged and unfolded; (ii) analysing the chronology of events with relevance for the development of Songdo; and (iii) providing a picture of the location's most relevant physical and organizational features. In the third section we focus on Songdo as an international business and knowledge location. The fourth section looks at Songdo as an integrated urban development project. In the final section we wrap up, pointing to critical development challenges and policy recommendations.

Songdo: context, history and management

Structures and dynamics: development foundations and institutional context

Geostrategic position and the evolving role of the Developmental State

South Korea is located in what is nowadays one of the most dynamic world economic regions – Northeast Asia. In the context of an ongoing hegemonic shift from Western economies towards Asia, Northeast Asia has become responsible for the lion's share of the world's economy and growth, particularly after the economic downturn of 2008–9 (OECD 2010).

The economic engines of this region are concentrated in a number of what Richard Florida and his collaborators (2008) call mega-regions: large extensions of urbanized territory defined in terms of contiguously (or very nearly contiguously) lighted areas as seen from space at night (ibid, p. 463). This indicator, though simplistic, is very illustrative and highly correlated with other more conventional measures like a region's GDP. With no surprise, it shows the highly uneven distribution of economic activity in a number of urban agglomerations in a spiky, far from flat world. South Korea has a well distinguishable place in this map; despite the differences within the country, according to Florida's methodology a large part of South Korea's territory forms a mega-region (roughly from Seoul to Busan), just like other Japanese and Chinese mega-regions, for example, the famous mega-agglomerations of Tokyo, Osaka–Nagoya, Shanghai, Beijing or Hong Kong–Shenzhen (see Figure 9.1).

South Korea's geographical location has been recognized as challenging. It is literally 'stuck in the middle' (Roach and Lam 2010) of two economic power-houses: the manufacturing giant China and the knowledge champion Japan. Dingli (2010) puts it very clearly:

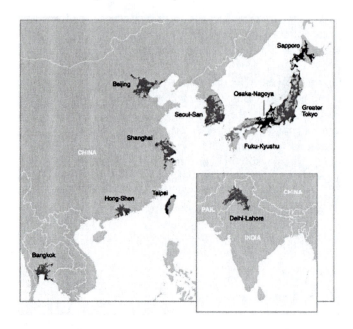

Figure 9.1   Asia's 'mega-regions'

Source: Florida *et al.* (2008)

> South Korea sits in a difficult neighbourhood. It has long competed with Japan, and compared itself to it. But Japan is richer, both in terms of money and in human resources. Now China is catching up. While Japan leads South Korea in high-tech prowess, China is narrowing its technological gap. And given that both China and Japan have many more people, it is unlikely that South Korea will ever match them in economic scale.
>
> (ibid, p. 19)

Thus, in the last few years, and especially after 1997's IMF stabilizing intervention, the Korean government has been pursuing structural reforms towards economic liberalization, flexible legislation, lower taxation and FDI attraction. Korea envisages developing an advanced services and 'high-tech' economy to complement and diversify its (still) *chaebol*-based industrial capacity. This 'globalization' strategy implies plugging into the evolving competition between world cities to attract mobile investments in spaces of economic, financial and labour flows (for example, Douglass 2000; Taylor 2000; Hill and Kim 2000; Wall 2009). Cities like Dubai, Hong Kong, Shanghai/Pudong or Singapore become, ironically, references and competitors for the attraction of similar types of international business and investment.

Simultaneously, the role of the national government slowly became more legislation-oriented, as a facilitator of private investments, an evolution *vis-à-vis* its role during the second half of the twentieth century, when government's active industrial policy and *chaebol* funding was famously called the 'Developmental State' (Wade 1990; Stubbs 2009, for a review). The rather visible hand of the state, by 'putting the prices wrong' (Amsden 1989), supported the emergence of national industrial conglomerates, 'too big to fail', for example in automotive, electronics, steel and shipbuilding. Famous examples are the *chaebol* Hyundai, Daewoo, Samsung and LG, nowadays world champions in their fields. Despite the state's role during the *chaebol* emergence and development, since the 1990s the stature of these companies evolved with their lead of global production networks, in which they plugged through, for example, mergers and acquisitions, disembedding themselves from the direct state support and becoming fully fledged global corporations (Yeung 2009).

However, and despite the ongoing structural reforms, the Developmental State seems far from dead. According with Yeung (2009), it evolved towards a 'new generation' Developmental State, with the supportive focus and main tenets now turned to 'pick the winners' in new high-tech and immaterial industries like ICT, nano- and bio-technologies. Moreover, with regard to the types of support from the different governments lately, it is noticeable that central government focuses on deregulation and tax incentives while municipal government tends to actively participate in numerous investment promotions encompassing 'providing the land at low cost' and other financial aids to lure in more businesses. Thus, the two governments or state levels have distinctive, though sometimes intertwined, roles in the field, with municipal support more direct and central more indirect.

The above-mentioned fundamental changes in South Korea – that is, economic liberalization towards the attraction of international businesses, and the emergence of a 'new generation', high-tech-focused Developmental State – are convergent and critical to understand both the emergence and developments taking place nowadays in IFEZ generally and in Songdo in particular. A third fundamental change is related to the national government's economic decentralization policy from Seoul towards other metropolitan cities, while nurturing the potentials of the capital region. We discuss this next, while framing the development foundations of Incheon in the context of Seoul's capital region.

Incheon and Songdo in Seoul's capital region – development foundations and context

Incheon is South Korea's third largest metropolitan city (2.7 million inhabitants), after the capital Seoul (only 30km away in the Han River, with 10 million inhabitants) and the southern city of Busan (3.6 million inhabitants, and among the largest seaports in the world). Incheon has always been geopolitically and economically important not only because of its port but also because of the proximity to the North Korean border and to the capital, Seoul. This proximity to Seoul, however, embodies a paradox: Incheon is a large metropolitan city, but at the same time it is too close to Seoul to claim full functional independence, namely for higher-level business activities and knowledge-intensive functions. Ducruet (2007) stresses that until the 1990s Incheon enjoyed the country's highest growth of industrial employment and rural migration. The population is ageing (in Korea generally), but Incheon is likely to keep attracting young workers from the rural areas. However, the city could not diversify its economy precisely given its proximity to Seoul, where core business and tertiary activities are concentrated. This situation poses challenges for the further development of Incheon and Songdo district.

Notwithstanding this integration, and as we can see by the commuting flows between Incheon and Seoul *vis-à-vis* other municipalities around Seoul (Figure 9.2), Incheon has a rather independent labour market and is far from being a simple suburbanized satellite of Seoul.

The economic muscle of this urban region is nowadays among Asia's and the world's strongest. The Han River area in general and Seoul in particular concentrates the headquarters, advanced manufacturing and R&D activities of the main Korean conglomerates and large industrial companies – among the world leaders in automotive, LCD TVs, electronics, mobiles, ships, steel, appliances and memory chips. These industrial competences accumulated over time to form a distinct set of available engineering skills, a large labour pool of very qualified technicians, adapted university and education curricula, but also industrial vested interests willing to keep the *status quo*, with influence in (industrial) policymaking. Again, government support was pivotal in developing and strengthening this economic and knowledge base over time, not only directly supporting national (export) champions, but also funding, for example, the military and defence industry and its appliances. Korean companies are nowadays among the world leaders in these industries. Some of them merged or established joint ventures with other global corporations. Daewoo Motors was integrated in the General Motors group, but kept its operations in Incheon; it recently announced a large investment in an R&D and pilot test facility in IFEZ. Simultaneously, national and local government nowadays strongly support economic diversification and the development of new high-tech activities, tapping into the skills and competences of national universities and R&D centres. Even if the service sectors are underdeveloped in South Korea *vis-à-vis* other developed economies (OECD 2005; Dobbs and Villinger 2010), Seoul still concentrates the most important and advanced share in the nation.

The economy of metropolitan Incheon, if statistically analysed without Seoul, represents approximately 4.7 per cent of the national economy (IDI 2010). In the last decade, despite the relative growth of tertiary activities proper to a metropolitan city (real estate, commerce, hotel and retailing and so on), a large share of Incheon's economy remained centred on industries like iron, steel, coke, light metals, plate-glass, textiles, chemicals and lumber, most of them organized in small and medium-sized companies (Ducruet 2007). Incheon's metropolitan city government has a clear vision to diversify its economy from traditional manufacturing towards the 'activities of the knowledge economy', and, aligned with National Government, directs funding for the development of ICT, biotechnology, nanotechnology, new materials and so on.

The knowledge base of the capital region is also very strong. The qualification level of South Koreans is very high by any international standard (OECD

2005; McKinsey and Company 2010) – around 95 per cent of Koreans attended high school, and 98 per cent are literate. During 2001–6, South Korea invested roughly 2.7 per cent of its GDP in R&D, the highest percentage for countries at similar development levels. This share is higher than in Singapore, Germany or even the United States. An important part of these investments became patented innovations. Specialization sectors in South Korea (electronics, mobiles, automotive) are particularly prone to register patents as innovation output; legislation is supportive and the results are globally impressive. In 2001, South Korea ranked world second in number of registered patents, Tokyo's mega-region being the first and Boston–Washington DC the third (Florida *et al.* 2008).

Seoul has the best research and knowledge infrastructure in the country, including R&D facilities of the largest industrial companies. Incheon city is also endowed with large universities and higher educational institutes in science and technology domains. Examples are the University of Incheon, Inha University-Technical College and Gachon Medical School – all of them developing brand-new premises and dedicated R&D centres in Songdo district. Notwithstanding this educational supply, Dobbs and Villinger (2010) note that an astonishing 30 per cent of the deficit in the services' trade balance of South Korea is associated with educational spending abroad. This reflects the decision of many families to send

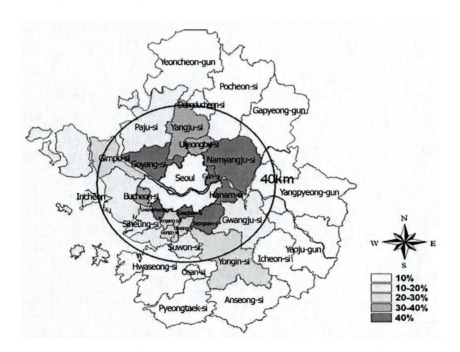

Figure 9.2 Commuting flows in Seoul – inbound commuting ratio

Source: OECD (2005), based on the urban planning bureau of Seoul's metropolitan government

young pupils overseas for primary, secondary and university schooling, because of the high value attached to education, and in particular to US degrees (Figure 9.3). As a result, a large share of PhD graduates working in Korea have experience working in overseas universities and companies, and a potential network of latent international contacts. The Korean highly-qualified diaspora has also proved to be an asset before, for instance for Samsung's technology search and related business in the USA in the late 1990s (Kuznetzov and Sabel 2008).

Incheon's international accessibility is excellent, especially after the opening of Incheon's international airport, already one of Asia's largest and growing passenger and cargo hubs (IDI 2010). The former international airport of Seoul (Gimpo), close to Incheon city, still runs and focuses on domestic and Asian connections. The new airport has been a central piece in the new Songdo district strategy. The new Incheon Grand Bridge, the seventh largest in the world (at 21km) recently opened and makes a 15-minute connection to the new international airport. Incheon also has a large sea port under expansion, and a new light port area is inclusively planned for Songdo; moreover, the new Gyeong-In waterway linking the River Han with Incheon (close to completion) may strengthen even further the city's logistical capacity and connectivity with Seoul. Incheon metropolitan city is well linked within and to Seoul through road, rail and metro lines. Songdo district has many metro stops and is highly accessible by all transport modes. This connectivity is likely to improve even further as new infrastructural investments are completed (see Figure 9.4).

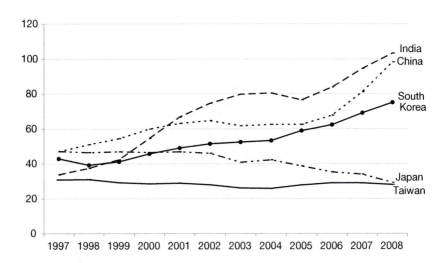

Figure 9.3 Number of foreign students enrolled in the USA, per nationality, thousands

Source: own elaboration, with data from Open Doors (n.d.), Institute for International Education, New York

Note: 1997 corresponds to the academic year of 1997/1998 and so on

Digital infrastructure – broadband, optical fibre – is excellent in Incheon and South Korea as a whole, often ranked as the world's best (Florida 2005; Kelly *et al.* 2003). Broadband penetration of households is close to 100 per cent and Korea is at the cutting edge of world broadband leadership. This makes the country, and some large regions in particular, perfect testbeds for new ICT-related innovations, as is the case of the development of u-city technologies and planning concepts in Songdo district (see following sections).

Incheon city has ambitious plans to achieve a balanced spatial development. The city representatives are aware of the potential detachment between IFEZ's new cities and the 'old' centres and districts of Incheon. Hence, the city plans a 2020 target for the development of new accessibility and revitalization plans for those city areas, in order to achieve a more equilibrated and polycentric development. These redevelopments are planned to be cross-funded with the real-estate profits generated by IFEZ. Yet, simultaneously, direct accessibility from the new cities to Seoul is likely to improve even further.

Incheon has all the market amenities typical of a metropolitan city, naturally complemented by higher order amenities and the cosmopolitan atmosphere of the city of Seoul, only 30km away: culture, leisure and so on. Incheon itself is not perceived as a highly vibrant city, but real-estate prices are much lower. The policy and promotional discourse of Songdo and IFEZ in general – 'a wonderful place where beautiful people live their interesting lives' (Songdo's Compact-Smart City Exposition) – is explicitly linked with the ambition to create distinctive

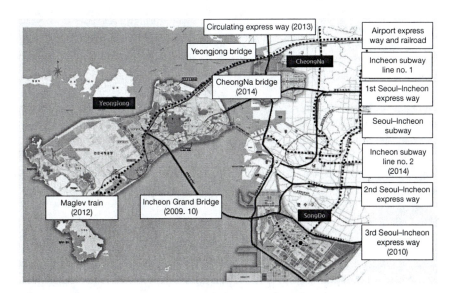

Figure 9.4   IFEZ – present and future accessibility infrastructure plans

Source: IFEZ (2009)

atmospheres, top cultural and leisure amenities and the vibrancy of an international business district, which has not yet materialized. Implicitly, Songdo targets the development of high quality living and office alternatives to a congested and expensive Seoul, to the benefit of Incheon, in a context of potential growing demands for quality housing and business space.

An important issue to look at is the diversity of people (in terms of background, culture and nationality), in Incheon and Seoul in general. Jane Jacobs (1969) had long mentioned the role of diversity in urban development and innovation. More recently, Richard Florida (2005) has associated the degree of cultural diversity of a city with the levels of tolerance, openness to new ideas, creativity and innovation; evidence (from the USA) shows that more socially and culturally diverse metropolises are also the ones with highest growth rates.

The South Korean population is culturally very homogeneous and social networks are rather strong and closed. For example, according to IDI (2010), in Incheon, only 48 thousand out of 2.7 million inhabitants are foreigners (less than 2 per cent). This condition does not seem to have hampered the impressive growth and development of South Korea in recent decades, which is in line with arguments that the diversity–innovation link needs to be contextualized to different industries and occupations. For example, Asheim (2009) convincingly argues that activities primarily relying on engineering skills – like the ones in which South Korea has excelled – tend not to require a large diversity of cultures, but stability, mutual understanding and even cultural and socially closed communities.

However, Florida (2005) stresses that to develop new types of industries and economic activities (such as ICT and media, creative industries, biotechnology) and to attract expatriate talent and investment from outside, diversity and cultural openness are important conditions, and those are still limited in South Korea. The perceptions of multinationals about South Korea as a place to invest, despite improvements in recent years, are still rather unfavourable (Kim and Lee 2007). The general business climate has been traditionally hostile to foreign companies, as well as the brand image of the country as a good place to invest *vis-à-vis* Asian competitors (Graves 2010). Florida (2005) comments that cities like Beijing, Shanghai, Hong Kong or Singapore are much better endowed with, for example, international hospitals, schools, English-language entertainment guides and English-speaking communities. This might endanger further attraction of talent and investment from outside – a prime objective of South Korea. Recent initiatives taking place in Incheon and Songdo, like the 'Incheon Free English' programme and the slogan 'smile in English' intend to raise awareness and slowly start changing this state of affairs.

As previously mentioned, the role of the state in economic and innovation policy has been and still is highly relevant in Korea. South Korea has been a fully fledged representative democracy since the late 1980s, and besides the national level, also at the local level is rather powerful and active deploying economic, innovation and spatial planning policies. Seoul has a special city status, but Incheon, since 1995, is considered a 'metropolitan city', with strong administrative and planning powers. The planning and development of IFEZ is an example of the influence and power of Incheon in the national context, but also of co-operation and policy articulation between different administrative levels. The city of Incheon has large planning departments and multi-disciplinary urban research units like the Incheon Development Institute, with a highly qualified staff (more than 30 PhDs), favouring an integrated approach to urban development and management. In the last eight years, the Mayor of Incheon, coming from the private sector, has been generally considered as highly proactive and one of the central orchestrators behind the recent developments in Songdo. The plans for IFEZ represent the Korean values of national pride and 'can do' spirit, nurtured during the last half century, and are at the core of the ambitious plans for the new Songdo district. We analyse those plans next.

Beyond the snapshot: story and background of IFEZ and Songdo

The first plans for IFEZ and new Songdo date from the 1980s. However, they evolved in a complex, nuanced and to a large extent unpredictable manner. Table 9.1 provides a chronology of key events, actors and changing landscapes associated with the changing strategies for Songdo, from the early 1980s until 2009.

From this evidence, two important observations stand out. First, more than two decades ago, the initial idea for Songdo's reclaimed land was rather different (focused on housing) and changed over time until it reached today's vision of a functionally integrated business and knowledge location. During this process the action's context and landscape changed various times (for example, economic liberalization, acknowledgement of the 'knowledge economy', Asian crisis, country's administrative structure) and several actors entered and left the process, influencing its strategic course (such as groups of experts, the mayor, external real-estate developers and planners, ministers). Thus, the present design and vision for Songdo has very much resulted from an organic process of development, in reality not in the hands of any single leader, but of a group of actors and orchestrators whose roles changed over time, as did their power and influence in the project. For example, it was probably unthinkable in the mid-1990s that a foreign private developer and foreign capital would have a powerful role in the design and development of the area. In 2003 the Mayor of Incheon Ahn Sang-soo took office and became an influential person orchestrating Songdo's development process, namely in attracting sound resources from the national government. However, the seed for Songdo's vision was defined previously, and will probably keep changing and being adjusted over the coming years.

Second, and related to the first observation, the district's development pace was rather erratic: it slowed down and accelerated during this roughly 30-year timeframe. In the early 2000s the project gained critical mass and become irreversible, as a number of actors and networks (such as the state, metropolitan government, external investors, advisors) became progressively aligned and legitimated, and discourse got entrenched within the main players and society as a whole (with visions of 'city of the future' and 'Northeast Asia hub').

Table 9.1 IFEZ and Songdo: chronology of associated events and actors

Period	Events and actors
Early 1980s	Incheon city decides to reclaim land from the Yellow Sea to build new city areas
1988	Korean government announces a massive housing construction plan in order to stabilize the housing market and real-estate rising prices (democratic reforms of Roh Tae Woo's administration; Olympics in Seoul)
1991	A basic plan for 'Songdo new town' is developed by the city of Incheon
1991–5	Housing prices stabilize and land reclamation process is delayed Growing acknowledgement of 'knowledge' in the post-Fordist model of value and wealth creation President Kim Young-Sam takes office in 1993 and starts a number of neo-liberal reforms, increasing trade and relations with China The construction of the new International Airport in Incheon starts
1995–6	Initial basic plan and vision for Songdo is modified towards 'knowledge, IT industries and global business'. City of Incheon promotes a 'tri-port' strategy and slogan – airport, seaport and teleport
1997–9	Asian financial crisis breaks in 1997 and the IMF intervenes for sharper market, regulation and economic reforms, pioneered by new president Kim Dae-Jung; large conglomerates restructure; government industrial policy becomes more FDI friendly Experts and ex-government officials first argued for the introduction of Special Economic Zones: the plan for Korea as a logistic hub in North East Asia National Government establishes the 1998 Foreign Investment Promotion Act, envisaging developing Free Economic Zones (FEZ) in different regions
2000–1	Ministry of Finance stresses the need to relax regulations hampering foreign competition in the service industry Investors argue that Korea cannot compete with China in manufacturing and propose the development of a financial hub International airport officially opens in March 2001 Kohn Pedersen Fox Associates, world leading architecture and planning company based in New York, is hired by Gale, an American real-estate developer, to start drafting the design of an International Business District in Songdo

Period	Events and actors
2002–3	Korean government starts to draft a Free Economic Zone law, in consultation with Incheon Metropolitan City and a number of experts (January 2002). FEZs are seen as a way to contour vested interests, regulations and mindsets that could hamper investment in new directions, like services activities (for example, only logistics or manufacturing-intensive activities)
	The city of Incheon grants POSCO E&C (subsidiary of the Korean steel conglomerate POSCO) the role of leading master plan developer for the first part of reclaimed land in Songdo district, under the condition of teaming up with a foreign developer, with the majority of interest in the venture (to ensure higher construction standards, international appeal, trust, attract foreign investors and financial muscle). A joint venture between POSCO and the American real-estate developer Gale Company is formed under the name 'New Songdo City Development LLC – NSC', with the support of the city of Incheon, later called NSIC – New Songdo International City (February 2002)
	Mayor Ahn Sang-soo takes office (June 2002)
	National Government authorizes a Free Economic Zone in Incheon, composed 3 sub-areas/new cities: Songdo, Yeongjong and Cheongna – Incheon Free Economic Zone (IFEZ). This is part of a larger National Government Plan from the Ministry of Finance and Economy called 'North East Asia Business Hub Plan'
	Designation of IFEZ, the first in Korea (port cities of Busan and Gwangyang followed). It is the first time Government designates an 'investment friendly' area for FDI (October 2003)
	The development of the International Business District in Songdo starts
2004	National Government's industrial economists sceptical of the viability and sustainability of the business hub and FDI per se; a complementary innovation clusters policy and industrial high-tech development are suggested for Korea
	The construction of the new Incheon Bridge directly linking Songdo and the new airport starts
2005–9	Progressive real-estate development and settlement of the first residents, firms and organizations in Songdo
	New foreign players' investment in the International District's real-estate development (Morgan Stanley)
	Songdo master plan receives a world award from the American Institute of Architects. The *New York Times* and the Urban Land Institute award Songdo with the first annual Sustainable Cities award, and, is chosen as a pilot programme for the US Green Building Council's LEED for Neighbour Development rating criteria (LEED: Leadership in Energy & Environmental Design©)
	New Korean Government takes office and champions 'Green Growth'
2009	First development stage in Songdo is concluded

Source: fieldwork plus Songdo TechnoPark (2010); Segel (2005); Wang (2007); Gale (2009); Korean Ministry of Finance and Economy (2002a, b) and Mortice (2008)

Goals, features and management of IFEZ and Songdo

As a result of previous events and developments, and due to the need to conciliate different actors' visions in a single district, Songdo became a rather complex and multifaceted project, composed of different 'villages' and 'knowledge locations' within. It is not the aim of this chapter to be fully comprehensive and examine in depth all its components (which are spread along more than 50 square kilometres, which is 60 per cent of the size of Manhattan). Instead, we retain the vision and main objectives, and punctually narrow down to analyse concrete examples of distinct sub-locations within Songdo. We look at it at three different but interrelated scales: macro (IFEZ), meso (Songdo district) and micro level (sub-locations within Songdo; see Table 9.3 and the next sections.

From a macro-level perspective, Songdo is one of the three 'new cities' comprising the Incheon Free Economic Zone (IFEZ). According to the phrasing and promotion lines of IFEZ authority (2010) and the Incheon Development Institute (2010), the aims of IFEZ are diverse and broadly refer to 'Building Northeast Asia's Centre for International Business' and 'Creating Special Economic Zones to Accumulate Technology, Human Resources, Companies, Finance and Logistics' and 'Strengthening National Competitiveness and Balanced Regional Development'.

IFEZ is a joint responsibility of the South Korean State/National Government, namely the Ministry of Knowledge Economy and the Incheon Metropolitan City. These two players are the public authorities and main orchestrators of the area's development. Under this umbrella, the development of IFEZ's specific areas and 'sub-locations' depends on partnerships between those government tiers and their own development corporations (see Table 9.2), as well as a number of private developers and large companies, most of them from the USA. Examples of those developers and companies, in the case of Songdo, are Gale (a real-estate development company based in New York), VaxGen (shareholder of Celtrion, a large biomedical company), Cisco and IBM, developing their own facilities. Researchers and planners from the City of Incheon follow and provide recommendations on the planning processes in articulation with the IFEZ authority, the city planning bureaus and the developers' own planners.

IFEZ aims to become a 'new-generation free economic zone', going beyond the more conventional manufacturing and office functions. It envisages a complete functional mix in dense and compact areas, integrating housing, working and leisure functions, as well as many amenities like parks, concert halls, hospitals, international schools and so on. IFEZ is the first development of its kind in Korea. The proximity to Seoul and to the international airport makes Incheon a 'natural' location for this type of development. Spatially, IFEZ aims to unfold in a poly-nucleated and non-contiguous new urban area (a total of 209km²), and hence the planning of three different and complementary 'new cities', with distinct vocations and ambitions. IFEZ business and population targets are clear, and they focus on attracting tertiary advanced functions, high-tech and science-based industries and the respective white collar 'knowledge workers', especially an international expat audience. Figure 9.5 depicts the three new cities where IFEZ unfolds (see also Table 9.2, for the main projects in each area). Their planned vocations are described as follows (IFEZ 2010):

- Songdo: hub for (i) international business and (ii) new high-tech industries (also with a new light port area). In the IFEZ booklet (2010) we can read that Songdo is planned to become a 'cutting edge knowledge industry city leading the global business community. ... It will bridge the communication between the future leaders.'
- Yeongjong: location of the international airport (also built on sea-reclaimed land). Its planned vocation is for air cargo and logistics, but also for the development of leisure resorts and tourism. Indeed, in the IFEZ booklet (2010) we can read that 'Yeongjong will also become the international tourist centre in Asia'.
- Cheongna: location planned to focus on international finance, sports, leisure and IT industry. In the promotion booklet (IFEZ 2010), it can be read that 'aiming to promote global finance and IT industry, Cheongna will also embrace the beauty of nature in your arms'.

To attract further business and investment, IFEZ authority (2010) provides a number of incentives:

- Tax breaks, including national and local taxes, ranging from full to 50 per cent exemptions during periods from 3 to 15 years;

Table 9.2 The new cities of IFEZ

New cities	Area (km²)	Planned population (2020)	Developers	Major projects (ongoing and planned, examples)
Songdo	53.4	253,000	Incheon Metropolitan City, Songdo Tecnopark, NSIC, Incheon Urban development corporation, etc.	International business district, knowledge and information industry complex, bio-complex, high-tech cluster, landmark city, global university campus
Yeongjong	138.3	169,000	Korea land corporation, airport co-operation, Incheon Urban development corporation, etc.	Airport, tourism complex, leisure complex, sky city, medi-city
Cheongna	17.8	90,000	Korea land corporation, Incheon Metropolitan City, Korea rural community and agriculture corporation, etc.	Global finance/business and leisure, sports, R&D centre, high-tech industry complex, robot land, floricultural complex
IFEZ	209.5	512,000		

Source: IFEZ (2010)

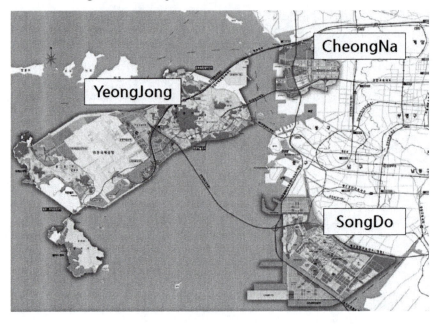

Figure 9.5 IFEZ: the three 'new cities'

Source: IDI (2010)

- administrative support, like financial services, 'one-stop' service and after-care and ombudsman services;
- provision of better living conditions and amenities like international schools and hospitals;
- rent and/or lease fee reduction incentives, for a maximum of 50 years, in property and land owned by the national and municipal government.

IFEZ's incentives have been planned to attract and support foreign investors, but Korean companies can also locate in the area (though not receiving the above-mentioned benefits), under certain conditions, namely (i) if they have strategic ties with foreign firms in IFEZ or (ii) if they belong to a policy-strategic sector, like ICT or biotechnology. The Incheon Metropolitan City and the Ministry of Knowledge Economy want to extend the incentives to Korean companies as well, but there is no consensus among the central government ministries as yet. Even without direct tax benefits, the strategy of 'opening the doors' to Korean firms increases the vibrancy of the area, which otherwise would have been difficult at an early stage, but is likely to generate relocations from other districts of Incheon, and eventually from Seoul. This raises the question whether a 'beggar the neighbour' phenomenon is already taking place nowadays in Songdo in relation to other Seoul capital region locations.

Songdo district nowadays

Songdo district (53.4km² on sea-reclaimed land) is the focus of this case study. Songdo is the IFEZ frontrunner, and its International Business District is currently among the largest private real-estate projects in the world (Ekblaw *et al.* 2009), if not the largest. As previously mentioned, the district envisages attracting global international business and 'high-tech' industries in order to diversify the regional economy and ignite new growth engines for South Korea. Moreover, Songdo is planned to develop as a highly functionally mixed urban area with residential space and amenities. Figure 9.6 provides a sketch of Songdo's planned 'components' in 2020, and Figure 9.7 is a real picture of the present development's stage at the time of writing (IFEZ 2010). Table 9.3 synthesizes Songdo's projects, partnerships and development stage.

We explore some of these projects in the next sections. We conclude now by looking into the land management processes and the present real-estate prices in Songdo. If we exclude public-driven investment areas (like the new Port) or amenities and facilities like green areas, theatre or golf courses, there are three major land use types in Songdo: (i) commercial (for example, office space for international business), (ii) industrial and R&D (for example, technopark offices and workshops) and (iii) residential. The fact that all the land in Songdo has been sea-reclaimed has important advantages. It is publicly owned and in principle there are no former laws and building restrictions (excluding technical ones); physical constraints to land redevelopment are also marginal (for example, there

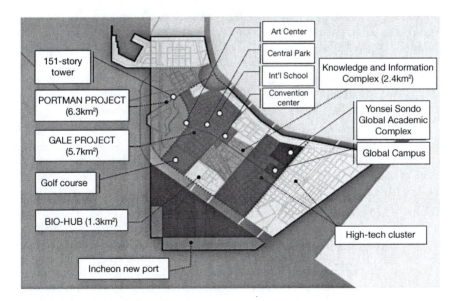

Figure 9.6 Songdo district

Source: IFEZ (2009)

Figure 9.7 Songdo – present stage of development

Source: IFEZ (2010)

is no need to clean brownfield site land); moreover, there are no residents or 'protesting' communities in the area – the land is physically and socially 'virgin'. This particular situation makes the area's development smoother, faster and under the control of governmental players, who can more easily manage the land prices and permits according to their strategic objectives.

As a result, the land development costs have been much cheaper *vis-à-vis* other previously built locations, for example in Seoul and even in Incheon (see Table 9.4). The city of Incheon sold the reclaimed land to the developers (for example, Gale, NSIC joint venture), both for residential and non-residential use, at a much lower price than the appraisal value.[1] In return, and since the development of residential units is more profitable in the short term (at an early stage, development of office space is unprofitable due to lack of demand and agglomeration), the contractual agreement between the City of Incheon and NSIC determined that NSIC would from the beginning develop office buildings as well.

However, the development of residential units (for example, apartment complexes) has been relatively dominant so far. This has advantages for the City of Incheon, since the sale of the land for residential units is the main source of IFEZ's direct revenue; moreover, the relocation of new inhabitants leads to the development of market amenities and creates urban critical mass. However, it is clear that it will take time until Songdo gets the vibrant feeling, functions and effective mixed land use of a real 'city'. Table 9.4 depicts Songdo's approximate land price levels at the date of writing. It confirms the fact that the demand for commercial

Table 9.3 Songdo district: main pieces of a holistic puzzle

Projects	Description	Main Developers	Status
Incheon Grand Bridge	12.3km bridge linking Songdo and the international airport	Incheon Bridge Co. Lda, Korea Expressway corporation	Completed
Tomorrow City	Promotion centre of ubiquitous technologies and Songdo's 2020 vision	Incheon Urban Development Corporation	Completed
Songdo Central Park	Urban and leisure park	NSIC	Completed
International School	All the education levels for international population	NSIC	Completed
RFID/USN Building	Building for radio-frequency identification/ubiquitous sensor networks' companies (u-IT cluster building)	Ministry of Knowledge Economy and Incheon Metropolitan City	Completed
Songdo ConventiA	Convention centre and new forum for international business	NSIC	1st phase completed
NEAT (Northeast Asia Trade) Tower	Business facilities and hotel rooms	NSIC	Almost completed
Incheon University	University campus	Incheon Urban Development Corporation	Almost completed
Techno Park Complex	Technological park	Incheon Metropolitan City Government	Almost completed
Jack Nicklaus Golf Course	Golf course	NSIC	Almost completed
Yonsei University International Campus	University campus	Incheon Urban Development Corporation, Songdo Internationalization Complex Development Co., Lda	Ongoing
Global University Campus	University campus; joint initiative of foreign universities to locate in Songdo	Incheon Urban Development Corporation, Songdo Internationalization Complex Development Co., Lda	Ongoing
Songdo Landmark Tower	151-storey office space tower for global business	Portman consortium (Portman, Samsung Corp., Hyundai E&C)	Starting
Incheon Art Centre	Cultural complex with concert hall and art schools	Incheon Urban Development Corporation	Starting
Science Village	Songdo Technopark expansion complex	Songdo Technopark	Starting

Source: adapted from IFEZ (2010), fieldwork

Table 9.4 Land and real-estate prices in Sondgo district (US\$/m²)

Land use	Development cost	Appraisal value (a)	Market price
Commercial	\$413	\$4,950	Lower than (a)
Residential	\$413	\$2,750	Higher than (a)
Industrial	\$413	\$1,925	Similar to (a)

Source: Fieldwork in Incheon Development Institute

premises and office space is still low (market price lower than appraisal price), while the opposite happens for residential uses, for which demand is higher.

From the side of industrial and R&D uses, IFEZ representatives believe that the land's low development cost will definitely attract many firms since they sell the land at the development cost, which is much lower than the market price. However, as previously suggested, many of these firms might represent displacements from other locations in Incheon or even Seoul. Moreover, some experts fear the emergence of adverse selection effects; for example, industrial manufacturing companies might move in, claiming larger than necessary plots, in order to obtain capital gains in the future. For example, it is estimated by the Incheon Development Institute (IDI) that land prices in the nearby Namdong Industrial Complex, a traditional industrial area with many manufacturing SMEs, is US\$1300/m², cheaper than the development cost in Songdo nowadays, but with considerably less quality. Simultaneously, the prices for premium office and R&D space are nowadays much lower in Songdo than in Seoul. IDI estimates that the land prices for office space in upscale high-rises in Seoul's Digital Industrial Complex offices can vary between US\$4,000–8,000/m² (*vis-à-vis* US\$4,950 in Songdo – see Table 9.4), increasing the attractiveness of Songdo as a business and knowledge location.

Songdo as an (international) business and knowledge location

Songdo aims to become (i) an important global business hub in Northeast Asia and (ii) a high-tech knowledge location, a cradle for new cutting-edge technologies. In other words, it explicitly targets clustering and agglomeration of a number of new advanced services, industries and skills, and, implicitly, the development of knowledge and innovation relationships between co-located players. In this section we analyse how far Songdo is in pursuing this objective, and how it has been taking place.

One first observation is that, at the time of writing (after the 2008–9 global economic downturns), Songdo already attracted a very significant number of foreign, but also national companies. Table 9.5 gives an overview of the key players that have negotiated a location in IFEZ in general, and in Songdo in particular. The targeted clusters in 'high-tech' and 'bio-pharma/medical device' fields have attracted a substantial number of important foreign corporations, whereas

Table 9.5 IFEZ (planned) clusters

IFEZ location	Selected clusters	Main partners (mainly FDI global corporative investors) at April 2010
Songdo	'High-tech'	IBM, Cisco, Boing, HP, GE, Gudel, Huneed Technologies, DynamicWave Telecom Inc., Semikron, NTPia, Fibox, Sanil Tech
	'Bio-pharma/medical device'	Celltrion, Crucell, i-Sens, Sartorious, Siemens, Stryker, Johnson & Johnson
	'Digital content'	Orix, SBS, Dongwoo Animation, CN, CNN
	'Alternative energy'	Yuzhnoye, NASA, Jaxa, Epoch
Yeongjong	'Aviation cluster'	Boing, Pratt & Whitney, ST Aerospace
Cheongna	'Vehicle cluster'	GM-Daewoo, Piolax, Saint-Gobain, Autoliv

Source: IFEZ (2010)

other firms in the field of 'digital content' and 'alternative energy' also invested, or are in the process of investing in Songdo. This leads us to a second observation: the sectoral focus of FDI attraction to Songdo has been so far rather broad, since, in the end, the IFEZ authority's bottom-line admission criteria have been rather open, requiring investors to be within a wide variety of 'high-tech' and somehow 'knowledge intensive' businesses; the definition of desired 'clusters' in the area seems to react accordingly, as new companies show interest in investing.

Moreover, Songdo has managed to attract a very large number of Korean companies and R&D units: SMEs (also with some 'knowledge' component), their R&D centres, as well as a number of start-up firms. These national investments in Songdo, supported by attractive land prices and other tax incentives (see the second section, above), also reflect the strong financial support of Korean science and technology policy, the new high-tech face of the supportive Developmental State (Yeung 2009). The complementary support of Incheon's City Government (such as funding R&D equipment and venture capital) increased the attractiveness of Songdo further and has been steering it as the natural new 'high-tech' location in Incheon, the place where the 'new economy' unfolds. The strong support from the mayor to attract the new Science Park to Songdo (see Box 9.1) helped make the location an increasingly natural recipient of the hard national funding, further supporting agglomeration and the clustering of new activities. Key examples of new activities agglomerated in Songdo can be found in the realms of medical and biotechnology (Box 9.2) and the development of new advanced sensor technologies (Box 9.3). Government officials often speak about a sort of 'holy trinity' of (broad) technological fields and 'clusters' to support: IT, NT and BT (information technologies, nano-technologies and biotechnologies).

The agglomeration and 'knowledge' densification strategy of Songdo (and of the national government) also includes the attraction of national and foreign universities. Large Korean universities have developed and are developing new premises in Songdo. That is the case of the renowned Yonsei University, scheduled

Box 9.1 Songdo Technopark

The recent Songdo Technopark, inspired by Western models, aims to host and support a diverse number of activities: electronics, biotechnology, new (nano) materials, precision instruments and mechatronics. These are in line with the priorities of the national government and the metropolitan city. The park provides all the typical facilities and services of a science park – office and labo-ratory space, support for technology transfer, business support services, incuba-tion, trial and pilot tests infrastructure, education and training, market studies, brokerage and so on. It is one of the most advanced technoparks in Korea. The park plays a critical role supporting the development of the broadly envisaged clusters of ICT, biotech and auto parts.

In 2009, the park hosted already 124 companies and 19 other organizations, representing more than 4,000 jobs in the area (Songdo Technopark 2010). Biotech start-ups locate in the park and attract venture capital and investments nationally and from overseas. In recent years, around 50 companies moved from Incheon city to the park; others moved from Seoul to benefit from the excel-lent facilities. The park provides six years of business support and premises for incubation. Besides, it facilitates access to government funds, business support, programmes to expand overseas and so on.

Recently, Songdo Technopark founded together with Inha University a specialized R&D centre for auto parts, to support an 'auto parts cluster centre'. This centre (now with 82 researchers) will be an extension of the Inha University and their centres working with auto suppliers for commissioned projects. The decision to locate the centre in Songdo was associated with the proximity to many other centres and research facilities, but primarily to the support of governmental and public agencies; the auto suppliers and main clients do not locate in Songdo.

The facilities of Technopark are presently being expanded into other zones of Songdo – the new Sondgo science village. This will take six years to complete. The new village is planned (see Figure 9.8) to facilitate the convergence of technologies and 'create a knowledge interchange market' (Songdo Technopark 2010). It will have several R&D, business and recreational zones. These include buildings focusing on specific 'clusters of activities' like IT, biotechnology and mechantronics (as well as the POSCO global R&D centre), but also dedicated areas for convergent research between the specialization areas of the park, pilots and other 'inner-city factories' where networking can also take place (Songdo Technopark 2010).

Different urban functions will also converge in this new area, namely R&D, accommodation and leisure. The 'inner avenue' area of the complex is planned to have joint facilities and (English-friendly) amenities like housing, studios, temporary accommodation, recreational facilities, theatre, mall, bookshops and pubs, music hall, food court, restaurants, fitness and sports centre, land-mark culture hub and so on. These functions are planned to be aligned with and complementary to the ones of the contiguous Yonsei University and Global University Campus.

Figure 9.8   Vision of the Songdo Science Village, or technopark expansion complex

Source: Songdo Technopark (2010)

Box 9.2 Songdo's bio-complex

Biotechnology is one of Songdo's spearheads. Together with multinational corporations (see Table 9.5) and national research facilities, the city of Incheon wants to develop a bio-complex in the area, and invests in related facilities, together with the national government.

One of the organizations involved in this project and already fully settled is the Lee Gil Ya Cancer and Diabetes Institute. Founded by Gachon Gil Foundation (which owns Gachon University of Medicine and Science), it develops state-of-the-art research and is endowed with cutting-edge technology facilities, namely the 'mouse metabolic phenotyping centre', an animal research centre and a 'genomics-proteomics' centre. The centre started in Songdo in 2008, with 80 persons and now hosts 170 employees, including foreign graduates. It has 19 full professors, including American, Canadian and Japanese, with a strong reputation and an extensive network of high-level contacts. The bulk of research funding comes from the government, but also partly from private sources.

The representatives of the centre acknowledge that the land to develop the centre's premises was much cheaper in Songdo than it would have been, for example, in Seoul. Also the infrastructure building was cheaper, and the area is very accessible. They expect that more facilities and biotech activities will locate soon in the area (FDI, foreign universities), creating a potent bio-complex. They have expectations of a coming 'subsidiary' of Johns Hopkins hospital for joint R&D (although it is unknown whether these functions will also be moved from the USA to Songdo). An American biotech company from San Diego located to the institute's 5th floor, due to the excellent infrastructure and previous contacts with the director of the centre. Bio-pharma factories and production capacity are located in the countryside. In the institute, fundamental R&D is the core activity.

Box 9.3 RFID/USN and MEMS technology centre

Songdo hosts one of the world's leading clusters of ubiquitous technologies and sensors, competing with the USA, Japan and Germany. This specific Songdo cluster ('u-IT') is anchored in the newly developed RFID/USN and MEMS technology centre (Radio Frequency Identification/Ubiquitous Service Discovery; Micro-Electro-Mechanical Systems). Around this centre there are fully settled 20 high-tech SMEs, with their own premises, plus 14 smaller companies inside the centre itself. Most of the firms are Korean, excluding one American and one Finnish sensor company. It attracts many users from Incheon, Seoul, Korea and even abroad, providing exclusive services and dedicated facilities for companies developing related technologies. Among those are testing and engineering labs, pilot facilities, training rooms as well as brokerage services, participation in events and several amenities. Moreover, the centre has a guest house for temporary visitors: researchers, customers and partners from abroad.

The government wants Korea to become world leader in this set of technologies, which have linkages with other objectives, like fostering green technologies as well as other established industries like automotive, ships and electronics. This spearhead is also linked to another national government strategy: the development of a network of ubiquitous cities (u-cities) in the country, where many urban services and functions are linked through wireless networking and RFID technologies (see next section). Songdo is planned to be one of the pilot pioneers of this futuristic system, and so new sensor solutions are being procured to feed it. By procuring u-technologies, the government also gives the supplying firms first-mover competitive advantages and a technological edge. There is a master plan developed by IFEZ/ National Government and Incheon Metropolitan City to provide the best conditions for RFIS/USN and MEMS companies to agglomerate in Songdo. Cisco is opening a centre in Songdo to tap into these u-city developments and provide ubiquitous network systems.

Figure 9.9 u-ITcluster and RFID/USN centre

Source: Ministry of Knowledge Economy (2009)

to relocate many courses and roughly 10,000 students from the city of Seoul; also the local (large) Incheon University is relocating its facilities from Incheon city to brand-new premises in Songdo. Moreover, a number of 'off-shores' from US universities will locate in an international campus, issuing US academic degrees, without the need for, but with the possibility of, study in the USA (see second section). The University of North Carolina is already recruiting the first students for the new Songdo Campus, and the State University of New York at Stony Brook is preparing to do so. Confident of the continued (financial) support and risk reduction by the Korean government, Delaware and George Mason University intend to open next year. The international campus is still under development and plans to offer a number of shared facilities such as libraries, student union buildings, sports, dormitories and guest houses. IFEZ authority puts strong efforts in attracting these universities, and there is a specific team devoted to this task in the organization. In addition, both national and Incheon government have been active in lobbying internationally for the location of transnational organizations in Songdo. That is the case of the United Nations Centre for ICT Promotion, located now in Songdo, with the mission of training Asian-Pacific policymakers in the use of ICT for better governance and policymaking. Incheon's Metropolitan Government provided financial support for land and facilities. The location excels in the required international accessibility, but also in digital infrastructure – essential for the centre's e-learning activities.

For the time being, and considering the still early stage of development of Songdo 'from scratch', it has already achieved remarkable results in the agglomeration of diversified business and high-tech, cutting-edge research and knowledge activities. However, whether innovation networks and interactions between co-located players have been (and will be) achieved is more debatable. We dedicate the rest of the section to some observations about the results of and potentials for knowledge networking in Songdo and clustering alignment.

At this stage it is not possible to assess or quantify the number or the strength of knowledge and innovation networks taking place in Songdo. We found evidence of interesting interactions and collaborations potentially conducive to innovations and knowledge sharing, for example in the shared facilities of the RFID/USN centre and in other shared biotechnology facilities and labs (see Box 9.2). These facilities have been precisely developed to facilitate collective efficiency by being co-located. On the flip side, we also found evidence of organizations located in Songdo whose main innovation interactions are outside the district; the same happens certainly for many other firms, and, naturally, there is nothing inherently wrong with that. The opposite would actually be surprising because of the newness and 'virgin' character of the location. One important question, however, is whether the global companies attracted to Songdo will become embedded in the district in particular, and in Seoul's capital region more generally. Some local firms and knowledge institutes show expectations that they can benefit somehow from the new global players that will co-locate in Songdo, for instance in the fields of ICT and biotech. However, the literature shows more cases of unsuccessful than successful integration and knowledge spill-overs.[2] Much seems to be dependent on the types of innovation, as well as the chance to establish cultural and social bounds allowing for fruitful and clean communication. The Korean 'conglomerate' tradition of in-house R&D (for example, Wang 2007) as well as the cultural, linguistic and working style differences *vis-à-vis*, for example, Western companies, may pose challenges to this desired interaction and the creation of 'relational capital'.

Recent literature has shown that these challenges are likely to vary according to the type of knowledge involved (for example, Gertler 2008). For example, in engineering activities where relevant knowledge is less codified (for example, automotive or mechatronics), meanings vary and client–user interaction is central, the challenges to co-operate and innovate across cultures are likely to be particularly high. The same is less true for activities where knowledge is more codified, like biotechnology or fundamental engineering, and that is probably why we already see some interactions with foreign partners in these fields (see Box 9.2 and Box 9.3). Moreover, the integration of the broad diversity of 'high-tech' activities present and planned for Songdo poses extra challenges to find the common integration points, in sectors whose types of knowledge are probably unrelated (Boschma and Frenken 2009), and thus where immediate branching and joint innovation are more difficult. In this context, the planned efforts to develop specific areas devoted to technology convergence in the new Science Village (see Box 9.1) are highly welcome.

Similar co-operation expectations are also directed towards the role of the foreign universities in the area. Some companies and organizations expect to co-operate with the faculty that will relocate in Songdo, for example in innovation-related issues. The extent to which this will happen is also a question. In our contacts with IFEZ authority, we found no evidence that the universities addressed by IFEZ to locate in Songdo show research or educational complementarities with the economic activities located in Songdo. Moreover, there is also no evidence that the relocated faculty is composed of researchers with applied research skills or an interest in co-operation with the industry. The off-shoring of international universities in Songdo may have big advantages, but there are challenges ahead. The development of curricula and the move of faculties from the USA are rather expensive, and previous experiences of off-shored campuses, such as in Japan, have failed; in Singapore this strategy has had mixed results. According to McNeill (2009), the first universities established in Songdo received US$1 million to adapt and implement their undergraduate courses; they expect few American students, at least in the first years. Moreover, McNeill (2009) also reports that the partial relocation agreement between Incheon Metropolitan City and Seoul's Yonsei University is facing sharp resistance and struggles from the faculty's staff and academic departments.

Before concluding, we briefly look at the alignment between the activities and clusters under development in Songdo, the city of Seoul and the inner city of Incheon. A cluster mapping exercise for the city of Seoul (OECD 2005) identified six spearhead clusters to foster: fashion and clothing, printing and publishing, three service-based clusters (financial industry, business services and IT) and one emerging industry cluster (digital content). At first glance there seems to be some overlap with the ambitions of Songdo, namely on what is referred to as IT, business services and digital. If Songdo offers irresistible conditions and support, some of these developing clusters may become spatially fragmented. The case of digital and media deserves particular attention. Moreover, there is a strong risk of competition between activities presently located in Incheon inner city and Songdo. For example, a large number of companies in the fields of IT, video gaming and virtual reality locate in the inner-city district of Nan-gu. Although the City of Incheon is very keen on supporting these activities (for example, by the supply of venture capital) and keeping them in the area, some companies have already expressed the desire to move to Songdo as well, to benefit from the excellent infrastructure and distinctive image. These issues should be taken into consideration, because they have implications for the balanced and sustainable urban development strategy pioneered by the City of Incheon. In the next section we turn our attention to the results and potentials of Songdo as an integrated urban development project.

Songdo as an integrated urban development project

As previously mentioned, Songdo's master plan recently received a World Award from the American Institute of Architects (AIA), due to the excellence and integrality of its urban design. In this section we analyse its features as an integrated urban development project, and also as a testbed for new urban planning concepts: as is the case of Songdo's u-city vision and the use of 'climate proof', environmentally friendly architecture. Moreover, we look at the integration of Songdo in the context of larger urban systems, namely within Metropolitan Incheon and Seoul's capital region.

The new Songdo district resembles what has been dubbed an edge city (Garreau 1991). This tag refers to new cities, usually emergent from rural areas in the previous decades, at the edge of large metropolises, but close to highways and transport infrastructure (such as airports). Edge cities emerged first in the USA with the advent of the car as a generalized transportation mode; often pedestrian-hostile, characteristics of these new cities are the presence of large shopping malls, high-rises and 'more jobs than beds'. Many examples can be found in the USA, in the metropolises' fringes, but also in Europe – for example, La Défense in Paris, Canary Wharf in London or Schiphol in Amsterdam. Similar types of edge cities are rapidly emerging in China and India.

As noticed by Mortice (2008), Songdo can be seen as an 'edge city to an edge city', if we consider it within the Incheon–Seoul urban system. However, there are important differences between the traditional American edge city and the planned Songdo district. For example, while many edge cities emerged rather spontaneously, Songdo was carefully planned by a team of architects and planners based in New York, in articulation with Incheon's urban planners. Songdo's design is clearly inspired by Western (read: American) reference models, hybridized for the Asian Korean context (Mortice 2008) – it assimilates much of the state-of-the-art in (physical) urban planning. Besides, contrarily to the dominant monofunctional, office-based character of edge cities, Songdo is planned to excel in multi-functionality – it combines housing, office space and plenty of leisure areas (see second section). Songdo unfolds around an International Business District, with strong density, high-rises, compact and 'smart growth': every function should be accessible within a five-minute drive. Landmark architecture and aesthetically 'beautiful' buildings are at the core of the whole concept.

Songdo can thus be seen as a 'new-generation edge city'. It displays a large number of (planned) amenities like golf courses, concert hall (inspired by the Sydney Opera House), urban parks (inspired by New York's Central Park, blended with references to Korean landscapes) and even water canals (like Venice) – see Table 9.3. Some amenities like urban parks are promising as spaces of conviviality, avoiding expats remaining closed in their residential or office space 'cocoons'. Furthermore, the steady functioning of the university campuses will very likely add to the vibrancy of the area, as students and faculty start to 'live' Songdo, create new atmospheres and attract new market amenities like restaurants, shops and the like. Boutiques and department stores are also expected to accrue to the area. The area will host international schools and hospitals. This encompassing set of amenities was certainly not planned in Songdo by chance – they have been consistently referred to in the urban literature as important for attracting and retaining the 'creative class' and the 'brains', the pivotal asset in the knowledge economy (Florida 2002; Glaeser *et al*. 2001, van Winden *et al*. 2007).

Economically, as the area's occupation unfolds and new activities start to operate, Songdo is creating new jobs both for the highly-skilled and for those with lower qualifications. Songdo's jobs and skills seem to come mainly from Incheon, its vicinities and capital region. Aware of the potential detachment between the 'old' and the 'new' Songdo city, Incheon plans to use the real-estate profits generated in Songdo to revitalize older neighbourhoods in the city, and in this way steer a more integral and balanced urban development (see second section).

Socially, the impacts on integration and cohesion cannot be fully accessed yet, but there are again important questions. Evidently, gentrification is not an issue in this case, since there are no local communities or former residents. However, the extent to which Songdo will become a socially balanced city is more debatable. Residential prices (see Table 9.4) so far indicate that the area is very attractive but potentially only affordable for the higher class. In the absence of other policy mechanisms, like the promotion of low-cost housing and rent control, social diversity in the area is likely to be limited. People from the middle and lower social status will likely commute to the area during the day to support the needs of the 'creative class', but will sleep in other locations. This may create a certain discontinuity and 'enclave' feeling *vis-à-vis* other locations in Incheon, which may be sharpened when high-class expatriates move into an area where they can access all urban functions without potentially stepping out into 'old' Incheon. This might hamper the desired urban mix and create a 'social island' situation, which seems at odds with the vision of opening Korean society to the world (see second section). The expected creation of the great cities' cultural atmospheres, vibrancy and buzz is also an issue to be assessed further on. There are no cases in the literature where those externalities have been created *ex novo* by importing amenities, though we found cases where those amenities were important to keep the area's diversity and growth (Storper and Manville 2006). The future dynamics of Songdo in this respect – namely cultural dynamics and community building – is a matter of further attention for IFEZ and the city of Incheon.

Environmentally, Songdo is presently the largest LEED© (Leadership in Energy and Environmental Design certification) development in the world. LEED is an international green building certification, developed by the US Green Building Council, ensuring the building's good performance in domains like energy saving, CO_2 neutrality, water efficiency and so on. Songdo has thus been considered a prototype of an environmentally friendly, climate-proof green city (Whitman *et al.* 2009). The buildings extensively use green materials and associated innovative techniques, making Songdo a testing lab for green building technologies. The recent National Government Strategy of 'Green Growth' (OECD 2010) will likely bring novelties in this respect.

Still in the realm of 'experimentation arenas', Songdo is among the pioneer Korean cities experimenting with futuristic ubiquitous-city (or simply u-city) concepts adapted to urban planning and management (Lee *et al.* 2008). A u-city is one where people can be connected to a large number of digital, web services any time and anywhere. Through, for example, video networking, Wi-Fi, radio frequency technology, sensors, telematics, other information systems and special management software, several activities in a city can be connected to and coordinated by a common network, such as safety and crime prevention, transportation, health care and the environment. These efforts have been supported by the u-Korea programme, a national level government strategy of the Ministry of the Knowledge Economy, together with local governments, willing to give South Korea a front-running position in the concept's implementation, but also associated technological advantages. There are thus many underlying objectives in this strategy, such as the development of further IT technological prowess, enhancing quality of life, attracting further FDI and balanced regional development and citizen empowerment. Songdo already hosts a relevant u-IT cluster (see Box 9.3), as well as a visitors' centre ('Tomorrow City') where the new technologies can be experienced in advance. IFEZ authority plans to demonstrate some of the new u-services in the forthcoming 2014 Asian Games in Incheon.

The full implementation of u-technologies has deep implications in the planning and functioning of the urban space, as well as its management (Lee *et al.* 2008). However, recent research (Shin 2009) is less optimistic about society's absorption of the u-city technological apparatus. Despite huge government investment in this strategy throughout Korea (US$300 million in the RFID centre in Songdo; US$60 billion in the first stage for all the Korean u-city pilots), Shin argues that infrastructure provision, technological and corporate interests have dominated the project so far. Korea developed a sound number of competitive related technologies, but with a very limited involvement of the citizens, potentially hampering the effective integration and use of these new technologies in society. Shin's research in the recent progress of u-city strategies in Korea reveal that none of the key actors involved – Ministry of Knowledge Economy, industry conglomerates and local government – have promoted a more inclusive and 'bottom-up' involvement of the citizens, focusing instead, respectively, on infrastructure development, technological capacity, cluster promotion, image and regional economic diversification.

Shin (2009) states that:

> ubiquitous computing infrastructure can be connected to a city's physical
> parts, such as buildings, roads, electrical infrastructure, manufacturing and
> residential establishments, but also, more importantly, it should be embedded
> into the fabric of social and cultural parts of cities.

This poses important challenges and opportunities for Songdo. So far, the
u-developments in Songdo have indeed been very much oriented by a 'tech-
nology-push' and the vision of high-tech clustering; simultaneously, the social
and cultural fabric of Songdo, at this stage, is still practically non-existent, so
the interaction between the technology and social system (where critical innovations may emerge) would in any case be almost impossible to attain. However, as
Songdo starts to be occupied and new companies and residents move in, there are
emerging opportunities to effectively test some of these new concepts. And here
lies probably one of the great advantages of Songdo – it may well play the role
of a protected and 'virgin' experimentation arena to foster larger socio-technical
transitions (Geels 2005; Rotmans 2005). Moreover, the type of users in the area
are likely to be demanding IT users, thus constituting an important test to the
potential applicability and implementation of the concept (despite the potential
drawback of lack of diversity). Songdo is flexible and 'new' enough to accommodate the infrastructure, although it is still to be seen whether the development
of the u-city concept will clash or not with the planned urban design.

Although many of the technologies required for the u-city concept have been
developed in the West, the Korean context of less expected privacy and safety
makes it a privileged testing arena, and gives Korea the opportunity to set the
standards of u-city concepts. Songdo, again, may play an important role in this
strategy.

Conclusions and perspectives

The scale and scope of Songdo as a new knowledge location has attracted the
attention of many commentators worldwide, rivalling other referenced and large-
scale developments such as Dubai. In the promotional material of Incheon's
Compact and Smart City Exposition (Incheon Metropolitan City 2010), Songdo
is referred to as:

> an international city of cutting edge knowledge. … Comprehensively
> equipped with advanced business systems, Songdo functions as one of the
> most beautiful, environmental friendly and effective cities in the world and is
> emerging as a true international city. Research complexes of world-renowned
> companies have been constructed here and are now in operation, contributing
> to a superlative complex of knowledge information industries.

In this chapter, guided by a number of research questions, a theoretical framework and recent empirical evidence, we tried to deconstruct this promotional

discourse and get deeper insight into the emergence and recent development of the district. We looked into the new Songdo district from an integrative and dynamic perspective in order to analyse its development and outlook as a 'knowledge location'. Throughout the case study, and on the basis of the analysis, we hinted towards some policy recommendations to take Songdo's encompassing project further – we will come back to some of them in this section.

Drivers and catalysts

The development of Songdo has been guided by a number of drivers and catalysts. The vision for Songdo's sea-reclaimed land varied over time, but, since the mid-1990s, the area's present shape has been driven by changes (and challenges) in the national and international landscape (such as the Asian debt crisis of 1997, emergence of the knowledge economy, increased globalization), which in turn gave rise to a number of national and local responses. The interesting phenomenon is that those responses found in Songdo an (urban) face: a 'virgin', flexible and protected policy arena to explore, test, demonstrate and implement those strategies, facilitated by the FEZ legislative flexibility, international image and appeal. The result of this process is the confluence in Songdo of many different urban functions, experiments and activities. Examples are FDI investment and international business attraction, indigenous innovative clusters, universities, promotion centres, English-speaking programmes, urban u-planning and technology experiments, landmark buildings and attractive amenities. All of them contribute to the creation of an image of a more open and investment-friendly South Korea, a 'Northeast Asia Business Hub'. Figure 9.10 illustrates this perspective and synthesizes the main catalysts and drivers beyond Songdo's evolution assessed in the previous sections.

More than through the action of established industrial vested interests in Incheon and Seoul, the strategy beyond Songdo originates in a rather top-down fashion, from the action of the national and local government, following economic diversification and new business attraction objectives. The government's vision – and that of their advisers and planners – dominated the discussion and implementation arena in the beginning. However, as Songdo took shape and new organizations started to relocate and gain legitimacy (for example, IFEZ managing authority), although the national and local government structures still had great power, the area's development started to be influenced by other players, such as the American developer Gale, research institutes, techno park and so on.

Critical development factors

The development of Songdo is still at a relatively early stage. Although it is speculative to make bold statements about its long-term success, some critical development factors are already noticeable. Some of them are highly context-dependent and hard to transfer to other cites; others, however, constitute important insights to bear in mind in the development of knowledge locations, and for urban management more generally.

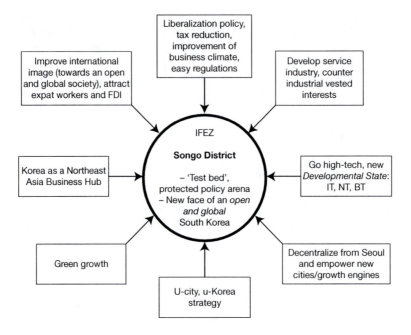

Figure 9.10 Songdo: at the crossroads of several strategies

Source: own elaboration

Starting with the former (hard-to-transfer critical development factors), three elements stand out.

First, there is the level of the state's commitment and (financial) involvement in the project, cutting taxes and providing the most diverse direct and indirect incentives for companies and organizations willing to relocate or start activities in Songdo. This support made agglomeration thresholds possible in a relatively short period of time; moreover, it made foreign investors and international organizations, like universities, more 'at ease' about moving to the newly developed area. Again, like in the conglomerate epoch, the state supported a project that seems to be too big to fail, counting on wide governmental support, image, and 'killing amenities' to feed the agglomeration process further. This catalyst lies at the centre of this story, but would be almost impossible to replicate in Western economies. This is the case not only because of the structural difficulties of the public sector sustaining such massive investment (whether with taxpayers' money, own resources or debt), but also because of strict competition policies in Europe, such as forbidding positive discrimination, 'picking the winner' funds and direct firms' support. The South Korean model of growingly liberal market organization, together with a refocused yet still strong new-generation Developmental State (see second section) is rather unique and cannot be found in Western neo-liberal and social-market economies.

Second, and related to the previous point, is the steady economic growth of Northeast Asia, more concretely in the Yellow Sea area, making this location extremely attractive for global businesses and, for example, university off-shores. China has been capturing the lion's share of foreign investments, but the high skills and technological capacity of the Koreans make it an attractive place for many high-tech investments as well, as legislation becomes more flexible: a prime objective of IFEZ and Songdo. Excellent accessibility (a brand-new international airport and a leadership in broadband) are also very helpful and distinctive attraction factors.

Third, the fact that Songdo's land was sea-reclaimed, and thus socially and physically 'virgin', clearly facilitated the development process. It made possible smooth and fast land and real-estate development (no community protests, no technical or legislative blockages), as well as an integral urban design (besides residential, also with office space and amenities from the beginning). This situation can be compared to some extent to greenfield developments (though with a lesser scope and scale) but not in the development of knowledge locations in previously urbanized areas. One interesting arena for further observation is the way government intervention will handle more complex situations that are already emerging, such as related to inner-city (re-)development in Incheon.

Four other critical success factors can be identified. When re-contextualized, these might have transferability potential to other cities and knowledge locations. First, Songdo benefited from the alignment between the area's high-tech objectives (biotech, IT, etc.) and the endogenous potential of skills, qualifications and knowledge production rooted in Seoul's capital region – which is not the case, for example, in Dubai. This makes the knowledge strategy of the area more sustainable and anchored.

Second, despite government's strong involvement, Songdo benefited from external sources of knowledge, such as the developer Gale, beneficial to bring new approaches to the area's planning as well as external visibility and resources beyond public support. We found some evidence that the role of Korean expatriates and highly qualified persons with working experience abroad (new firms' CEOs, research professors, etc.) located in Songdo might have played an important role in attracting new external companies and investments, but this is an issue requiring further investigation.

Third, an important success factor so far has been the clear alignment between the different government layers involved (national, local). Moreover, also important has been the creation of a specific managing authority for the area (IFEZ authority), with power and flexibility to manage daily and strategic issues working in close articulation with other stakeholders.

Fourth, the orchestrating role assumed by Mayor Ahn (now former mayor of Incheon) was relevant in the latter dynamics of the area, but should not obscure the organic development behind Songdo's project, which dates from before his administration. A certain 'adaptation capacity' to changing landscapes, emerging challenges and new actors' strategies, while keeping the project on track – keeping the grand vision – was an important success factor, and reveals the capacity to manage in complexity. We hint that this has been largely due to the skills and capacity of a number of highly qualified actors involved in the process, in the technical departments of the government and city administration.

Songdo as an (international) business and knowledge location

So far, and despite its early development stage, Songdo has done well in attracting an important critical mass of international and national companies and organizations (universities, science park, specific clusters' infrastructures and complexes – biotech, sensors, IT). For the attraction of international companies, Songdo's image and flexibility have been paying off. Moreover, the possibility of participating in and closely monitoring front-running developments (such as u-technologies) is attractive for global IT companies like IBM or Cisco: the co-presence in Songdo, with brokerage from other organizations (for example, IFEZ authority) may facilitate virtuous exchanges.

However, despite these particular cases, the extent to which other knowledge and innovation networks are emerging or will emerge in the future is debatable. The diversity of players and technologies accruing to the area may be too high to fruitfully co-operate and learn from each other. Although everything seems to be 'high-tech', there are sound differences between the business and innovation modes of, say, biotechnology, materials and auto-parts companies, or between a North American Corporation and a Korean SME. In this context, English training and other initiatives to mitigate cultural and social barriers between foreign companies and Korean players are welcome.

To overcome or minimize some of the potential 'networking' blockages, further attention should be paid to clarify the definition of cluster policies in Songdo, avoiding general banners like 'high-tech'; those policies should be probably less sectoral (such as biotech, IT) and more 'platform'-oriented (such as bio-sensors), in order to find the convergence points between different technologies present in the area. The role of competent brokers (for example, Koreans with experience in different technological fields and cultural contexts) might be particularly important here. The initiatives and physical infrastructures planned for the 'science village' are promising in this respect.

The potential complementarities between these clusters and the universities (national and international) located in Songdo should be assessed further. There is nowadays a big hype that those universities will co-operate in research with Songdo's research institutes and companies, which might not necessarily be the case. Finally, it is important to avoid the idea of Songdo as a 'knowledge island' and find ways to plug Songdo's national and international firms with other players in Incheon and Seoul. This can be a way to avoid or at least minimize fragmentation between ongoing cluster initiatives in different areas of the capital region.

Songdo as an integrated urban development project

Songdo has been planned as a highly integrated and multi-functional, almost 'perfect' city. It follows international best practices in urban master planning, adapted to the Asian-Korean context. The ongoing experimentation of u-city strategies and 'climate proof' construction gives Songdo the 'cherry-on-the-top-of-the-cake' of their smart city strategy. Moreover, the former experimentations are linked with the dynamics of Songdo as a knowledge location: many foreign corporations in Songdo are willing to participate in the 'u-city development' supplying technologies. Songdo's u-IT cluster is also aligned with the city's u-strategies.

Furthermore, Songdo envisages an extensive number of high quality (of life) amenities. Indeed, there are nowadays good arguments for, and evidence that amenities, quality of life, skills and urban growth go hand in hand (for example, Glaeser *et al.* 2001), even if they seem to be insufficient to ignite agglomeration, innovation and growth (Storper and Manville 2006). In this context, the 'creative class' thesis of Richard Florida (2005) has been challenged by many commentators as being too eager to provide off-the-shelf and amenity-based policy prescriptions. However, his recent writings in an essay about South Korea suggest more moderation and a nuanced approach:

> Competitive cities and nations in the 21st century will be those that are open, dynamic, and aesthetically inspiring. Talented, mobile workers are attracted by the opportunity to be around other highly engaged and intelligent talent in arenas that are beautiful and authentically lively. They like densely populated cities where they can meet organically through street scenes filled with cafes, restaurants, bookstores, music clubs, and other unique social and commercial spaces. So smart urban development is essential; it is also difficult to do. One needs to thread a fine line between encouraging entrepreneurs to grow such places and yet not succumb to the temptation to create artificial environments.
> (Florida 2010)

Agreeing with the previous point, it is important to stress that Richard Florida touches upon one of the critical factors in Songdo's future, probably the least tackled so far, but likely to generate unbalances: the potential sense of artificiality of the area. This is a flip side of the 'virgin' character of Songdo's developed land. It still lacks the identity, cultural and social fabric of other places. It is not clear whether this will be a plus to attract mobile workers (it makes the potential cultural clashes less evident) or a negative feature (a feeling of artificiality). In any case, this issue deserves further attention, considering that the type of 'atmospheres' that make a world city lively and vibrant (such as a distinctive cultural scene) are not yet present in Songdo. A related issue has to do with community building and social involvement: will Songdo become an enclave for the well-off or an integrated and diverse community? The second option might require complementary investments and regulation to support low-cost housing and policy controlled rents.

To conclude, we stress the need to carefully consider the integration of Songdo in its reference urban system, that is, within Incheon and in the capital region. A risk is that Songdo becomes the 'window' and entry door to Seoul, overtaking Incheon. It is thus important to avoid the possible physical, social and economic division between 'new' Songdo and 'old' Incheon. The plans of the city of Incheon to cross-fund the revitalization of 'old' Incheon with profits from Songdo are a good idea, but might require additional funding sources, complementary soft measures and permanent monitoring.

10 Munich: Maxvorstadt

Introduction

The city of Munich is one of Europe's most renowned knowledge cities (see for example van den Berg *et al.* 2005). It is home to innovative companies (such as BMW, Siemens and Linde AG), several higher educational institutes (HEIs) and a number of public research institutes (for example, Fraunhofer-Gesellschaft and Max Planck Institute). Famous inventers, such as Rudolf Diesel (inventor of the diesel engine), Carl von Linde (refrigerator), Georg Simon Ohm (theory of electricity), Rudolf Hell (television and communications) and Albert Einstein all spent part of their life in Munich. Nowadays, it is generally recognized that knowledge has become the prime source of growth in advanced economies. Knowledge development in the Munich region is increasingly strengthened; for example, key firms like BMW still contribute significantly to innovation in the Munich area. One of Munich's inner-city districts, Maxvorstadt, is one of the key locations of the city's knowledge infrastructure as it includes a wide variety of cultural and educational institutions. However, various stakeholders feel that Maxvorstadt's potential is not fully exploited, and therefore an evaluation of the area as a knowledge location is taking place. The district and its unique combination of knowledge and cultural institutions have been described as a 'gift not accepted', or as an 'undiscovered treasure'. Current efforts focus on bringing actors together to formulate a strategy to develop the district further, and to exploit the area's potential. An important part of this strategy is to integrate marketing of the different museums in Maxvorstadt in order to attract more visitors to the district. Policymakers, as well as other stakeholders, such as representatives of museums and universities, are aware of the need for an integrated development plan for Maxvorstadt. Therefore, the city of Munich has started a discussion (referred to as the 'Maxvorstadt discussion' in this report) with other key stakeholders to explore whether the integration efforts for the Maxvorstadt museums can function as a stepping stone towards an integrated development plan for Maxvorstadt. This chapter seeks to provide guidance for this discussion. Therefore, we provide insight into the potential of and barriers to further development of Maxvorstadt. Moreover, we give suggestions for management for further development of Maxvorstadt. Hence, we analyse the stakeholders involved, their interests and co-operation or conflict among them.

The remainder of this chapter is organized as follows. The following section describes the urban-economic context of Munich. Insight in this context is needed in order to understand the dynamics of Maxvorstadt. The third section introduces Maxvorstadt, while section four deals with current dynamics that influence the development of the district. The next section describes the actors involved in the development of Maxvorstadt and argues for the need for an integrated development or master plan. Moreover, the following section gives suggestions for the management and the master plan. The last section concludes and provides policy recommendations that may help to develop a master plan for the district.

Munich's urban economic and political context

Munich, the capital of the Free State of Bavaria, is the third largest city in Germany with a total population of 1,360,867.[1] It is only surpassed in number of inhabitants by the cities of Hamburg and Berlin. The city and its surrounding urban region, which consists of eight municipalities, have a total number of 2.5 million inhabitants (Hafner *et al.* 2007). The population of Munich can be considered diverse: 22.6 per cent of the population in Munich consists of people with non-German citizenship. In 2008, Munich's population grew by 1.02 per cent, mostly due to net migration (0.76 per cent), which includes regional migration.[2]

As it is impossible to understand the development of a location in isolation without knowing the wider urban economic context, this section briefly describes Munich's urban economic context.

Munich is one of the most prosperous regions in Germany. It has a dynamic labour market, a low unemployment rate,[3] a dynamic service sector, high purchasing power and high GDP per capita[4] (Hafner *et al.* 2007). Moreover, 'Municon Valley' is one of the leading regions in the knowledge economy with high scores on various knowledge and R&D indicators[5] (Castells and Hall 1994). It acts as a magnet for visitors[6] as well as for (foreign) companies that open a business in the Bavarian capital. Moreover, it is considered one of the most attractive cities in Europe in which to live and work. Munich is known as a big city and a small town at the same time. Each district, like Maxvorstadt, can be seen as a small town with its own facilities such as a church, bars and restaurants. Within the districts there are strong, informal personal relations, and a warm atmosphere. These characteristics, in combination with a rich variety of cultural assets in the city and natural assets in the region, create a distinct quality of life in Munich making it one of the most attractive cities in Europe.[7]

Like other cities, Munich is affected by the economic downturn. The unemployment rate increased from 4.4 per cent in August 2008 to 5.0 per cent in the same period in 2009 (Landeshauptstadt München 2010). However, according to our interview partners, Munich's real-estate market is not yet affected by the economic downturn as real-estate prices remain constant and in some cases are even still slightly rising. Rent levels for real estate (residential) are growing at a stable pace, and are at €13 per m² higher than in other German cities like Hamburg (€12.50) and Stuttgart (€11.90) (Landeshauptstadt München 2010). Thus, the real-estate market in Munich continues to grow, albeit at a slower pace.

Previous studies give various explanations for Munich's success. First, the city has undergone a relatively late industrialization. Therefore, it was able to directly invest in modern sectors and it did not suffer from the decline in old heavy industries as has happened in other industrial areas. Second, Munich benefited from the relocation of various companies and industries from Berlin after the Second World War. Third, Munich has a highly diversified economic structure – known as the Munich Mix – with a good balance between various sectors, between large multinationals and small and medium-sized companies, and between international and local firms. Finally, Munich has a strong knowledge base that is strongly linked with the business sector (Castells and Hall 1994; van den Berg *et al.* 2005; Hafner *et al.* 2007; van Winden *et al.* 2010).

To remain competitive as a knowledge and economic centre, a strong regional knowledge base is crucial. Higher education institutes (HEIs) and private research institutes play a key role in the development and continuity of the knowledge base. Munich has a strong knowledge base with eleven HEIs in the city or its immediate range, as well as other public research institutes and research departments of private firms.[8] The HEIs differ in size (see Table 10.1). It is important to note that the two universities, TUM and LMU, can be seen as complementary to each other. A very rough division can be made, where TUM as a technical university focuses on beta sciences, while LMU is more involved in alpha and gamma sciences. Both TUM and LMU are considered among Germany's finest universities. TUM and LMU were selected in the first German Excellence Initiative as Clusters of Excellence. This national programme strengthens cutting-edge research and promotes top-level as well as young researchers.[9]

Munich's success also has a downside. As van den Berg and Russo (2004) note 'Munich is just too good' (p. 301). Due to its popularity, there are problems in managing accessibility and different functions conflict with each other, while there is a risk of losing lower-income groups who cannot afford to pay the high (real-estate) prices. The presence of well paid knowledge workers creates specific criteria for provisions in the city such as residential space in the higher segments and high-class leisure facilities. Munich's specific labour market has consequences for its demographic structure. Currently, over 50 per cent of the households in Munich are single households,[10] with a high share of highly qualified young people especially in inner-city areas. The city government fears that as the demographic structure evolves (single households become dual households and dual households eventually become families), Munich may be unable to retain its knowledge-intensive labour force inside the city, losing citizenship, expenditure and tax revenue. According to our discussion partners, initial effects are witnessed in that families leave the city centre of Munich as they are unable to find suitable housing or the amenities they require. Moreover, lower-income and in some cases middle-income groups cannot afford to live in Munich any more, which may lead to a shortage of specific types of labour needed for essential services, such as healthcare, cleaning and other public services. In the interviews it was expressed that Munich is clearly polarizing as there is an increasing difference between the highly skilled and the un(der)educated workers. In addition, the resulting high

Table 10.1 Students enrolled at higher educational institutes in Munich for 2007

University	Students
Ludwig-Maximilians-Universität LMU	46,203
Technische Universität TUM	19,887
Hochschule München	13,037
Universität der Bundeswehr	2,903
Stiftungsfachhochschule München	1,688
Hochschule für Politik	936
Hochschule für Musik und Theater	757
Akademie der Bildenden Künste	689
Hochschule für Philosophie	447
Hochschule für Fernsehen und Film	386
Munich Business School	152
Total	87,085

Source: own elaboration; data from: www.statistikdaten.bayern.de

real-estate prices have implications for Maxvorstadt which is becoming too expensive for students.

The increased real-estate prices also have consequences for Munich as a business location in certain sectors (like the media industry), as there are signs that firms move to other locations with lower real-estate prices, such as Berlin. However, for other sectors, like high-tech industries, Munich remains the leading location in Germany. Finally, a recent study shows the importance for Munich in creating a specific identity of Munich's knowledge landscape required to attract and keep students and researchers to the city (Astor *et al.* 2010). This specific identity building process may start from the campus locations and can be extended to the metropolitan region as whole. Maxvorstadt, which is home to various HEI campuses, seems to be a suitable location to start an identity building programme.

To conclude, Munich has a strong knowledge base and a favourable economic structure for knowledge-intensive activities. However, its success also has a downside in the form of high real-estate prices which influences Munich's competitive position as a place in which to live and to do business. The political structure, with a division between the state and the city which have different 'political colours' may lead to hindrances for development of the city. One of the major locations for knowledge-intensive activities is Maxvorstadt, which houses several HEIs as well as a high concentration of cultural institutes. In the next section, we describe this district in more detail.

Maxvorstadt: district of education, science and culture

Maxvorstadt is an inner-city district in the city of Munich which is directly located to the north-west of the old city centre. Figure 10.1 shows that the area is bordered to the east by the English Garden and the Königinstraβe. In the north the quarter is bordered by the area of Schwabing, in the west by Neuhausen, in the south-west by the main railway station area. In size, the district is roughly comparable to the city centre (429ha). The district is characterized by historic locations, such as the Königsplatz and the university area of the LMU. Throughout the years, the district has offered a mixture of residential, education, research and cultural functions. This section describes the area's history, education and culture – two major functions in the district, the accessibility of the area and its integration with the rest of the region.

History of Maxvorstadt

Maxvorstadt was established in the early nineteenth century by the Bavarian king Maximilian I Joseph as a first expansion of the historic centre of Munich. Development in Maxvorstadt expanded after 1825 by royal decrees of King Ludwig I, who attracted world-class artists to the area. Ludwig I's development vision for Maxvorstadt can be captured by the phrase: 'a new Athens on the Isar River', referring to the public life on streets and squares in ancient Athens. The patronage of this early nineteenth-century king, and his successors, was instrumental in the development of Maxvorstadt and gave the district its current shape and ambience. Architects Leo von Klenze and Friedrich von Gärtner were charged with these developments. Klenze and Gärtner developed the Ludwigstraße with the Bavarian state library (BSB), a university (LMU), the Victory Gate, the Königsplatz, the Glyptothek, the Basilica of St Boniface and an art gallery. In the second half of the nineteenth century development continued with the construction of more common functions such as residential and commercial buildings.[11]

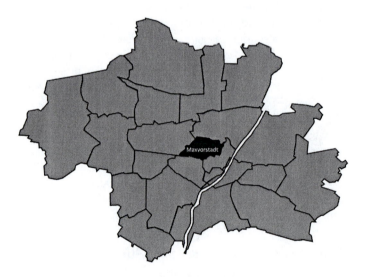

Figure 10.1 Location of Maxvorstadt

Source: www.maps.google.com, own elaboration; December 2009

Maxvorstadt is a district with a strong history. It was home to famous artists and scientists throughout history. In the early twentieth century, the city of Munich attracted many famous writers and poets (among others Thomas Mann) (Stegen and Streit 2003). This group of writers created a specific atmosphere and were called the 'Schwabing Scene' after the district of Schwabing. In fact the most important meeting points for this scene were actually located in Maxvorstadt, and not in the neighbouring district of Schwabing. Moreover, various famous engineers, like Carl von Linde, worked at the Technical University in Munich that was opened in Maxvorstadt in 1868.

During the inter-bellum, the Nazi Party seized power, changing the face of Europe over the coming decade, and greatly influencing urban development in Maxvorstadt. Substantial property in the district was acquired by the NSDAP and the prominent Königsplatz was converted into a 'celebratory square for the movement', as 22,000 granite slabs covered the lawns created by order of King Ludwig I. Additional property around the square was acquired by the NSDAP and transformed into the seat of power for the Nazi Party. In the later stages of the Second World War (July 1944), carpet bombing by the Allied forces destroyed the inner city, including Maxvorstadt. After the war, an essential decision was made to restore the old building style. TUM professor Hans Döllgast was responsible for the reconstruction of characteristic buildings such as the Alte Pinakothek, the Monastery and Basilica of St Boniface and the old northern cemetery. Architect Alexander von Branca rebuilt the 'Neue Pinakothek', breaking with the old traditions and standing on the brink of post-modernism.[12] History, and key decisions during the period of rebuilding, have shaped the district of Maxvorstadt. The tradition of art, culture and science is still very much alive in and around the buildings restored to their former grandeur. Therefore, many discussion partners characterize Maxvorstadt as the true heart of Munich.

Education, science and culture

Culture, education and science continue playing a major role in Maxvorstadt, and the district is a key location in Munich's knowledge and educational infrastructure. It houses the main campuses of the two large universities (LMU, TUM) as well as the University of Applied Sciences (HM) and two smaller universities. A large share of the total students (87,085; see Table 10.1) attends classes in Maxvorstadt and the surrounding areas (50,000 estimated in interviews).

The district is also a major part of Munich's cultural product. It houses many art- and culture-related institutions, such as the Alte Pinakothek, the Neue Pinakothek, the 'Pinakothek der Moderne', the Lenbachhaus, Siemens Forum, the 'Grafische Sammlung', the Glyptothek, the Museum Georgianum, the Brandhorst Museum, the Academy of Fine Arts and the University of Music and Performing Arts Munich. Although this can be considered an impressive array of art and culture institutions, there is consensus among our discussion partners that, with only 100,000 visitors a month, Munich has so far been unable to realize the full potential of this area. Visitor numbers differ substantially between the different museums (see Table 10.2). Additionally, the district houses the Oskar von Miller

Forum, a meeting place and guest house for students and visiting scientists. It is dedicated to promote a holistic image of construction engineering across multiple disciplines.[13] Furthermore, the Bavarian State Library is located in Maxvorstadt, a successful cultural amenity with over 1 million visitors in 2006. This amenity is currently successful because of the longer opening hours of the main reading area (08:00 to 24:00 hrs every day).[14]

Urban centres often contain a large number of urban amenities making it attractive surroundings for knowledge workers (Glaeser *et al.* 2001). Moreover, downtown areas offer the right atmosphere for face-to-face contact and the spread of unintended information spill-overs (Strorper and Venables 2004). Also Maxvorstadt can be seen as a vibrant downtown district. Besides the educational and cultural facilities, the area has attracted specific facilities for students and (young) knowledge workers, such as bookshops, galleries and bars, which is also expressed as the 'C&C (Coffee and Copy shop) Culture'. Many specific and often unplanned happenings are organized in the district, like fashion shows, readings and music shows. As expressed in the *Süddeutsche Zeitung* (23 June 2010): 'Nowhere in Munich is more happening than in Maxvorstadt'. Another article mentioned the importance of the variety of shops and restaurants in the surroundings of the university as well: 'Here [in Maxvorstadt], desires of intellectuals and other parts of the upper class are satisfied. No other quarter in Munich has so many second-hand bookshops, galleries and bookshops as Maxvorstadt' (Stegen and Streit 2003, p. 124). However, rising real-estate prices may threaten this specific atmosphere as the area may become too expensive as a place to live for students and low-income knowledge workers (for example, emerging artists). We discuss this gentrification effect in more detail in the fourth section.

Table 10.2 Museum visitors in Maxvorstadt

Museums	Yearly visitors			Monthly average
	2006	2007	2008	2008
Alte Pinakothek	272,646	218,386	225,231	18,769
Neue Pinakothek	152,592	204,016	192,732	16,061
Pinakothek der Moderne	370,366	448,982	368,812	30,734
Städtische Galerie im Lenbachhaus	174,034	170,144	311,171[1]	25,931
Staatliche Antikensammlungen	49,922	62,430	41,366	3,447
Siemens forum	n/a	n/a	n/a	n/a
Glyptothek	119,217	115,418	107,766	8,981
Total	1,138,777	1,221,383	1,249,086	103,923

Source: Statistisches Amt München, 2010

Note
[1] Note that the number of visitors of the Städtische Galerie im Lenbachhaus was higher in 2008 due to a successful temporary exhibition

Accessibility of Maxvorstadt and connection with other locations

Districts do not develop in isolation and are functionally and/or physically connected with other parts of the region and with other regions. This is especially true for an inner-city location, such as Maxvorstadt, which combines various functions that are complementary, but sometimes also overlapping, to those of other districts. These mixed functions generate flows of people within, but also between, districts. The size of these flows makes Maxvorstadt dynamic: on a daily basis almost 50,000 people visit the area to study, work or visit the museums. This number is roughly equal to the total population (47,771 in 2008) of the district. Due to the substantial visitor flow inside the district and the mobility of its inhabitants, accessibility is an important issue in Maxvorstadt (City of Munich 2008). Although accessibility is at present adequate in Maxvorstadt, it remains an important issue. For instance, accessibility by car in Munich's Maxvorstadt is characterized by some interview partners as inadequate, especially in locations close to the city centre. City officials state that further development of roadways is not an option because of the lack of space. Therefore, solutions for accommodating future growth are sought in the field of public transport. It is believed that the provision of high-quality public transport connections will ensure continued accessibility. In 2006, a new subway ('U-Bahn') connection was developed to connect the TUM Campus Garching in the north to the inner city (see Figure 10.2) and it would be possible to extend this line (U6) to Neufahrn, a station of the regional railway S1 to the airport or to the university campus near Freising. However, there are no concrete plans to realize this at the moment. The same U6 as well as other subway connections link Maxvorstadt with other major knowledge and university locations such as the LMU Grosshadern Campus in the south-west. Connecting districts or regions with other districts may lead to concentration or to the spread of activities. There is no consensus on the possible effects of improved public transport connections on the functioning of Maxvorstadt. On the one hand Maxvorstadt's improved connectivity to the rest of the network may make the district more accessible, drawing more people to the area. On the other hand Maxvorstadt's improved connections may make other non-central locations more accessible, decreasing the need for a central knowledge location such as Maxvorstadt. An important development in this respect is the state decision to move substantial parts of TUM and LMU to locations on the periphery of Munich. Without proper policy measures, this may decrease Maxvorstadt's position in Munich's knowledge network. Moreover, the district is not considered suitable for slow-moving traffic such as pedestrians or cyclists because of substantial, fast-moving car traffic. Additionally the connectivity between certain parts of Maxvorstadt, such as the museum quarter and the rest of the city, is a point of attention, as the entrance to the quarter is facing away from the city centre.

To conclude, Maxvorstadt is a crucial location for Munich's cultural and scientific product. It has good public transport connections with other locations. Major remaining questions include:

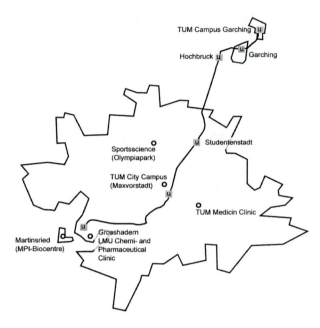

Figure 10.2 U-6 subway line connecting the different university locations

Source: www.mimed.mw.tum.de

- What is the functional link between the various functions within Maxvorstadt?
- How are the functional links with other locations?

We discuss these questions in the next section, placing them in the context of the major contemporary developments in Maxvorstadt.

Maxvorstadt: current development and dynamics

Maxvorstadt is a mixed, inner-city area characterized by diversity, prosperity and a rich tradition in culture and education. These characteristics are shown in the physical composition of the district. Cultural and educational institutions form the heart of the district, while commercial and retail functions dominate the south-western part of the area (which is close to the city centre). Residential functions dominate in the northern parts of the district. In this section, we analyse these functions and major developments of Maxvorstadt in more detail. First we discuss how various functions in Maxvorstadt influence the real-estate market and what initiatives are taken to cope with the high real-estate prices. We then discuss the potential of Maxvorstadt as a business location and its position in knowledge networks, followed by an analysis of the idea of linking culture with science. The last two sub-sections investigate two major contemporary dynamics in Maxvorstadt: spatial dynamics of knowledge institutes and the development of Maxvorstadt's museum quarter ('Kunstareal').

Mixed functions and real estate market

Cities increasingly develop into mixed environments, where living and consuming are combined with other functions such as leisure and business. However, space is scarce in central areas and different functions compete for it. This results in higher real-estate prices, making the central areas less affordable for certain target groups. This is the case in Maxvorstadt. In this section, we analyse the competition for space in Maxvorstadt with special attention to the potential for and barriers to student housing in the area.

Commercial functions have started replacing residential functions in Maxvorstadt. This effect is strongest in the parts adjacent to the city centre. The increased commercial activities in Maxvorstadt lead to rising real-estate prices and Maxvorstadt has become one of the more expensive areas of Munich. As a consequence, some inhabitants are unable to afford the high real-estate prices and move to other districts. For instance, inhabitants with middle incomes (that is, an annual income of approximately €40,000–€50,000) can no longer afford to live in Maxvorstadt. The trend is that mainly people with a double income and no kids ('dinkys') can afford to live in Maxvorstadt. Many of these people leave when they have children, because of the shortage of suitable housing for families at affordable prices. For example, an apartment with three rooms costs about €1000 per month or more, depending on its size (based on interviews). In 2009, new rents for an 80 to 100m^2 flat amounted to €13.90 per m^2 excluding energy costs; this was the fourth-highest level out of 33 local areas for which this information was collected (Landeshauptstadt München 2009).

Besides the fact that commercial functions move into Maxvorstadt at the cost of residential space, there are a number of other reasons for the rising real-estate prices, which are all related to increasing attractiveness. First, the district is developing a 'bohemian' culture; students, artists and other bohemians move to Maxvorstadt as they can no longer afford to live in locations with even higher real-estate prices, such as the Glockenbachviertel. They choose to live in Maxvorstadt because the district has an inherent spatial quality and a rich history. Second, the squares and other public spaces, such as the Königsplatz and the Alte Pinakothek, are attractive meeting places in summer time. These meetings in public space contribute to a vibrant ambience in the district. Third, certain commercial functions have been developed in the areas that bring flair and vibrancy to the area. For example, various fashion boutiques are moving into the area and café-kiosk retail is expanding (*Süddeutsche Zeitung*, 14 July 2009).

Student housing

A special target group which is influenced by the high real-estate prices is students. Students can contribute to the vibrancy of an area, but also have specific demands, such as low-cost residential space. A previous Euricur study has shown that the student community is not integrated in the Munich community because of the shortage of low-cost housing and bureaucracy. Moreover, the study states that Munich misses a real student atmosphere (van den Berg and Russo 2004). This latter was confirmed in our interviews as it was argued that the proportion of students in the total population in Munich is limited.

Maxvorstadt has dual potential as a student district. On the one hand, the district houses a large number of educational institutes. So, students are in the district to study. Moreover, the district has many student facilities, such as book shops, and has a vibrant atmosphere. Students may increase this vibrant atmosphere. However, worth mentioning is that not all students are attracted by a vibrant city centre. A distinction should be made between different types of students, as beta students seem to be more interested in a campus with good research facilities and participate in small specialized networks, while alpha and gamma students tend to prefer a university in vibrant urban surroundings with open social networks (van den Berg and Russo 2004). On the other hand, the city of Munich (including Maxvorstadt) has problems housing students (see also van den Berg and Russo 2004). As real-estate prices are high, students can often not afford to live in the city. Although some student housing can be found in Maxvorstadt, the district is not particularly suited for student housing. Rents are prohibitively high. Some students cope with these rents by sharing apartments, but in reality most students do not live in Maxvorstadt. Most students live even outside the city of Munich in the surrounding metropolitan (functional) region. This region is more or less delimitated by the train (S-Bahn) network. It should be noted that many students and professors, especially foreigners, do not perceive Maxvorstadt as a separate location. These people come to Munich – the metropolitan region they perceive – and do not base their location choice on individual characteristics of locations such as Maxvorstadt or Garching. With good public transport connections, they are able to travel through the region and exploit the assets of each individual district.

Policy measures and initiatives

In order to retain residents with lower incomes and students, the City of Munich takes various measures, among others subsidies on social and student housing. Through the so-called Munich model young families are supported in order to keep them in the city. Support for students in the form of subsidized housing is more difficult and in the interviews it was argued that it is not possible for the city to support students financially on a continuing basis. A solution might be to build student houses, but this is difficult because of high land prices.

The city and state government also jointly attempt to develop affordable student housing in Maxvorstadt on a limited scale (*Süddeutsche Zeitung*, 27 October 2009). The city has clearly expressed its ambition to increase the available student housing, but it depends on the state, which has the resources to develop the required real estate. Currently, co-operation between the state and city level in the field of student housing might be improved. A barrier for further development is that state resources are scarce and are also needed elsewhere. Some interview partners have suggested that private actors, such as insurance companies, or other major firms (such as Siemens) may contribute to investment in student housing. From the viewpoint of corporate social responsibility and marketing this may be interesting for these companies.

Other interview partners have expressed doubts whether student housing in the city is needed and whether providing it would be effective. Time and resources would be better spent on ensuring cheap and effective public transport for students. Public transport for students is a point of attention. Currently available student tickets do not cover the entire public transport network of Munich. For instance, it is not possible to travel from TUM's Maxvorstadt campus to its Garching campus, as the current ticket is not valid this far outside Munich. Sound infrastructural accessibility (primarily by public transport) seems to be a more efficient solution than investment in student housing, and it may be sufficient for students to just frequent Maxvorstadt for study, shopping and recreation.

Knowledge networks and Maxvorstadt as a business location

The high real-estate prices of Maxvorstadt and the traditional function as a living quarter also have an influence on Maxvorstadt as a business location. Apart from consumer services and specific student services, Maxvorstadt has hardly any other businesses. Due to a shortage of space, Maxvorstadt is too expensive for business with low profit margins (for example, the location is not suited for certain artists),[15] while businesses with higher profit margins (such as financial institutes) prefer more central locations in proximity to other businesses, rather than the mainly residential, educational and cultural function of Maxvorstadt. This does not mean that Maxvorstadt is irrelevant as a location for business. In particular, the presence of the universities might be of great value for firms' knowledge and innovation networks.

A key issue for knowledge locations is the existence of knowledge networks between relevant institutes and industries, and the geographical dimension of these networks. In other words, to what extent does the physical proximity of firms and knowledge institutes in one area matter? At first glance, this question does not seem to be relevant for Maxvorstadt as the district is mainly a living and university area without major (industrial) companies. Furthermore, as most of the HEI locations in Maxvorstadt are used by alpha-oriented faculties, less interaction with (industrial) firms may be expected. This is in large contrast with other locations, such as Garching (which, for instance, attracted the European R&D centre of General Electric, and Siemens has a major R&D and training centre in Garching). The campus in Garching strongly benefits from the presence of TUM. Another example is INI.TUM, an establishment of TUM at Audi's main site in Ingolstadt set up to do joint research projects for the luxury car manufacturer (see van Winden *et al.* 2010).

In addition, for most of the HEIs in Maxvorstadt, the geographical scale of knowledge networks is much wider than the inner-city location. LMU, TUM and Hochschule München all have relations with key firms in the Munich region (such as BMW, Siemens and Audi) and benefit from the diversified economic structure of the region. Furthermore, co-operation is fostered with firms in other regions of Germany (for example, Hochschule München is doing research projects with Porsche in Stuttgart). The character of the industrial co-operation differs widely, from permanent co-operation in special foundations (such as BMW and TUM having jointly set up a special research foundation) to project-based co-operation based on personal contacts (such as the co-operation between Hochschule München and Porsche). It should be noted that both TUM as well as LMU have special departments that deal with formal relations with industry; however, personal relations between firms and professors also play a role. It is also worth noting that there are relations between the universities and other knowledge institutes. For example, throughout Germany each Fraunhofer research unit is headed up by a university professor. These university professors ensure a link between the (upcoming) labour market and the Fraunhofer-Gesellschaft.

Linking culture and science

Although the potential for HEI–industry interaction is limited in Maxvorstadt, there is space for interaction between HEIs and cultural institutes. This interaction is not directly related to knowledge development, but has a number of benefits for universities, the cultural institutes and society as a whole. First, the interaction can make science and innovation more visible to the general public. This shows the public what knowledge is available in Munich and what is possible with science. For instance, the department of architecture of TUM shows (student) concepts in the Pinakothek der Moderne (which hosts the Museum for Architecture of TUM). Similarly, an exhibition of the Hochschule für Film und Fernsehen has been shown in the Pinakothek der Moderne. In addition, firms also show science and innovation in their own museums, such as BMW Welt (outside Maxvorstadt) and Siemens Forum. These initiatives on the micro level work well. For instance, BMW Welt is a huge success. Interview partners have suggested that the potential of these individual initiatives may be improved. This could be done by linking the individual initiatives to achieve a common product such as specific tours, in which various companies are visited, combined with other tourist attractions such as museums. It should be noted that there is a limit to the extent companies are willing to show their activities; they are not likely to show basic research for reasons of secrecy, despite the trend to open innovation (Chesbrough 2003).

Second, and related to the first, showing science has an important educational function and can help to make people enthusiastic to study a science subject. This may help to prevent (future) shortages of qualified researchers in certain areas. Therefore, as an example outside Maxvorstadt, the German Museum shows a number of research projects of the Fraunhofer-Gesellschaft. These exhibitions are aimed at making children up to the age of 18 (just before these children choose their university majors) enthusiastic for natural sciences and so prevent a (future) shortage of qualified researchers. It should be noted that this example illustrates that university–museum co-operation is not limited to the borders of Maxvorstadt. Within Maxvorstadt, the Siemens Forum aims at social engagement, education, research and innovation in the fields of technology, arts and culture.[16] Third, the museums as well as the Bavarian State Library may function as important meeting spaces for students as well as other groups of society.

With some major exceptions, like the Doerner Institute (which focuses on the preservation of art) and the co-operation between TUM and the Pinakothek der Moderne, many co-operation projects between museums and HEIs are of a temporary nature. From the interviews it becomes clear that there is a demand for more permanent spaces to display contemporary science. Furthermore, most museums focus on fine art, which is not always complementary to science, and therefore, an interview partner stressed the need for the opening of a museum that focuses exclusively on science. A recent initiative by the city of Munich worth mentioning in this respect is the 'house of science'. This idea was initiated by the private sector. The plan includes the transformation of a former monastery into a place to exhibit products of all types of sciences. The building should be open to the public in order to make science available to the general population. Additionally, it may link between different scientific disciplines. In general, the house of science is planned to serve two functions: (i) as a platform for discussion; (ii) a place to show science to the people (Landeshauptstadt München 2008). The project is still in a planning phase and, although our interview partners are generally positive about this project, the expectation is that it will not be implemented because of a lack of resources. Aside from this project, there are only a very few shared projects between industry, museums and universities. One other initiative is the Day of Science, where universities open their doors to the general public, but despite this being a success, it happens only once a year. Some interview partners suggested that universities may be opened more often to the public. However, universities are not likely to function as a museum, and tend to focus on their core business (doing research), but can have their own (separate) museum. A good example is Harvard University in the USA, which has its own museum showing science to the public via exhibitions and lecture series. Another initiative is a cultural walk (KulturGeschichtsPfad) that recently has been set up in Maxvorstadt. This walk shows the cultural potential in Maxvorstadt via guided tours in the form of a pocket-size book that takes you along highlights in different areas of Munich. For each highlight extensive information is provided in the book. Recently such a book has been developed for Maxvorstadt.[17]

Spatial dynamics of knowledge institutes

Universities play an important role in urban development. This role has widely been addressed in academic literature, both in terms of its role in knowledge and skill development in regional innovation systems (for example, Coenen 2007; Benneworth and Hospers 2007) as well as the physical and social development of cities due to the presence of university buildings and student communities (for example, see Phelps 1998 and van den Berg and Russo 2004). At the same time, universities compete with other urban functions for space, and in various cases urban university campuses relocate to suburban locations (Hall 1997). This is also the case in Munich, where certain faculties at inner-city campuses in Maxvorstadt and other central locations have been (re)opened at suburban locations.

In recent decades, Maxvorstadt has been confronted with a displacement of university functions, especially of faculties in the beta sciences. This process started with the establishment of a centre for nuclear research in the neighbouring town of Garching in 1975. For obvious reasons this centre could not be established inside the city of Munich. Further displacement has taken place since then. This was due to growth of the universities and competition for space with other urban functions that needed more space, such as museums. The displaced university functions have moved to municipalities within the metropolitan region, but outside Munich's administrative borders. Figure 10.3 provides an overview of the current (academic) university locations in the Munich region. It should be noted that more relocations may be expected, although different interview partners contradict each other on the extent of further relocation. Some interviews indicate a move of up to 80 per cent of the university hospitals to locations outside the city. Despite the fact that these clinics are not in Maxvorstadt, and plans for relocation are still unclear, the close proximity of these clinics and the discussion on relocation influence the future development of Maxvorstadt. Although most HEI movements have been from the inner city to regional campuses, the reverse also happens. A recent and promising development is the attraction of the Hochschule für Film und Fernsehen (HFF) to the Maxvorstadt area. In late 2009 a new building was constructed to house this HEI. The HFF shares the building with a museum for Egyptian art. Moving HFF to Maxvorstadt will enable students to interact with the city environment; this has a number of benefits. First, the students are able to use the inner-city environment for their projects, adding to the value of their studies. Second, the presence of students in this part of Maxvorstadt may increase the vibrancy of the district. Third, in co-operation with student associations the HFF may be able to organize small and larger events showing 'local productions'. Overall, the attraction of HFF to Maxvorstadt can be viewed as highly positive and beneficial for both HFF and the Maxvorstadt district.

Opinions on the implications of the relocation of HEIs for Maxvorstadt differ. On the one hand, the Maxvorstadt area (LMU main campus and TUM Arcisstraße) is still rich in faculties, especially in the alpha and gamma sciences (see Figure 10.3) and university representatives have clearly stated their intention to stay in Maxvorstadt, although more relocations cannot be excluded. The interviews have also made clear that there is no need to bring faculties back to the city centre and that such an effort would be too expensive and ineffective. On the other hand, the relocation of the universities raises some concern among urban policymakers. The fear is that plots that might become vacant would be commercially developed without proper attention to the area at large, which may go at the cost of the spatial quality and urban variety required to guarantee a prospering city area.

The city has limited influence on the relocation of the universities and the resulting use of land, as university real estate and land are owned by the state. The developments of the campus locations in the region need to be financed. As a consequence, the land holdings of the state in the city need to be commercially exploited in order to contribute to the financing of the outside-campus locations. This leads to different interests of policymakers on the local and on the state level. So, on the one hand there are the financial constraints under which the state operates and on the other hand the ambition of the city to ensure urban spatial quality.

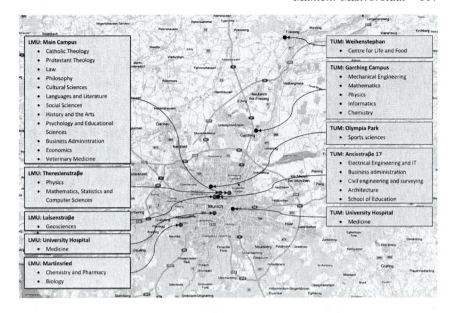

Figure 10.3 University presence in the Munich region, overview per faculty

Source: www.maps.google.com, own elaboration

Expansion and development of the 'Kunstareal'

Cultural, or art, districts (or quarters) play a key role in economic development, for instance in revitalization of old neighbourhoods, or as a tourist attraction. However, research has shown mixed results with successful and less successful cases of cultural districts. Management of cultural districts is difficult because of the presence of various actors with their own interests and there is not a 'one size fits all' solution (for example, Hitters and Richards 2002; Mommaas 2004; Lavanga *et al.* 2008; Van der Borg and van Tuijl 2010).

The management and further development of the museum district 'Kunstareal' in Maxvorstadt is also a major challenge. Despite Maxvorstadt's rich collection of museums in geographical proximity to each other, there is not a single cultural cluster yet that acts as a common (tourist) product. Most of the individual museums function as 'silos' and work on their own. A major explanation for this is a difference in ownership of the individual museums: 80 per cent of museums are public owned (divided into state-owned and city-owned museums), and the other 20 per cent are privately owned. Moreover, and despite physical proximity of the different museums, the museums function as separate attractions instead of forming a common and larger tourist product. A single brand or ticket office for the quarter is lacking. Therefore the area is not perceived as an integrated quarter but as a collection of separate museums.

Another point of attention is that the museum district is insufficiently integrated with the inner city. Proper signage is missing, and from an architectural perspective the orientation of the area might be improved as currently the museum quarter is facing away from the city centre. Furthermore, connections to public green areas like the Old Botanical Garden in the south, have to be improved.

There is awareness of the need to join forces in order to develop a more common product, to solve practical problems (such as a shortage of storage depots) and to attract more visitors. Therefore, various initiatives have been taken. A major one is the formation of the foundation Pinakothek der Moderne (PdM) which has been set up by private actors with the aim to develop and manage the Pinakothek der Moderne, a new museum developed in Munich's Maxvorstadt. The Pinakothek der Moderne is a building housing four major museums which feature fine art, graphic arts, architecture and design. Aside from its permanent collection, the Pinakothek der Moderne also has various temporary exhibitions on display.

PdM has joined forces with the department for urban planning of TUM in order to develop ideas to improve the quality and number of visitors in the museum district in Maxvorstadt. This resulted, first, in a joint strategic conference on the future of the Maxvorstadt area. Second, it led to the establishment of a forum on the future for the art district ('Kunstareal') Maxvorstadt. This forum took place in April 2009. The conference focused on a number of key issues for the art district: visibility of the collection, capacity for storage, integration of the museums with the rest of the district, and networking between universities. This resulted in an approach based on three pillars which involves a joint programme for the museums, integration of public space and a general vision and strategy for the area (Pinakothek der Moderne 2009). One of the key issues identified during the conference is the lack of art storage space. Such storage space can take the form of (common) depots, shared by a number of museums. Additionally, a lack of common exhibition areas for temporary exhibitions was identified. Furthermore, the forum led to a discussion revolving around the question whether the strategic co-operation and planning in the museum area could be developed further, perhaps into a strategic development plan for the entire Maxvorstadt.

In addition, a project group headed by the Bavarian Minister for Science, Research, and the Arts and the Lord Mayor of Munich was established in 2009. During 2010 and 2011 various stakeholders which might be interested in co-operation for the further development of the Kunstareal (like representatives of universities) have been invited to participate in a development process.

Stiftung Pinakothek der Moderne (2009) and interviews give suggestions about the exploitation of the museum quarter's potential. First, there is an opportunity to develop a common tourist product by promoting the area as one Museum Quarter ('Kunstareal') Munich. This museum quarter should have a common brand and offer the option of having a ticket that gives access to all museums in the quarter. Moreover, a map that depicts all museums could help visitors to move through the area. This might also help in a second way, opening up of museums, as currently the buildings look forbidding and closed. Third, there is a potential to create a stronger link between 'art' and 'science'. Co-operation takes place already on a limited scale in some projects, but could be done on a more permanent basis. A permanent exhibition space of student productions in museums could increase interaction between culture and science. Fourth, the opening hours could be extended in order to attract a broader target group. Finally, engaging Web 2.0 development would ensure a strong presence for the entire museum area on the web. However, many suggestions are difficult to realize because of budget restrictions. Currently, various stakeholders are investigating how improvements can be made with limited budget and how a shared vision supported by many stakeholders can be created.

Governance and policy: towards a master plan

The previous sections have made clear that there are several joint initiatives and plans for the development of Maxvorstadt on a micro level (for example, regarding one function or building). There is no master (or development) plan yet for the development of the entire district, building on the strong knowledge infrastructure and the specific features of the Kunstareal.

Developing an integrated master plan is a complex process, that involves many stakeholders all with their own interests and with limited available resources. Van 't Verlaat (2002) shows that optimization of development plans is dependent on three 'variables' which are: spatial quality (the observable quality of the built environment); market quality (demand by the end-user); and available resources. Tensions occur between each of these elements. Through careful and informed policy these tensions can be managed, resulting in better plans for all involved. Although theoretic in nature, this model has proved its validity in various empirical case studies (Van 't Verlaat 2002; Urlings 2007; Van Randeraat 2006). Other studies have shown that successful area development can only take place if public–private co-operation is organized and implemented in a successful way (see for example Deloitte 2008; Franzen and De Zeeuw 2009).

The Maxvorstadt discussion also includes many stakeholders each with their own responsibilities and interests. This section first briefly describes these actors, then discusses arguments for the need for a master plan, and finally provides some suggestions for the management of further development of Maxvortstadt.

Actors involved and their tasks

The previous sections have made it clear that many stakeholders are involved in the development. All have their own interests, as well as their own responsibilities and resources. These are the main actors.

- The *City of Munich*, whose primary concern is to guarantee urban and spatial quality. Major issues for the city include creating a vibrant district and the presence of the universities and students is seen as a major requirement for this. Furthermore, the city aims to ensure a balanced supply of residential space for different income groups.
- The *State of Bavaria*, which is a major owner of key facilities in Maxvorstadt (for example, museums and universities) and is a major investor in the area. It

also has the resources to do this. However, resources are limited due to the fact
that these are also needed at other places in Munich and other parts of Bavaria.

- The *museums and HEIs* (including students) are major users of the area
  and require a certain market quality. These actors can also contribute to
  the spatial quality and vibrancy of the area. A key actor for the development of Maxvorstadt worth mentioning is the foundation 'Pinakothek der
  Moderne' (PdM), because it was among the first actors to set an agenda
  for Maxvorstadt (concerning the future of the Kunstareal Maxvorstadt) and
  to join forces with other actors (TUM). However, PdM's role is limited to
  the art district, although it may help to bring actors together. HEIs play
  in this way a key role as a bridge between the city and state government,
  for their physical presence, local involvement in the city and connections
  with the city government,[18] but have a financial dependency on the state. In
  particular, TUM has strong local ties and is aware of its role for the direct
  surroundings, but also has access to the state government. It should be
  noted that despite the awareness of HEIs of the importance of local development and the willingness to contribute to this, the primary concern of
  universities, and increasingly polytechnics as well, is to do research since
  top research is rewarded with financial incentives.
- *District Council Maxvorstadt* is an actor with limited power, but it represents the interests of inhabitants and it has local knowledge with regard to the
  development of and more practical problems of inhabitants and other stakeholders in the district. So, this actor is crucial to develop and keep societal
  support at the local level.

Towards a master plan

All stakeholders are aware of the need for an integrated plan for the future
development of Maxvorstadt, and are willing to contribute to such a plan. This
study has given various reasons for the need of such a plan. First, the district
has various functions which complement each other (such as universities and
student housing), but also compete with each other for space, which is scarce.
Major contemporary dynamics in these functions include the displacement of
the universities and the development and/or extension of the museum district.
Second, there is the potential and ambition of linking different functions, especially culture and science. It is important to show science to (local) society. This
may have different advantages including making youngsters enthusiastic about
technology, the potential of creating new combinations and to create discussion platforms between different disciplines. Moreover, museums can function as places to apply science as well, for instance for art restoration studies.
Third, and related to the others, the high real-estate prices may lead to gentrification with the risk of losing certain functions. A key issue for the master
plan is how to keep the necessary functions available, either by keeping them
in Maxvorstadt or by ensuring good (public) transport connections with other
areas. Fourth, both the Lord Mayor of Munich as well as the Bavarian State
Ministry for Science, Research, and the Arts have made further development of

Maxvorstadt their priority. So, there is political support from different political layers; the city and the state are willing to join forces, despite possible political barriers (such as differences in budgets and interests). Finally, Munich aims to host the Winter Olympics in 2018. This is a shared goal that can bring actors together and to give Maxvorstadt its own function and a face (for example, the cultural centre) in the total 'product Munich'.

The development of a master plan cannot be done by a single stakeholder alone, but requires the support of many stakeholders. Major questions are how the development can be managed and which stakeholder takes the lead and brings actors together. The city is seen by many stakeholders as the actor to take the lead in the development of a master plan for Maxvorstadt, although some argue that the state is better equipped for this task due to the availability of resources. Other actors have stated their willingness to support a good master plan and may be able to bring stakeholders to each other, but cannot take the lead. Although stakeholders agree that central leadership in developing an integral development vision for the area may be beneficial, some question the possibility of managing an entire city quarter.

A master plan is a complex plan covering many topics. Based on the interviews, we are able to give suggestions for two of these topics: (i) marketing of Maxvorstadt and (ii) the integrated use of public space.

Regarding the marketing of the area, it is important to create a balanced marketing plan that is integrated in the total marketing plan of the Munich region. Our interviews clearly show that the potential of Maxvorstadt lies in its central location, its specific urban quality for inhabitants as well as commuters and visitors, and the presence of the rich variety of cultural and educational institutes. This might be a central part in the marketing plan and Maxvorstadt might be branded as a 'hotspot where art and science meet'. An important question which needs to be raised for the development of the marketing plan is whether the brand Munich and/or a specific brand Maxvorstadt will be used. As noted in the previous sections, many (potential) city customers (like students) do not distinguish between individual locations such as Maxvorstadt, but live in, consume in, or visit Munich. Therefore, and especially for international markets, as one of our interview partners suggested, Munich should be used as the common brand as a focal point for knowledge and culture, with its epicentre within the city of Munich in Maxvorstadt. Individual locations, such as Maxvorstadt can be used as sub-brands. For, instance, the museum quarter can be branded as 'Kunstareal Munich-Maxvorstadt'. Also other knowledge locations in the region can then be branded in such a way, like 'University of Munich @ Garching', recognizing both the brand of the region as well as the local setting.

Concerning the integrated use of the public space, some of our interview partners suggested making more public buildings easier to access as these now look forbidding and closed. This includes using squares and streets between the buildings for public events. The relocation of the Hochschule für Film und Fernsehen to Maxvorstadt can be seen as an opportunity in this respect. Public spaces can also be made more attractive by using art and science. These public art works might also have an educational function in some cases.

Conclusions and recommendations

Munich has a rich tradition in knowledge development. The city houses famous innovative companies (such as BMW, Siemens, Linde AG), many research institutes, and was home to famous inventors such as Carl von Linde and Rudolf Diesel. It is a leading city in the knowledge economy, with high knowledge indicators and a high quality of life. The success has also a downside in the form of high real-estate prices and competition for scarce space, which negatively affects Munich's demographic composition and its competitive position for certain industries. For instance, lower- and middle-income groups cannot afford to live in Munich any more, which may lead to a shortage of labour needed for essential services, such as healthcare and public safety.

Munich wants to continue its tradition in science and research in order to distinguish itself from other cities and to keep a leading position in the knowledge economy. One of the key locations in Munich's knowledge economy is Maxvorstadt. This district houses a substantial number of HEIs and forms the cultural heart of the city with its large collection of museums. The district suffers from a scarcity of space, and different functions (education, living, culture and others) compete for this scarce space with higher real-estate prices as a consequence. The City of Munich has started a discussion with other stakeholders in order to safeguard and stimulate the potential of the area as a knowledge location. Furthermore, involved stakeholders have discussed the development of a strategic plan for the future development of the area.

Our study has analysed current dynamics in Maxvorstadt – including the development of a museum cluster; geographical dynamics in the location of HEIs; linking culture with science; and rising real-estate prices as a consequence of a shortage of space – and aims to give insights for further development and management of the area. This section summarizes our main findings and gives some concrete recommendations to develop Maxvorstadt further.

A first conclusion is that Maxvorstadt has a number of key assets. Its major asset is the relatively unique concentration of museums and HEIs in one city district. This asset has not been fully exploited yet, but there are opportunities to do so. First, the museum quarter 'Kunstareal' can become a major part of Munich's tourist product. It can diversify the tourist product, next to other strong images of the city such as beer, football and the green surroundings. An important and related asset in this respect is the central location and the proximity to the city centre. Nevertheless, the connection with the city centre might be improved by better information provision (such as signing) or improved 'passages'. Another challenge is the development from a collection of single museums to a museum cluster that functions as a common (tourist) product. Some suggestions about this are the introduction of a shared entrance ticket and joint marketing of the district. Second, there are opportunities to link culture with science, whereby museums show science developed by HEIs and/or firms. Maxvorstadt already has some major examples of this, including the Doerner Institute and co-operation between the Pinakothek der Moderne and the Department of Architecture of TUM. Linking science with education has a number of benefits, such as an educational function (science has been shown to society), a recruitment function (people can get enthusiastic about science and start studying it, which may prevent future labour market shortages for certain disciplines) and it may link different disciplines. Moreover, museums can function as places to apply science, like art restoration. There are also some critical remarks to be made on the extent to which science can be linked with culture. First, companies, but also HEIs, are not likely to show basic research for secrecy reasons. Second, with some major exceptions like Museum Reich der Kristalle (Bavarias mineralogical collection), most of the museums show fine art, which is not directly complementary to science. Therefore, a solution might be to start a new museum focusing on science or join forces with the museum which is the closest to science. Fourth, HEIs are not likely to function as a museum on their own and tend to continue focusing on their core business, which is doing research. However, HEIs may open their own museums. A best practice in this sense might be the Harvard museum in the USA.

Despite the large number of HEIs, we have no evidence that Maxvorstadt functions as a key knowledge location for local business–university relations. For many firms, Maxvorstadt is not attractive due to the scarcity of suited space and the high real-estate prices. Therefore, firms are located in other places and see the entirety of Munich as the relevant region. Similarly, HEIs in Maxvorstadt have networks with firms crossing the entire Munich region and other parts of Germany. In other university locations of the Munich region, which focus on other disciplines, co-location of universities and firms does matter, such as is the case of the Garching Campus.

A related conclusion is that Maxvorstadt is just one of the various locations in Munich. Many actors do not see Maxvorstadt, as with other districts, as a specific location, but live, work, consume or do business in the entire Munich region benefiting from the specific assets of the individual districts. This has at least two major consequences. First, in marketing plans, the brand Munich should be used, while Maxvorstadt may serve as a sub-brand (for example, Kunstareal Munich-Maxvorstadt). Second, and although Munich's (public) transport network functions well, further development and maintenance are essential to link the various districts, enabling the various city users to exploit the assets of the single districts. Moreover, the accessibility of the district for pedestrians and cyclists may be improved.

A good working transport network is also crucial for another development, the geographical dynamics in the location of the HEI campuses. The relocation of HEIs can be considered as a natural process in which HEIs try to find optimum locations with the right facilities for different disciplines. Some disciplines move to more suburban locations as there is a need for more calm surroundings, sufficient space and good research facilities. Others benefit from a vibrant inner-city location, such as Maxvorstadt. A good example of the latter is the relocation of the Hochschule für Fernsehen und Film to Maxvorstadt, which may also increase the vibrancy of the district.

Maxvorstadt, with its central location, rich cultural assets and other urban amenities, and the main campuses (management function) of two major universities and several other HEIs, may act as a spider in Munich's educational and science network. The district may also be attractive to various target groups related to the educational institutes, such as students, visiting researchers and conference participants. Many interview partners agree about the contribution of students and the other mentioned target groups to the vibrancy of the district, although there is no consensus about the necessity that they also live in Maxvorstadt, as the district may be too expensive for them (especially students). Moreover, it has good connections with other districts where students and the other target groups can live. Another point which should be made is that just like different HEIs, groups of students and researchers are not homogeneous; they are not all attracted by a vibrant city centre. Some prefer calm and green surroundings in the suburbs instead.

Final conclusions can be drawn regarding the stakeholders involved and the management of the area. Many stakeholders are involved in the 'Maxvorstadt discussion', each with their own interests and, sometimes conflicting, tasks. Therefore, co-operation is sometimes difficult. Another barrier for co-operation is Munich's success. There is no common threat that brings stakeholders together, as happened in the regions of Eindhoven and Helsinki in times of deep crises. Munich can try to find a common opportunity to bring stakeholders together. The bid for the Olympic Games might be a good opportunity for this. On a smaller scale, the development of the Kunstareal, may also be seen as an opportunity for this.

A positive sign for further development of Maxvorstadt is the willingness among all stakeholders to co-operate and the awareness of the need for an integrated development plan. A major question remains: Who takes the initiative for such a plan and how the plan is guided during the rest of the process? There is no agreement on who has to take the lead as both the city and the state can take this role. Most stakeholders, however, suggest the city is the most suitable actor to fulfil this role. Other actors cannot take the lead due to limited (financial) power, but can play a role as bridge between other actors (for example, universities can bring the state and city government closer together).

Recommendations

In the previous sections we have described drivers and barriers for the development of Maxvorstadt. In this final part, we end with some concrete recommendations that may help to develop Maxvorstadt further.

A major recommendation is the need for the development of a master plan for the entire district which covers various themes, including development of the campuses, development of the Kunstareal, Maxvorstadt as a district to live (dealing with real-estate prices and housing problems), and the integration of science and culture. Specific detailed plans can be made for the different themes. It is crucial to integrate these detailed plans into a single master plan. Similarly, the master plan of the entire district should be integrated into visions and strategies for the larger Munich region (for example, the development of the Maxvorstadt campus cannot be seen without the development of other HEI locations). It is especially important to integrate Maxvorstadt with other inner-city districts to prevent overlap and competition.

Regarding the development and implementation of the master plan, more recommendations can be given.

First, we provide recommendations for the management of the area. All key actors (universities, cultural institutes, City of Munich and State of Bavaria) should take an active role and co-operate on an equal (non-hierarchical) basis in order to realize a shared vision. Important for the co-operation is the mentioned role of universities to link the city with the state. The current development of the Kunstareal can be seen as a best practice for the new way of co-operation. Moreover, a suggestion might be to introduce a form of area management to guide further developments in Maxvorstadt. This can only be done after political consensus has been reached on the future of Maxvorstadt. This area management can be organized by an independent accomplished process manager whose main task is to identify common interests and to define a programme of requirements for the area. At a later stage, the area manager can be charged with the establishment of a partnership organization (with representatives of all major stakeholders) which is responsible for the development and realization of a master plan. It is important to prevent an imbalance in power which may hinder development of the area as is the case in Eindhoven (see Chapter 7, Eindhoven).

We can also give recommendations regarding the marketing and accessibility of the area. Regarding the promotion of the area, we suggest using Munich as a main brand and Maxvorstadt as a sub-brand. As mentioned, the location may be branded as a 'hotspot where art and science meet'. So, it can contribute to the identity of Munich as a knowledge city by concretely showing the meaning of art and science for the wider society and visitors. Furthermore, it is important to investigate the wishes and roles of different target groups, including students, universities, museums, inhabitants, companies and visitors. For instance, research can be done to find out how and to what extent the specific target groups are related to culture and science. Moreover, potential overlap and conflicts between different target groups should be mapped. Finally, regarding accessibility, as earlier mentioned, connections with other areas are crucial. Especially important are improvements to the visibility of the area. This can be done by improving the physical passages to other parts of the (inner) city, improving the entrances of public buildings, and development of a proper (digital and physical) information system for different target groups, including proper signing and development of specific maps.

11 San Sebastian: PI@

Introduction

San Sebastian is well known as a distinctive seaside location in the north of Spain and as the host of a top international film festival. Tourism is thus, and for a long time has been, the city's central economic engine. However, driven by the implementation of the public Basque TV in early 1980s, San Sebastian has also developed a relevant productive system associated with film and other audiovisual activities.

Presently, fundamental trends in global audiovisual markets are imposing many challenges on this system. Its former driver of growth (that is, Basque TV procurement and government support for the film industry) slowed down, and a large number of established audiovisual activities reached maturity. Simultaneously, although new technologies, such as virtual reality, and more 'democratic' (internet) distribution channels created room for new entrepreneurship and innovative combinations of activities and skill, this virtuous process has not yet taken off. In this setting, the City of San Sebastian recently launched an initiative called PI@ – Audiovisual and Digital Innovation Pole – a 'silver bullet' cluster strategy (that is, targeting a very specific activity) to support the sector through a wide array of services. Part of the strategy is the creation of a new physical hotspot for the industry, in a location at the outskirts of San Sebastian.

This chapter analyses the development of San Sebastian's audiovisual cluster over time. Based on this analysis, it reflects on the new cluster policy, with a specific focus on the creation of the 'hotspot location'. It starts by briefly analysing the socioeconomic context of the city, and its governance traditions. It continues by sketching the main global trends in the audiovisual industry and assessing its organizational, social and geographical modes of organization. Subsequently, from an evolutionary perspective, a central part of the chapter analyses the driving forces behind the development of this cluster of activities in San Sebastian, and identifies present trends and challenges. We argue that the cluster is in a transition stage, in which public policy might play an important role. Next, we assess the baseline characteristics of PI@. Finally, we draw conclusions and present a number of suggestions for the continued development of PI@ as a hotspot for the local audiovisual industry.

Socioeconomic context of San Sebastian

San Sebastian, or Donostia (in Basque), is situated in Gipuzkoa, a province of the Basque country, one of the politically autonomous regions of Spain. Together with Bilbao and Vitoria, San Sebastian is one of its most important cities, with roughly 180,000 inhabitants. The three cities form an urban triangle at a distance of some 100km from each other; San Sebastian is roughly 30km away from the French border. San Sebastian's population is ageing, and migration has increased slightly.

The economic base of the city is highly dominated by tourism and service industries. The region is strongly industrialized, however: the Basque country has some of the most industrialized regions of Spain, with strongholds in aeronautics (Airbus), and electrical machinery. In the last decades, besides engineering-based industries, the Basque economy and San Sebastian have also developed smaller productive systems, such as activities related to film and audiovisual.

San Sebastian is home to important universities and knowledge institutions, namely units of the public Basque University. In early 1980s, the decline of among others the metal, chemicals and shipbuilding industries, led the Basque government to set up the foundations of a Basque network of strong industry-based research centres. Nowadays those centres are an important part of the region's research backbone and work closely with the industry in order to promote its diversification towards more knowledge-intensive sub-sectors (such as through the use of new materials, energy sources or virtual reality engineering). Together with Madrid and Catalonia, the Basque country is one of the most knowledge intensive regions of Spain.

The Basque country is export-oriented. Bilbao has an international airport, and there is a small airport in San Sebastian. There are, however, few direct air connections to Europe. Concerning digital infrastructure, the city is presently working to expand its fibre optic network. Quality of life attributes and amenities are considered rather high. Lacking the buzz and vibrancy of a big metropolis, the quality of the public space, limited congestion, a strong identity and a seaside location and relatively low cost of living compared with other Spanish and European cities have been playing a role in the city's attractiveness as a residence.

The population is at present ethnically homogeneous: less than 6 per cent of the residents originate from outside Spain. The majority of migrants come from Latin America. As part of the Basque country, San Sebastian has a strong cultural identity and concentrates a large percentage of Basque speakers. The Basque country enjoys strong political autonomy, and has many degrees of freedom to implement economic and innovation policies. It was one of the first regions to design 'Porter style' cluster policies in the early 1990s (Arbonies and Moso 2002). Recently, the Basque government has been active in designing new cluster initiatives, like the Basque audiovisual cluster.

Besides general support for entrepreneurship, training and office space provision, the city recently selected three spearhead industries: green technology, assistive technology (medical technology to support the elderly and people with disabilities), and the audiovisual industry. Each industry is to be supported by integrated programmes encompassing service provision and in some cases infrastructure development.

Institutions and organizing capacity

The city of San Sebastian has a long tradition of active local economic policy. Fomento de San Sebastian was established in 1902 to support, manage and promote the construction of hotels and public real estate, such as the hippodrome. Its tasks increased in scope over time; for example, it now includes the promotion of the city's many festivals, and various types of support for local firms.

In 2004, the Department for Economic Development, Employment, Commerce and ICT was incorporated as a publicly-owned (100 per cent) private company, and turned into Fomento San Sebastian. This helped to increase its management flexibility. It reinforced its involvement with private companies and allowed the department to assume new roles, including the provision of external consultancy services, the organization of training and brokerage, job fairs, subsidizing entrepreneurship, providing office space and the provision of accelerator programmes. Moreover, Fomento elaborates economic strategic planning exercises and is working on monitoring and evaluation systems to assess the outputs and results of its actions.

Fomento has roughly 50 employees and manages an annual budget of €25m. It has developed into an institution with substantial capacity to deploy economic policies at the city level. Its staff encompass a diverse set of skills, strategic management capacity and experience in the field. Fomento shows indications of internal learning capacity. Moreover, and probably most important, it is seen as a trustworthy and active partner by other stakeholders, able to intervene and actively support local economic activities (as was proved during our research visit and interviews).

Why did Fomento select the audiovisual industry as a spearhead sector? For one thing, Fomento had stepped up contacts with local firms, by organizing general discussion meetings, surveys, employment monitoring schemes (such as the 'jobs of the future' initiative). The relevance and challenges of the sector popped up in this process (note that the audiovisual industry hardly shows up in general industrial statistics). For another, the participation in the INTERREG IIIC network CINeSPACE allowed Fomento and the city's film commission,[1] to capitalize on other cities' experiences (such as Venice, Glasgow) and to start reflecting internally on a way to support the cinema- and audiovisual-related activities in San Sebastian. The PI@ project – Audiovisual and Digital Innovation Pole – described in the fifth section of this chapter, results from these previous efforts.

Twice a year, Fomento organizes a forum with local actors in the audiovisual sector (such as TV, producers, media firms, knowledge institutes and associations) to discuss and reach consensus on the development of projects and competitiveness initiatives for the sector. The city has also been active in developing spaces for the needs of the 'new economy'. Fomento is continually in touch with local companies, running surveys to identify, for example, new services to provide. Besides PI@, the city is developing (in partnership with research institutes) a building to accommodate temporary foreign researchers and a dedicated helpdesk.

The audiovisual business: changing practices and global trends

This case study focuses on the evolution of a localized audiovisual cluster and on the policies under development to support its transition towards new rounds of innovation and competitiveness. However, first it is important to clarify what is meant by 'audiovisual', framing it in the context of its evolution towards a broader set of 'digital content' activities.

Fomento commissioned a study in order to identify new business opportunities in 'audiovisual' (Rodriguez *et al.* 2009). In this study 'audiovisual' is understood as a hybrid sector comprising different subsectors. Grabher (2002) argues that the transient nature of new media activity 'confounds any systematic empirical efforts because the research object does not constitute a crisply demarcated sector' (p. 1912). Still, he refers to some specific activities usually considered under this umbrella, namely providers of internet applications, the 'infamously famous' dot-coms, new digital providers of music, TV shows or film, web design and a diverse range of new content producers.

As we will see later, some of the subsectors identified as 'audiovisual' are reaching (or have already reached) maturity, and are in a process of diversification and integration with other fast-growing niches. For the sake of this study, we find it useful to group them in four different sets of activities:

- TV and radio distribution, as well as cinema, video and music (audiovisual in a narrow and more conventional sense);
- internet and new software applications (for example, search engines, social networks, online publications);
- videogames;
- production of digital contents (for example, mobile contents and services, online digital publications).

Despite the particularities of each subsector, there is a rich body of literature (emanating at the crossroads of economic geography, management studies and sociology) that allows us to understand fairly well the organization of production and geographies of 'audiovisual', 'content' or 'new media activities' (from now on we will speak simply about audiovisual, considering the ensemble of the four sub-niches previously mentioned). For example, recent work of Harald Bathelt (2002, 2005) and his co-author (Bathelt and Gräf 2008) analyse in depth a group of clustering experiences in media, film and TV broadcasting in Leipzig and Munich (see also van den Berg *et al.* 1999). Also very insightful for our study is the work of Gernot Grabher (2002b) on organizational practices of new media, which frames an evolving research agenda on project-based economic activities, like media or audiovisual (see also Sydow *et al.* 2004). This literature stresses some typical features of the audiovisual industry to keep in mind:

- The project based nature of the business. The 'product' is usually developed outside the boundaries of a single firm, implying co-production and co-operation between a set of providers and specialists, often through functional teams. Core capabilities of a firm are often the skill to mobilize internal and external resources towards the development of specific projects or portfolios of projects. The film industry is the extreme example with 'one-off' projects, but it also happens to a lesser degree in other types of production (such as documentaries, TV shows). It is not rare that one firm has five or six permanent workers and hires fifty other freelancers and temporary staff for a project. This puts rather high demands on project organization skills, but also on risk management and assessment (such as financial, but also on the temporary staff's skills). In the TV industry, we see a similar dynamic. TV stations often outsource a great deal of the creative production to other smaller, and more flexible, production firms, which in turn combine permanent and freelance staff to satisfy the client's demand.

- Regular and intense collaboration between users and clients in product design. In many cases, projects and new products are not developed *for* a particular client, but *with* the client (Neff and Stark 2003, quoted in Grabher 2002a). This puts a strong focus on the proximity to the client during the product development process. With the increasing involvement of the client in multiple media platforms and demands of total connectivity, this practice is likely to become bolder. As we will see, this is the reason why some indigenous web design and publicity firms of San Sebastian opened offices in more expensive locations like Madrid, Bilbao or Barcelona, where important clients are located.

- Relevance of 'economies of recombination', that is, balancing the provision of a one-off solution with the ability to develop portfolios of similar products towards efficiency, recombining previously deployed skills and techniques. This is frequent in web design and other types of consultancy, but also, for example, in special effects (FX) companies, which may provide similar services for a film production company and for an advertising company.

- Significance of a specialized labour pool and networks of reputation. As Grabher (2002b) illustrates, 'the average small size of new media ventures, the temporary nature of projects, and the imperatives to reconfigure firms in short project cycles puts a high premium on access to a local pool of potential project collaborators' (p. 1919). Using freelance creatives and technicians is thus a regular working practice, such as for editing, postproduction, artwork, special FX, packaging, music composition, camera and lights and so on. They flow from different projects and create what Grabher calls 'latent networks'. Personal contacts are more important than job fairs; CVs are dominantly portfolios of projects and productions rather than a set of formal qualifications. This has direct consequences for entrepreneurship policies: more than supporting start-ups, the provision of on-the-job and in-house training assumes central relevance to plug new ventures and creatives in a small world of contacts and reputation. Together with 'know-how', 'know-who' assumes central relevance. Moreover, networks tend to become rooted in previous practices and well established contacts and 'institutions' (Sydow and Staber 2002) – thus, co-operation and joint projects between older established entrepreneurs and new generation firms won't flourish immediately.

- Large metropolises 'have it all'; associated with the presence of the most important clients, successive rounds of circular and cumulative causation lead to the concentration of specialized labour pools, large firms, their spin-offs and specialized providers in large cities. Moreover, these cities have a particular ability to attract talent from outside (van Winden *et al.* 2007), particularly due to the quality and distinctiveness of their labour markets for audiovisual careers. This set of conditions constitutes fertile ground for the emergence of new combinations, related combinations and innovation in large cities. In smaller cities, the emergence of similar clusters tends to be initially associated with a single large player or client (such as broad-casting TV), government action, or content producing specificities related to language or regional culture.

- Role of spatial proximity in fostering knowledge spill-overs. In the creative industries (of which audiovisual industries are part) face-to-face contacts (F2F) and 'buzz' are assumed to be critical for innovation (Asheim *et al.* 2007). F2F is still the essence of project-based work: despite the opportu-nities opened by ICT, the critical moments of production and organization still tend to require meetings and personal interaction. The 'buzz' generated by this ecology of contacts (Storper and Venables 2004) and in some cases the fact of simply 'being there' exposed to many sources of 'noise' and non-systematic information (for example, Gertler 2003; Grabher 2002b) allows for better monitoring and benchmarking about what other firms are doing, essential market and regional political trends, the availability and reliability of potential collaborators, and ease in finding specific pieces of information. Being part of this type of close ecology of contacts allows a more effective and efficient filtering and interpretation of information. The question remains on what spatial level this 'buzz' takes place: is it the street, the building, the café, the city or the metropolitan area? And, what possibilities are there for 'global buzz', for example through internet platforms (Jones *et al.* 2010)?

Global trends

A study from the OECD (2007) describes some key trends in the audiovisual and digital content industries for the years to come (see also the study of Rodriguez *et al.* 2009). Without claiming to be comprehensive, we sketch in the next points some of those central global trends:

- Market structures: as in many other sectors, one may expect (and can already see happening) an increasing concentration, through mergers and acquisitions, resulting in very large media and audiovisual conglomerates. Simultaneously, public assets (like public TV stations) are likely to become at least partially privatized. Audiovisual market structures witness two parallel trends: concentration and presence of large players, determining the level playing field, together with the atomization of small independent firms and producers.

- Distribution: a 'democratization' of distribution channels (namely through internet) and an increasing role of the consumer as the 'king' (from 'lean back' to 'lean forward'), with more and more diversified demands; personally produced and distributed contents are emerging fast (for example, MySpace; YouTube), just like on-demand TV and new ways of cinema like stereoscopic and 3D.
- Changing allocation of advertisement budgets (for example, from TV to internet), opening opportunities for smaller content providers to benefit from this budget, if they manage to attract audience and users (such as Facebook and its external content providers, like Zynga, the firm who developed the FarmVille application). This trend will generate new training and educational markets for specialized providers and e-learning, for example, in graphic design and digital content production.
- While post-production services are likely to decrease (people can do it with their own PC), own TV broadcasting is likely to emerge in firms and government bodies.
- Convergence of contents (audio, video and data), platforms (PC, TV, games console) and distribution channels. One key example of almost full content convergence is in our own cell phones or mobiles; Skype and VoIP (voice over IP) is an example of integration data-audio-video; also emergence of new platforms like the e-book.
- New consumer demands and 'banalization' of established technologies raising new demands for applications of 3D or special FX in industries like cinema, TV or videogames; traditional economic sectors are likely to demand new audiovisual technologies: machine building (image screens), tourism and heritage (GPS systems) and so on.
- Developments in breakthrough technologies like augmented reality (for example, when pointing a smart phone at a building displays extra information about its shops, restaurants and so on).
- Decline of generous subsidies for the European film industry.

This study of Rodriguez *et al.* (2009) identifies growth activities worldwide, as 'audiovisual business of the future': (i) telescopic and 3D cinema; (ii) videogames (online games, games for mobiles); (iii) low-cost exportable films and mini series; (iv) digitalization of content for e-books, archives, public libraries and so on; (v) e-learning; (vi) mobile contents; and (vii) a diverse array of internet services like streaming services, cloud computing, social networks, virtual worlds and geolocalization. After these general considerations concerning the organization and the future of the audiovisual sector, in the remainder of this chapter we 'come back to earth', zooming in and looking at these trends from a specific and localized perspective, that is, through the analysis of concrete evolution and challenges ahead in San Sebastian's audiovisual cluster.

Development path of the audiovisual productive system in San Sebastian

Before the 1980s, the Spanish audiovisual sector was almost exclusively concentrated in Madrid and practically non-existent in the Basque country and San Sebastian. In this section, we analyse how the cluster developed during the 1980s as a consequence of the Spanish regional autonomy law of 1979. Under this new institutional frame, the political regional autonomy of the Basque country and its strong nationalistic identity were behind two convergent events that ignited the spark for clustering to take place: (i) the emergence of a (strongly subsidized) Basque film industry and (ii) the implementation of the public Basque broadcasting TV.

The Basque film industry in early 1980s

After decades of Franco's dictatorial and centralistic regime, a regional autonomy law was issued in 1979 giving important political powers and financial resources to the different Spanish regions. The first years of the 1980s thus implied significant changes in Spanish political organization, especially in the strongly nationalistic Basque country. By this time, as a way to promote the Basque nationalistic identity *vis-à-vis* Madrid, the Basque film industry had started to emerge, largely subsidized by the Basque Government (Department of Culture), and typically through co-productions with other countries. It was also during this nationalist peak that the International Film Festival of San Sebastian was managed by a Municipal Foundation, and became rather inward-looking. It lost the competition category in 1983, and during the 1980s the festival gave a strong focus to Basque productions, many of them produced in San Sebastian.

De Pablo (1999) sees a link between the Basque co-productions of the early 1980s and the strategic objective of promoting the national identity of the Basque country in Spain and abroad. He particularly analyses two documentary co-productions with France and Great Britain of the early and late 1980s, produced by the San Sebastian's companies Frontera Films: *Euskadi hors d'Etat*, in 1983 and *Eresoinka* (Guernica) in 1987, with a lot of shooting taking place in the Basque country and implicit and explicit political messages about the autonomy and identity of the Basques. These documentaries never tipped in national TVs or abroad, but they involved the establishment of projects between external directors and local staff, scriptwriters, actors and producers, reinforcing Basque identity and creating demand for local audiovisual and cinema skills (even if highly subsidized).

Simultaneously, another segment of the Basque film industry started to develop in the early 1980s: the production of animations and cartoons. San Sebastian hosted the first Spanish animation company, and the first Spanish animation movie in 1985 was produced there. Reacting to the emerging opportunities, new entrepreneurs and freelancers started film- and animation-related activities (post-production, audio, video, etc.) in San Sebastian.

The establishment of the public Basque TV

Also in the early 1980s, the Spanish Government and the new Basque Regional Government released funding and provided the legal framework to establish the Basque public broadcasting TV – EiTB. By that time, very few audiovisual companies and skills were located in the region. Thus, Basque staff received training and learned from established broadcasting TVs in Madrid and abroad (for example, USA, UK). Freshly qualified technicians and other staff started their work for Basque TV. The establishment of Basque TV created new business opportunities in the region through its procurement and outsourcing policy. A number of production and post-production companies emerged in the region to supply the TV with small movies, documentaries, fiction, TV shows, advertising clips and many other audiovisual services and products.

From the beginning, San Sebastian was an important pole for the audiovisual industry. EiTB has had production centres in San Sebastian since 1987. An important reason to locate production facilities in San Sebastian was the fact that the Basque language is relatively dominant in the city and the Guipuzcoa province.

Despite the importance of Bilbao as a regional capital, it is estimated that San Sebastian still concentrates 40–45 per cent of the total audiovisual industry in the Basque country. An important share of the production and post-production audiovisual companies that started in the early 1980s are still active today in San Sebastian, and still have Basque TV as their main (if not only) customer. While the EiTB production centre of Bilbao concentrates on news and informative programmes, San Sebastian has the lion's share when it comes to TV shows, film and other creative productions.

The involvement of private local and regional audiovisual companies has been strong since the beginning of Basque TV. EiTB assumed early on the role of 'spider in the web', organizing an 'extended enterprise' of providers, buying broadcasting products and their copyrights. Local companies still get contracts for the production of creative pieces to fit the TV's schedules (usually defined twice a year, for winter and summer season). These contracts can take more than 1–2 years, such as the production of a TV show of hundreds of episodes. Each of the shows and productions requires a large number of freelance technical and creative services, audio, image, production and post-production, management and so on. Presently, EiTB, in its San Sebastian production centre, works on a regular basis with eight or nine production companies ('first-tier' suppliers) based in the city, generating work for related audiovisual services of other companies and freelancers (many of them originating from spin-offs of the incumbent audiovisual companies).

The audiovisual cluster nowadays

Over time, San Sebastian has accumulated a number of audiovisual activities and related skills (technicians, directors, creatives, photographers, scriptwriters and so on). As previously mentioned, the agglomeration dynamics were spurred by the convergence of two events: the emergence of a Basque film industry and the implementation of Basque public TV, associated with the outsourcing of audiovisual content and services.

EiTB has nowadays an annual budget of €25m for its production centre in San Sebastian. This budget has been quite stable during recent years (until 2010, when it started to shrink due to the economic downturn and financial crisis). The company has an in-house staff of 147 persons, plus roughly 60 for the radio section. Externally, EiTB requires the services of roughly 150 creative jobs (firm staff or freelancers) plus around 200 professionals working as actors, singers and so on. To these numbers can be added approximately 30 persons working with lighting, audio, changing plateaus, secretaries and security. EU regulations require that at least 5 per cent of the TV outsourcing budget should go to European producers. Basque producers are potential suppliers, but often in association with other countries. San Sebastian has four other broadcasting channels (small ones), to which Basque TV issues broadcasting licences. Their growth potential is limited. Moreover, the number of hours outsourced by EiTB in San Sebastian seems also to be stable (see Figure 11.1).

Recently, EiTB launched EiTB.com, the internet platform, and it has plans to add more diversified platforms and contents, video, audio, interactive platforms and so on. However, this transition is happening at a slow pace.

Nowadays, according to Fomento, San Sebastian hosts approximately 123 companies working in the audiovisual field. Of these, 54 are production companies (cinema, TV, fiction, animation, documentaries). Out of these 54 production firms, 5 are considered 'big' (with more than 15 employees), working directly for EiTB on a regular basis in production and post-production. The rest of the firms are quite small, typically with a central entrepreneur and few more staff. Many of

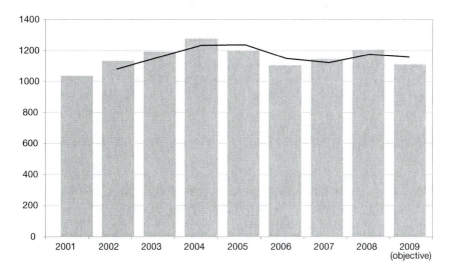

Figure 11.1 Number of outsourced production hours in EiTB's production centre in San Sebastian, 2001–9

Source: EiTB, own elaboration

these, together with freelancers, work for the larger firms on a project basis. Some of these firms are spin-offs of former EiTB and other firms' employees.

Historically, San Sebastian is relatively specialized in the niche of animation (two out of five animation movies in Spain are from San Sebastian, compared with ten out of 130 total movies). The film industry is still nowadays much based on independent and experimentation movies and co-productions between Basque and other countries, of relatively small dimension (€1.5–2m) and highly subsidized, despite their recognized quality (there were Basque films nominated for Oscars in recent years).

During the last decade many production firms pursued downsizing strategies, giving rise to spin-offs and external content providers. One case is precisely in the animation niche. During the 1980s and 1990s the firm's internal staff numbered more than 50 employees; besides writing the dialogue, it was necessary to draw several sequences of cartoons. Nowadays, although the creative definition (scripts, characters design and so on) is still done in San Sebastian, many production tasks and computer drawing, as with many other simple manufacturing activities, have moved to lower-cost locations. The internal staff's downsizing led, however, to an increase in freelancing activities (technicians, creatives and so on), on a project basis.

Still, other companies followed an expansion and diversification strategy. One example is ARISTA. It started in San Sebastian in 1995 with five persons as an informatics and web design firm and evolved towards the publicity, advertising and branding niche. Nowadays ARISTA employs 230 persons in their four offices of San Sebastian (115), Bilbao, Madrid and Barcelona, providing individual and tailor-made solutions to clients like Nestle, Warner, Repsol and other large multinationals. Being in big cities is considered essential to be close to clients for permanent interaction in product and services development. However, important parts of the creative work are done in San Sebastian. Salaries are 25 per cent lower than in Madrid and it is not difficult to hire creatives. ARISTA recently founded a spin-off in San Sebastian (TAK) for the market of e-learning and training and intends to provide training courses for the audiovisual sector, capitalizing on its experience and foreseeing the market trends of production's democratization.

Institutional infrastructure

Since the 1980s, and as the clustering process evolved, San Sebastian and the Basque country as a whole developed a specific institutional infrastructure for audiovisual activities. To a large extent, the sector has been organized since the early beginning around the Basque Ministry of Culture (film subsidizing) and the EiTB. This has led to the tacit establishment of norms, routines and institutionalized behaviours organizing players' action in the cluster (for example, contracting procedures of EiTB, the 'status' of established independently-working and pyramidal producing firms, the rise of a cultural gap between old and new generation entrepreneurs, reputation). Moreover, since the late 1980s, intermediary organizations have been created, like independent producers and actors' associations, audiovisual sector entities (for example, Egeda, Aisge and Media Antena), municipal film commissions, and, more recently, networking and external promotion initiatives supported by the Basque government (Eiken audiovisual cluster). Universities and R&D centres developed a working tradition with some of these players (especially the TV industry), and provide relatively aligned courses and specializations for the sector's needs.

More recently, local and regional chambers of commerce started to pay extra attention to the audiovisual sector. They organize trend-watching conferences and provide information about global developments in the industry. Specialized courses from the local educational infrastructure and private training providers contribute to the provision of an adequate supply of skills. Recent locally based initiatives – like the 'package of support' under development for an Audiovisual and Digital Innovation Pole PI@ (see later section) – can also be understood as part of a larger co-evolutionary process between firms, organizations and institutions towards promoting the long-term competitiveness of the audiovisual cluster in San Sebastian.

Like in other processes of cluster evolution (see, for example, Maskell and Malmberg 2007) and after the initial spark of the early 1980s, the emergence of a supportive institutional infrastructure in San Sebastian and in the Basque country provided fertile ground for the development of the audiovisual cluster. However, we can see indications that some components of this institutional structure might be hampering the transition towards new stages of development. We will elaborate on this later. Before that, in the next section we analyse some of the most recent trends and challenges of the audiovisual cluster in the Basque country, and specifically in San Sebastian.

Trends in San Sebastian's audiovisual cluster

In this section we critically analyse the most recent trends that affect the development of the Basque audiovisual cluster. Some of them are rather emergent, but may gain dimension and configure important opportunities.

Market restructuring

On the one hand, like in many other sectors, also audiovisual and TV companies are passing through diverse mergers and acquisitions towards more efficiency and resource sharing. Worldwide, the bulk of production is increasingly dominated by powerful players (for example, the BBC). Also in Spain, large conglomerates have been acquiring shares and control of other companies, resulting in a larger market concentration. For example, part of EiTB has been recently bought by an international conglomerate; other producers in the Basque country and San Sebastian have been partially acquired by the large Spanish audiovisual conglomerate MediaPro.

On the other hand, local and Basque firms have also been restructuring their operations to cope with the client's demands (for example, EiTB procurement). Though it is not a generalized trend (many firms prefer to remain independent), some companies created production chains and reorganized internally. These moves are reinforcing a certain gap between a small number of relatively powerful players and a large number of micro-activities and companies. Low cost home-made productions are likely to increase, steered by fierce competition and access to more democratic distribution channels like the internet; TV will likely see reduced publicity income due to its spread in many other distribution channels. New training companies (for example, e-learning) are developing fast in San Sebastian – there are growing market opportunities to provide training for old and new small producers.

Despite the emergence of other niches (for example, videogames), the growth of the audiovisual cluster, and also its diversification towards the production of new contents, will still be highly dependent on the procurement policies and strat-egies adopted by EiTB (who recently changed its board) – for instance in procure-ment for internet content. It will be increasingly difficult for smaller producers to access the large contracts and the 'big money' available in the near future in the Basque country. Basque TV has a potential audience of around two million persons in the Basque country – it is a rather regional reality. The big TV business in Spain is in Madrid and Barcelona. This will determine the need for firms to diversify to other products and markets in order to grow.

San Sebastian has firms and skills in creative production, ICT, 3D and videogames, but they have not yet converged into new products and integrated contents. Different sectors have their own clients, their specific incentives and institutions (for example, Malerba 2002) and links are relatively few. On the other hand, some knowledge on virtual and augmented reality, rather relevant for the videogame niche, is still concentrated in Basque excellence research centres. The incentives to invest in growing sectors and new portfolios of innovative contents, games, 3D and so on, are still limited, due to: (i) the presence of captive markets (EiTB) for larger firms of production; and (ii) the overall small and fragmented dimension of the rest of the audiovisual sector in San Sebastian. However, the potentially diminishing resources of EiTB are likely to generate changes in the market, new opportunities for entrepreneurism and challenges for established ones.

New rounds of external knowledge and 'brain circulation'

The genesis of the audiovisual cluster in the Basque country and in San Sebastian in the early 1980s was associated with the access to external knowledge and skills from Spain and from abroad. Also nowadays, an important part of new audio-visual entrepreneurship dynamics taking place in San Sebastian is associated with the return of creatives working and studying in other renowned audiovisual hubs worldwide, for example Los Angeles/Hollywood, San Francisco, Houston, Canada, London and Madrid.

These new ventures are bringing a fresh perspective, knowledge and new clients to the cluster. On the one hand they bring state-of-the-art knowledge and experi-ence in new activities, such as 3D technologies, virtual graphic design or special FX; on the other hand, they bring a vast network of contacts worldwide which are relevant for their own activities (such as new partners for co-production, clients, updated knowledge and access variety, contacts with world market trends) and potentially for the cluster as a whole.

In parallel, Basque research institutes and their most internationalized staff members have accumulated relevant knowledge and have links with many knowledge 'pipelines' and external contacts related with audiovisual technology (such as 3D, animation, graphic design, videogames, augmented and virtual reality) through contracts with global firms, former students and government agencies (for example, ESA). Some of these centres have long-standing experience in working with the different types of industries, and are well prepared to fulfil the role of brokers between different sectors, and also between academia and new business creation. However, the market applications of these new technologies have not yet taken off in San Sebastian. For these developments, proximity to final users and clients, permanent interaction and business understanding are essential.

Timid emergence of research-led new combinations and converging product platforms

Some of the research groups (for example, TECNALIA) have been developing research projects internationally in the fields of 3D and videogames in close co-operation with world audiovisual giants like Disney in Orlando, with a permanent research unit there. Moreover, they control 3D technology and have dedicated in-house infrastructure.

Some training firms in San Sebastian (for example, SYNTESIS) have the technology and skills in 3D, graphic animation and videogame industry. However, as previously mentioned, the transition between traditional audiovisual production towards other integrated platforms of products mixing ICT, graphic design, 3D and augmented reality have not yet emerged. Basque TV, through its new distribution channel EiTB.com, is a potential client for new and more interactive contents.

The videogame industry is also a promising niche, though without a significant presence in the Basque country. There might be possible interesting combinations between new 3D developments and the established creatives working in animation in the city;[2] still, it is central to developing the necessary networks to permeate the big markets and supply world leaders or other partners working with, for example, Sony or Nintendo, at distance. The provision of niche contents, such as for mobiles and the internet, might be a more feasible niche to plug into, bearing in mind the difficulties of specific contents to flow at 'distance'.

Companies from other sectors in San Sebastian and its immediate region (not only from TV and audiovisual production, but also from construction or industrial machinery) are training in 3D and digital graphic design. Architecture is intensive in graphic design and 3D visualization technologies, and all the machinery more and more requires image technology and visuals, for example for their dashboard and interface devices. This puts in evidence important new markets and clients for audiovisual and graphic technologies that might be emerging in the region, and whose joint development tends to require strong physical proximity between client and provider (Asheim *et al.* 2007). Recent investments from the Basque 'Filmoteca' – digitalization and reconstruction of former Basque short movies – are providing room for experimentation of new techniques and technologies, just as some new requirements of communication from public and private entities.

Box 11.1 TECNALIA – technological corporation

With more than 1,500 researchers spread across several locations in the Basque country, TECNALIA is a non-profit research centre, publicly and privately funded. Despite the support of the Basque Government, a substantial part of their income (around 50 per cent) comes from private sources and co-operation with the industry. Some of their main clients are in the fields of aeronautics (AIRBUS), energy (IBERDROLA), telecommunications (TELEFONICA, IKUSI) and new materials, but also works closely with the broadcaster TV EiTB. TECNALIA is structured in five divisions: Sustainable Development, Industry and Transport, Innovation and Society, Health and Quality of Life, and ICT-ESI division. Within the ICT-ESI Division, the MEDIA Business Unit takes care of all technologies related to the 'new media' sector.

The MEDIA Business Unit, integrated into the ICT-ESI division, has around 50 collaborators, most of them graduates and PhDs, divided into four units: Virtual Reality, Television, Virtual Engineering and Information Systems. Most of its internal competences and external networks are of central relevance for the development and transition of the audiovisual and digital cluster in San Sebastian and in the Basque country, namely to bridge competences towards new combinations of products and services that may respond to the present market changes. The MEDIA Business Unit manages a large network of international contacts and is active in many fairs and events worldwide, namely in ICT and software breakthroughs and applications, 3D and videogames (for example, the renowned world meeting in Las Vegas). Moreover, resulting from a previous co-operation agreement with Mercedes and local authorities in Vitoria, the MEDIA Business Unit has a dedicated virtual technology and 3D graphic centre in their facilities. The Unit has also longstanding knowledge in working with the TV and the 'virtual/digital' business and is aware of the state-of-the-art technology and new challenges of the sector.

The MEDIA unit has provided consultancy to Fomento in defining the top ten facilities to invest in for the new PI@ building and in fine-tuning the concept (prices, markets, companies and so on). Presently, the MEDIA unit is expanding its activities and moving a research unit to the PI@ building. The new PI@-TECNALIA Innovation and Development Unit will advise in innovation and technology to audiovisual and digital companies. This Unit will provide innovation diagnosis to the local companies, support the design of new projects and present them to regional, national and international funding calls, looking forward to promote synergies between companies.

Is there a role for the International Film Festival in the local audiovisual industry?

The International Film Festival of San Sebastian (see Box 11.2) takes place every year in late September and is presently one of the top (A category) European competition festivals together with Cannes, Berlin and Venice. It first took place in 1953, by the initiative of a group of local commerce companies wanting to 'extend summer' and touristic activity in the city. From the 1960s until the late 1980s the festival passed through turbulent times. Until the late 1970s, Franco's dictatorial regime used the festival as a tool to support the image of Spain and the regime abroad. San Sebastian nationalists reacted and in 1977, after Franco's death, a Municipal Foundation assumed the festival management, with implications on its vision – it turned into a more 'closed' festival, 'for the city', and as a result, in 1983, it lost the competition (A) category, quality, international exposure, and became a rather inward-looking event.

In late 1980s, a new management team struggled to bring back the international appeal of the Festival and launched efforts to attract again international films to competition. In 1988–9 the festival won back the competition category (A). By this time, a new society had developed to manage and organize the festival, headed by the city of San Sebastian in association with the Spanish and the Basque Government and the Deputation of Guipuzcoa.

At first glance, the business interests of the festival (cinema industry) and the local audiovisual industry seem to converge only by chance. Competition is international, and no link seems to exist between the festival and local and regional production. It is, however, interesting to return to the fact that the beginning of Basque cinema production is associated with an 'international retraction' of the festival, putting in the spotlight some emergent co-productions. In an unintended way, the festival provided exposition and opportunities for emerging companies.

Nowadays there are interesting trends (some of them latent or potential) worth mentioning concerning the link between the festival and the audiovisual production system in San Sebastian:

- The local procurement of audiovisual services before and during the festival (plateaus, cameras, lights, TV, audio, interview stages, plasma, projectors and so on), fully absorbed by the festival, although this procurement is not reflected yet in new technologies and innovations.
- The role of the festival in creating 'temporary buzz' (Maskell *et al.* 2006) and a platform of meetings and networking between international and local producers and firms, activating previous contacts and establishing new ones.
- The recent establishment of a parallel co-production forum for buying and selling during the festival. A group of producers (mostly local but also from

---

Box 11.2 San Sebastian's Film Festival: the city and the global cinema industry

The renowned San Sebastian Film festival (SSFF) is a large cinema 'bazaar'. The management of the festival identifies five different stakeholders for their activities:

i   Citizens, even those who do not visit the festival or attend sessions: autograph collectors, fans, people at the door of hotels to see the stars, day trippers and so on.
ii General audience (95,000 tickets were sold in 2009 and there were 170,000 people in the audience, plus organized talks, speeches, workshops and so on),

including aficionados travelling from the entire world to visit the festival, attend sessions with the directors and so on.

iii Juvenile audience and children (attending cinema mornings, educational sessions, etc.).

iv Press, with regular presence of more than 50 international channels, conferences, international press, guests and so on.

v Cinema industry (the real 'business' and core of the festival).

A large festival has multiple impacts in a city, and the SSFF is no exception. The main interest of the city in the past has been linked with direct tourism revenues (hotels, restaurants) and image building; thus, it was very much focused on the consumption side and opportunities generated seasonally. In reality, there are good reasons for not putting the 'spill-over expectations' to high. The 'business' of the festival and of the cinema industry tends to be much more footloose and sees the festival in a different way: as a competition platform, a temporary cinema industry hub, part of a global circuit of other festivals where movies are exposed and, hopefully, sold. For example, as the production director of SSFF puts it, 'for the cinema industry and for the business of the festival it's irrelevant if Brad Pitt comes to San Sebastian (it's only a local event), but it is "big news" if an exhibited Korean movie sells its exhibition rights to ten different countries'. It's a buying and selling point, a temporary spot where supply (movies and its producers) and demand (country, region distributors) meet.

The core of the festival of San Sebastian is organized around the competition between approximately 50 new movies. Other retrospective films are also shown, but these 50 are the centre of the festival for the industry. Film producers from throughout the world propose their movies to be evaluated for the SSFF by a first peer review committee (50 movies were selected out of 1,800 applications in 2009). The ones approved will enter the official competition in San Sebastian and will receive international exposure. These are usually divided in different categories (fiction, action, documentary and so on). Cannes and Berlin are still the big European festival hubs and the best productions try to be selected by those first, but San Sebastian comes afterwards, in strong competition with Venice. Only the big production houses of Hollywood (for example, Paramount, Universal, Warner), with their own distribution channels and cinemas, are not so active in the film festivals.

The main objective of the producer is usually to sell the film to the country and region distributers. Besides the competition stages, there is a sales office where producers and distributers meet. Film festivals are then ranked according to their status for the industry as buying and selling points (for example, whether there will be many distributors and buyers, whether the festival has a good reputation for competition). The more a festival sells, the higher it is ranked, the more distributors and buyers it will attract and also the better movies it will attract, in a cumulative causality fashion. In this sense, keeping up the quality of the movies is essential to keeping the festival status and its interest for the industry.

The SSFF is the most important 'gate' for Latin American cinema. Besides specific sessions in some particular categories (for example, Basque and Spanish movies, surf, animation), the festival is active in attracting new platforms for eastern European producers and African cinema. However, these categories are not usually at the competition core.

the EU and abroad) are invited to present their productions (short movies, etc.) and are offered the chance to meet with the TV and other buyers to sell it.

- The position of San Sebastian as the third most popular urban setting in Spain in which to shoot movies (after Madrid and Barcelona), but especially to shoot publicity short movies because of tax incentives. Shootings from external directors are also common. One of the reasons is the sunlight and sunset in September, the festival month – a visiting card for potential directors. Many directors attending the festival consider returning to shoot parts of movies (for example Woody Allen, in an agreement with MediaPro). The city film commission tries to find local suppliers and partners, but there seems to be room for a more integrated and proactive approach. It is estimated that the city attracts €4.6m in shooting investment in 2008, a 25 per cent increase since 2007.

- The internet and video conference diffusion is likely to have an effect in the way the SSFF is organized. It becomes possible to watch the films and press conferences of directors through the internet, as well as participate in meetings at distance through ICT; also new digital content provision may provoke changes in the way a festival takes place. Although not completely, these trends are likely to endanger some of the *raisons d'être* of the presence in the festival. For this reason, in their strategic plan for the coming years the festival may give more relevance to the linkages with the city in order to provide the visitors, namely producers and distributors, a more integrated supply of services (besides integrated offer of horeca, for example, also innovation showrooms – like in Hollywood, 3D innovations and so on).

Summing up: positioning the background of action of PI@

From the previous discussion it becomes clear that, over time, the procurement of EiTB and the emergence of a small, independent film industry in the Basque country in the early 1980s sparked the clustering of an audiovisual productive system in San Sebastian. This cluster shows nowadays well known agglomeration characteristics typical of many other clusters analysed in the literature: presence of specialized providers, anchor players (for example, EiTB), localized knowledge and information spill-over through labour market dynamics (for example, freelancers), firm spin-offs and relevant input–output relations. These dynamics co-evolved with the emergence of an infrastructure of supportive associations and organizations (Maskell and Malmberg 2007; Boschma 2004), but mainly of 'soft' structural institutional features organizing the system, like specific business routines, culture, reputation and power (for example, Cumbers *et al.* 2003). Figure 11.2 helps us to frame and understand the present state of San Sebastian's audiovisual cluster and the challenges that lie ahead.

Almost 30 years after the initial spark of the early 1980s, a first round of the cluster's development seems to have reached maturity. At this stage, saturation of more traditional business models (such as conventional audiovisual production) and challenges imposed by a number of higher order trends in the industry (see third section,

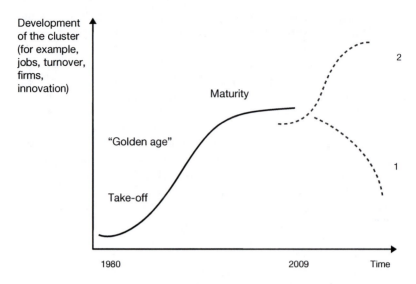

Figure 11.2 An evolutionary view on San Sebastian's audiovisual cluster

Source: own elaboration, adapted from Maggioni (2006)

above) are opening a period of transition and discontinuity. At this time (2009) direct and indirect dependence of the cluster from EiTB and government subsidies is overall high, while the growth rates of firms, jobs and turnover are limited; the market take-off of new innovations is almost non-existent. Simultaneously, new entrepreneurs are adding novelty to the cluster, for instance by bringing external (tacit) knowledge and access to new technologies and clients applying, for example, 3D technologies, FX and virtual reality (with growing applications worldwide); others are developing contents (such as documentaries) for external markets, based on new external networks of business contacts. In Figure 11.2, this latter phenom- enon is represented by the dashed line that started to emerge below the bold line: a first but still incipient response to the new industry trends. However, all in all, new private ventures and new applications have not yet generated the 'wave of entrepreneurship' and exploration needed to spur new rounds of innovation and profits in San Sebastian, central to making the dashed line (2) emerge and develop (for example, through new variety and 'Schumpeterian' activity re-combinations, development of new markets or plugging-in niche platforms).

In this context, and considering the global industrial challenges ahead, the relative decline of the audiovisual cluster (represented by dashed line (1)) is a risk. It is more the case as the cluster shows signs of entering a stage of lock-in (Grabher 1993; Martin and Sunley 2006) in their present competences and clients (traditional TV and cinema production). A group of important players enjoy stable and rather captive markets and new entrants lack the structure to compete on the same business models. This is hampering the development of new activities' portfolios and delaying investments and responses to new challenges and trends. Institutionalized behaviours, culture and an understanding gap between new and former entrepreneurs may hamper the development of new related combinations and transition towards new audiovisual activities.

In this critical stage of the cluster's evolution, research has been clearly arguing that 'policy matters'; but the prescriptions are far from straightforward. 'Ready-to-use' cluster policies are likely to be misleading (for example, Orsenigo 2006; Wolfe and Gertler 2006). In this context Carlsson (2006) asks how policies can be designed 'when the desirable outcome lies decades down the road and cannot be specified?' (p. 272). The case of audiovisual in San Sebastian shows how a structural policy decision (autonomy law of the Spanish regions) created markets and institutions for the development of this cluster, yet in a rather unintended way. In this case, the cultural background of the city (for example, the Basque language) determined the concentration of creative activities after the TV and cinema public spark.

However, concerning entrepreneurship promotion, policy action is more difficult (even more so in a specific sector where the role of reputation and job market functioning is rather distinctive). Nevertheless, as stated by Wolfe and Gertler (2006):

> it [new entrepreneurship] seems to be a key element of cluster development in the third and last stage of cluster emergence, particularly to provide an environment conducive to the entering of second and third generation start-up firms. At this *stage* [emphasis added] government polices to sustain the entrepreneurial drive are perhaps the most important.
>
> (Wolfe and Gertler 2006, p. 261)

This is the precise stage where initiatives like PI@ come in. We will come back to policy analysis and recommendations in the last section, but first we will look at the specific baseline characteristics of the PI@ project under development by Fomento in San Sebastian. We look to the soft and hard policies under development, with a particular focus on the setting up of a physical location for audiovisual activities.

The PI@ project: baseline characteristics

The City of San Sebastian is developing a specific location for the audiovisual and digital industry: the PI@ building (Box 11.3). It is located at a business park close to the city centre.

The PI@ building is to become a physical concentration of audiovisual and digital activities. Fomento has secured loans for the building from the government; the loan has to be paid back in fifteen years.

Fomento has a long tradition of developing real estate for particular economic activities in the city. The organization owns, manages and participates in a number of specific buildings and premises for different types of activities. Examples are the Miramon technology park (a business park for high-tech firms) and the ZENTEK building (for ICT firms).

There was a key reason why Fomento was keen to develop another special building, this time for the audiovisual and digital industry. The conclusions of the interviews made by Fomento with the local companies in 2005 were clear in this sense. The city has the ambition to further promote this cluster, and it believes that PI@ can provide a contribution. The PI@ building is being developed on a plot of land owned by the local government. The project – budgeted at €20 million – will be financed by San Sebastian Town Council, which was granted a €17-million loan with a 0 per cent interest rate and a €623,000 subsidy from the Spanish Ministry of Industry, Trade and Tourism in the context of Plan Avanza. The Spanish Ministry of Territorial Policy also finances the project with €3 million for the technological adaptation of the building. The building's first stone was laid on 23 September 2008 and the largest part of the construction work was concluded before late 2011. The first companies are settling in the buildings at the time of writing.

PI@ is planned to become the central place for knowledge creation and innovation development in the audiovisual and digital industry. It should offer an innovative space, inviting to collaboration, and endowed with particular facilities for SMEs. Moreover, it should play a role in fostering co-operation between local technological institutes and companies.

In the next concluding section, we reflect on these goals, and complement them with insights based on the evolution of the local industry and global developments in the audiovisual sector.

Box 11.3 What will the PI@ building be like?

The building will be located in Zuatzu Industrial State, a business park outside, but with good accessibility to, the city centre. Two buildings will be developed on a plot of land owned by the local government. They will eventually house about 60 companies in the audiovisual and digital industries, which will rent the spaces featuring common state-of-the-art equipment. In a 19,000m² surface area, the PI@ building will offer a number of facilities:

i   room for about 60 companies in the audiovisual industry;
ii   underground car park;
iii new town archives;
iv   childcare facilities;
v   audiovisual equipment for companies, including control rooms, dressing rooms, and real and virtual sets; a pitch room to screen film projects as in a small cinema theatre; a 3D stereoscopic auditorium; a video library;
vi   card access control system.

In the PI@ building, bioclimatic architecture is applied, which involves the use of geothermal energy to achieve thermal comfort inside, the exploitation of sunlight, the production of solar energy using photovoltaic panels, the capturing of energy and the transformation of CO_2 by means of wall coverings, small wind turbine and many other techniques.

Figure 11.3 Projection of the PI@ buildings

Source: Fomento San Sebastian

Functions of the buildings

PI@ is set to be more than just another building where firms can rent premises. In the official brochure of PI@, the following functions are envisioned:

- organization of activities that help to dynamize the audiovisual industry and attract film directors and producers so that they shoot in town;
- renting suites to audiovisual companies at reduced rates, including common rooms and state-of-the-art technology;
- R&D+I (innovation): setting up a Research Unit for the audiovisual industry, thus strengthening the connection between marketing and science;
- carrying out activities to encourage innovation among audiovisual companies;
- fostering networking and internationalization through contacts with other organizations, co-operation agreements and promotional activities at the international level, among other measures;
- designing and carrying out a financing plan for companies in the audiovisual industry;
- drafting an audiovisual training plan and setting up a Training Unit;
- creating an Audiovisual Job Exchange, meeting specific sectoral needs;
- establishing an Audiovisual Observatory collecting indicators of industry evolution;
- providing specialist advice to companies that need it: company co-operation and networking, business management, marketing, merchandizing, new markets, legal issues and so on.

Conclusions and perspectives

Key conclusions

In the previous sections, we analysed the development of San Sebastian's audiovisual cluster (from an evolutionary perspective) over the last two-and-a-half decades. This cluster is not starting today 'from scratch'; it presents a story of evolution over time and a distinctive path produced by the complex interplay and co-evolution of agents, organizations, institutions and routines. The PI@ initiative itself is a recent visible face of this co-evolutionary process.

Moreover, we argued that the audiovisual cluster is presently in a critical transition stage. Thus, from a policy perspective, the challenge is not to support an *ex novo* clustering process but to facilitate the transition from a stage of maturity towards new waves of entrepreneurship and the development of novel activities with growth potential. It is up to firms and entrepreneurers to be the engines of this transition, but there is an important role to play for public policy to facilitate this process.

When looking to this audiovisual cluster in San Sebastian it is possible to identify at least two different subsectors: one related to film and TV (more mature, with lower growth potential of its own), and one related to new image, motion applications, 3D and virtual reality (much smaller, emergent, but with higher growth potential), not only for conventional TV and film but also for industrial facilities relying on image technology, and services such as, for example, publicity or web design. We know nowadays from the literature that the two niches do not have exactly the same spatial sensitivity to distance from clients and partners for innovation, and their clients and organizational modes are different (for example, Asheim *et al.* 2007). Moreover, they might respond to different incentives and different sector institutional frameworks for innovation (Malerba 2002) – this is probably why the convergence between both niches towards joint innovation platforms and products has not happened yet in San Sebastian. This fact brings complexity to the cluster's structure and relevant policy challenges.

Overall, the city of San Sebastian, through Fomento, has been able to mobilize the relevant stakeholders for the PI@ project. PI@ apparently has strong political and social supporters, ranging from firms, R&D institutes and other organizations and associations. They see it as a 'face' or the 'address' of the cluster (and of the local policy for the cluster), an anchor and a meeting point. Expectations are high concerning its role to support firms' development and impulse for new entrepreneurs in innovative activities. However, departing from this general and hardly questionable vision, it is important to discuss the more fine-grained dimensions of PI@ in the context previously described.

It is important to stress that understanding clusters from an evolutionary perspective is not the same as applying the famous 'Porter Diamond' (for example, Porter 1990, 2000), and is likely to derive different policy prescriptions of 'scripts' of action. From a theoretical and empirical perspective, recent literature in economic geography and urban studies has been sceptical about the use of 'standardized' cluster policies (for example, Martin and Sunley 2003). A central pitfall is a tendency to ignore rooted and self-constructed institutional frameworks, paths and contexts that condition the success of any development strategy. Moreover, practice shows the problems of deploying 'one size fits all' policies, whereby the same prescription would equally fit a biotech, shipbuilding or an audiovisual cluster, whether in a small city, a large metropolis or even countries as a whole.

Recent contributions on cluster policymaking (for example, Orsenigo 2006; Wolfe and Gertler 2006; Maggioni 2006; Carlsson 2006) have argued that policy interventions should be based on functional requirements and multi-level policymaking rather than on too focused and targeted policies. It is too difficult and complex to identify beforehand which activities will develop and where. Carlsson (2006) suggests, for example, general improvements of the knowledge base, the creation of transparent incentives, promotion of experimentation, guaranteeing appropriate market conditions, or promotion synergies between players.

Wolfe and Gertler (2006) also refer to policies for clusters in more mature and transition stages, which tend to be more focused and tailored to the specific cluster's conditions. After reviewing a large number of cases, the authors suggest policies to facilitate:

- development of strategic planning exercises, in order to evaluate progress, develop shared understanding of the city/region specific assets, external threats and opportunities, identify gaps, steer mindsets and prepare the field for co-operation between involved partners;
- upgrading of innovation capacity within existing firms;
- technology absorption and diffusion;
- development of networks and better links among firms, brokerage and mentoring activities.

We would also add:

- Facilitate the permeability to new and related variety in the region (Boschma and Iammarino 2009) for example, through knowledge of new entrepeneurs with working or studying experiences abroad.

What policy lines can thus be suggested to facilitate the development of the audiovisual cluster in San Sebastian? What components and specificities should the PI@ project count with?

A 'script' for PI@

It seems clear to the involved stakeholders that PI@ should be rather more than 'a building'. Some stakeholders in San Sebastian's audiovisual industry stress that developing 'a firms' hotel' is even undesirable, in the sense of a top quality (and expensive) facility, closed to the outside and with residual interactions between their tenants.

This is not to say that the ergonomics of the PI@'s physical environment (such as meeting and common areas, 'plug and play' areas) should not be well planned

– its design might actually be essential to the development of new networks, experimentation, unexpected encounters and 'buzz'. It is indeed important to take into consideration the specific working practices of the sector (such as the balance between closed offices and open areas, studios, plateaus and so on), and to reject the growing 'one size fits all' architecture projects of technological parks throughout the world.

PI@ – as a building area and site – can be understood as instrumental to a more encompassing strategy rather than an end in itself: it is part of a larger strategy and a portfolio of specialized services and actions to guide the transformation of the audiovisual cluster in San Sebastian towards new growth and innovation stages.

More concretely, PI@ may assume the following, sometimes overlapping roles (at the time of writing, many recommendations were already taken on board by PI@).

First, it should become an engine for collective efficiency of the audiovisual industry, where firms (located in the building or not) can access technical resources, share efforts and access specialized services; especially those services and facilities that otherwise would be way too expensive to be acquired by a firm alone (for example, besides law and accountancy services and dedicated broadband, also licensed software, plateaus, 3D technologies and other sets of facilities). Moreover, since it is difficult to specialize in parts of the audiovisual value chain locally – the local market is rather small – PI@ could act as a facilitator of an 'extended enterprise' model, fostering horizontal and vertical division of labour towards efficiency and more specialization. These and other efforts should be pursued under a clear alignment between different cluster initiatives at different territorial scales – for example, the alignment between the (cluster) policies at the Basque and local level to support audiovisual activities is not totally clear yet.

Second, PI@ should contribute to create 'chemistry' between different types of activities and generate innovation. It should encourage creativity and experimentation. The decision of TECNALIA to move part of their research facilities to the PI@ building is good news: it constitutes an important technological 'anchor' that may break ground for the emergence and acceleration of new combinations and spin-offs of new activities. This clearly needs to be complemented with the right mix of incentives, not only from PI@ but mainly from the Basque government's innovation policy. Thus, PI@ should find the right articulation platforms to take part (and possibly influence) policies at other spatial levels with impact in the audiovisual cluster. No less important is the definition of 'entry criteria' for PI@. It should be narrow enough to guarantee a certain cognitive proximity but open enough to allow for desirable synergies between audiovisual related activities, clients and technology providers, and avoid the selection and lock-in in certain types of activities or sector 'silver bullets' – these might reveal themselves to be not the most promising in the medium and long run.

Third, PI@ should facilitate the connection of the cluster to external knowledge. It should encompass strategies and efforts to help local firms to plug into external knowledge networks, access external clients (whether in creative or 'industrial' sectors) and encourage the entrepreneurship of professionals with experiences abroad or outside the Basque country (such as working with 3D, FX, virtual and augmented reality). This will help to add variety to the cluster, and to avoid risks of lock-in. Moreover, PI@ should facilitate the access of innovative audiovisual firms to demanding clients, namely for niches where co-development between client and provider is essential (such as image technology for specialized equipments), whether or not within the city's administrative limits;

Fourth, PI@ and the City of San Sebastian should consider a strategy to use the International Film Festival as a platform for creating 'temporary buzz' for the local audiovisual cluster, and as a way to strategically connect local entrepreneurs to external contacts. One example could be promotion of PI@ as a distinctive unique selling point (USP) for directors willing to shoot in the city, complementing and strengthening the present work of the film commission. It can be very appealing for an external producer if in one single location he or she can access a variety of advanced services, and eventually pay a 'single bill'. This would include expanding the work nowadays developed by San Sebastian's film commission, and integrating other actions already rendered by Fomento, like the organization of national visits to local companies (for example, to national TVs).

Fifth, PI@ should become an incubator and cradle for start-ups. It should reduce the start-up risks for small entrepreneurs and freelancers, and help to foster and broaden their knowledge and business networks. Providing financial incentives *per se* is insufficient in a sector where the job market and the game of acquiring projects are based on reputation and previous on-the-job training. Traditional initiatives like job fairs are unlikely to be the mechanism used by firms to hire and access skills for their activities. Thus, PI@ should combine traditional start-up incentives with a programme of internships in local firms and talent identification, as well as incentives for co-operation with other players locally or outside.

Sixth, PI@ should become a recognizable 'face' of the local audiovisual industry, with a physical address. PI@ should promote a marketing and communication strategy in articulation with the city and with other regional initiatives. It should directly involve local firms and communicate the strategy of PI@ for local and international stakeholders, namely for potential clients.

Seventh, PI@ should constitute a platform where members can share information, develop joint projects and innovations, and create a joint strategy. PI@ and Fomento should continue a permanent dialogue with the stakeholders in the audiovisual sector. This is important to avoid redundancies and permanently assess the cluster's needs. Keeping the development of intelligence and sector vigilance of global trends is a worthy activity. Moreover, despite the permanent need to monitor and adapt the strategy, it is important that the portfolio of services and expectations with PI@ are well defined and aligned with the actors' needs (present and future) from the beginning. Strategies of 'let's go and let's see' might create wrong expectations and make the project lose momentum, support and interest. The project and services in practice should not be dissonant with PI@'s vision and communication of the project. There are many examples of knowledge locations that raised high expectations and grand visions but got lost in the daily condominium and financial management of simple business park infrastructures.

Finally, other general urban policies can impact on the cluster. Besides good jobs and career opportunities, provision of good housing and the quality of public space are proven to be important in the attraction and retention of skills. San Sebastian has both, associated with a strong urban identity. Moreover, the city should by no means put all its efforts in retaining recent graduates. There is evidence that a certain 'brain circulation' can be positive for a cluster's development (for example, Saxenian 2007). The case of San Sebastian suggests the same, with the returning from abroad of professionals in their thirties who start their audiovisual ventures, driven by family ties and affectivity, a driver often forgotten in urban and regional studies.

Part III

Synthesis of the findings and theoretical reflections

12 Key findings from the case studies, policy and practice

In this chapter, we synthesize the results of our study. In the first four sections we present a number of findings, structured along the main constructs of our theoretical framework (see Chapter 4). A number of comparisons are drawn and cross-case patterns are identified, illustrated with examples and practices from the cases. A number of associated policy implications and lessons for the planning of knowledge locations are pointed out, as well as issues deserving further research.

Catalysts, actors and institutions

Knowledge locations do not develop out of the blue: they are driven by a number of catalysts or sparks that ignite or speed up the (re)development process. The cases analysed in this book show various catalysts – often associated with deeper societal changes – that influence the planning decision of a new knowledge location. This planning endeavour is taken up by a number of actors, whose behaviour is bounded by a number of previous planning practices, production and innovation institutions.

What have been the catalysts for developing new knowledge locations?

A first catalyst relates to the perception of urban policymakers of an increasingly global competition to attract mobile talent, business and investments in knowledge-intensive activities. Not surprisingly, cities put a focus on new growth sectors, such as ICT, multimedia, design or biotechnology, and develop knowledge locations to give those spearheads a 'face'. This is very much visible in the promotion strategies of Arabianranta (Helsinki), labelled as an 'art and design city', Strijp-S (Eindhoven) dubbed a 'creative city to attract the creative class', PI@ (San Sebastian) as a hub for the audiovisual sector and the Digital Hub (Dublin) as a world-class location for digital media. Songdo (Incheon) is a rather extreme case. For the Korean government and the City of Incheon, Songdo is a tool to attract international investments and expatriate workers to grow a 'knowledge and business hub in East Asia'.

Another major catalyst for the development of (mixed and urban) knowledge locations is the perceived change in lifestyles and working preferences.

In many sectors, especially in the creative industries, private life and work are becoming intertwined; working hours are no longer 'from nine to five'; many meetings combine pleasure and business and are 'on location'. As a response to these changes, many cities have invested in multi-functional sites that combine work, living, educational and recreational functions. Most essays in this book deal with the development of such sites, focusing on specific areas within a city. They range from downtown areas (Munich and Dublin) to first urban expansion zones (Eindhoven, Helsinki). In the chapter on Songdo, we discuss the development of an entire new edge city *vis-à-vis* 'old' Incheon, in the shape of a new-generation Free Economic Zone mixing housing, offices, industry space and leisure. The City of Eindhoven envisages a more metropolitan feeling with Strijp-S in order to attract and retain the workers who prefer to live and work in a vibrant urban surrounding.

A related catalyst is the increasingly project-based character of innovation and the economy as whole. Many industries more and more work on a project basis and not (only) on permanent structures, combining different disciplines and skills. Often, research and development (R&D) is no longer carried out by single researchers in a closed lab, but through an open and interactive process between different partners, including clients, suppliers, competitors and/or research institutes. This requires new flexible working spaces, meeting rooms, shared and specialized research facilities and a new generation of 'open campuses'. Cities try to accommodate these trends by investing in new knowledge locations that provide these types of facilities. Examples include the PI@ building in San Sebastian, the former NatLab in Eindhoven, Dublin's Digital Hub or Songdo's inner-city factories. An innovative example is Maxvorstadt in Munich, where museums and research institutes join forces, among other things, to use museums as places to create, apply and expose new knowledge and art–science combinations.

Cities also invest in knowledge locations as a response to macroeconomic challenges. For the city of Helsinki, one of the major reasons to develop Arabianranta as a multifunctional site – and not as a green area as originally planned – was the necessity to create jobs to fight the deep crisis which hit Finland in the early 1990s. Similarly, in the Digital Hub the focus on a new and more regionally anchored ICT branch (multimedia) has been chosen in order to reduce Ireland's dependence on FDI. Songdo, in contrast, has been developed to increase Korea's openness to foreign capital.

The development of mixed-use knowledge locations – especially in Europe – is also associated with the availability of space due to the closure of manufacturing sites of large companies, such as the former Philips site in Eindhoven, the old Guinness brewery in Dublin or the Arabia porcelain factory in Helsinki. Despite the high costs for cleaning the soil (as a consequence of previous industrial activities), it is still beneficial and profitable to redevelop these sites because of the high demand for scarce space in urban locations. Moreover, there are often financial resources available for urban regeneration. In Europe, cohesion policy is a major source of funding, aimed at levering the participation of other players in the development of such sites. But in Asia also there is considerable funding for knowledge locations – many of these projects (like Songdo) are seen as national flagships and benefit from substantial national funding.

Finally, there is a political catalyst. Peer pressure and exposure to international networks of best-practice exchange play a role in igniting the development of knowledge locations, for example, endowing policymakers with legitimation, discourse building and 'catch-the-wave' behaviour. For example, the development of Songdo was inspired by Dubai's model of high-quality Free Economic Zones; in Europe, city networks for best practice exchange and the diffusion of 'success models' have clearly influenced the strategies of many cities in developing new knowledge locations, now seen as a widespread local economic development tool.

Cities may learn from each other's experiences: fostering best-practice exchange is actually a central objective of our study. However, best-practice should not be taken at face value, but must be deeply contextualized in its spatial-economic context. In fact, the cases presented in this book are more or less successful precisely because of the context-specific conditions and assets, which cannot easily be replicated. In a time when the development of knowledge locations has reached the status of a new local planning orthodoxy, urban polices should strive to do contextualized benchmarking and assessments, paying attention to the processes of development of locations rather than basing new projects exclusively on snapshots and 'off-the-shelf recipes'.

The entrepreneurial mayor, the visionary planner: on the role of public administration's players

As a response to the previous catalysts, who takes action for planning and designing knowledge locations? Traditionally, the local government and elected policymakers take the lead, often inspired and supported by the insights and ideas of other agents such as local civil servants, heads of municipal departments, regional development officers, consultants and developers. City governments often have a strong role in planning, decision-making, mobilization of relevant stakeholders and lobbying for financial resources.

However, the degree and type of government involvement differs. In some cases cities enthusiastically support the project and play an active role through the action of many departments. The case of Songdo illustrates the strong involvement of the city of Incheon in comprehensively planning and orchestrating the development of the area, in close collaboration with the national government. The former Mayor of Incheon, coming from the private sector, had a strong role pushing the project, involving consortiums of developers to execute the master plan, as well as key foreign investors. Also in Munich, the development of Maxvorstadt has been supported by many municipal departments and their directors – they aim to mobilize a diverse group of stakeholders – and the mayor shows nowadays strong commitment to the district by heading some major related working groups. In Helsinki, the shape of Arabianranta was influenced by the vision of a planning director, who steered city decisions towards what was seen at the time as a rather innovative planning approach. Moreover, the large span of the intervention required joint efforts of many departments like urban planning, public works, social affairs, culture and economic development.

In other cases, commitment is looser and only parts of the local administration become involved in the project. For example, in Eindhoven, despite the strong support of an alderman, commitment for the development of Strijp-S is looser and only some departments of the city are involved. There is a gap between the interests and visions of the city council and public officials. These differences slow down decision-making and the development of Strijp-S in general.

Broad support from the city government can be decisive in the speed and integrality of the development of knowledge locations. However, the role of key persons in the public administration – whether endowed with political or technical power and legitimacy – is pivotal. It is frequently up to these individuals to influence others with their ideas, which eventually gain support and become flagship projects.

When universities and companies influence the location's vision

Notwithstanding the role of local government, it would be misleading to attribute to cities and their representatives a monopoly – or even dominance – in the development of a knowledge location (although it may look like that at first glance). Universities, companies and other actors from local production and innovation systems often play a decisive role, for example, influencing the vision and strategy of a knowledge location: they not only contribute with financial resources and act as anchor tenants, but also frequently influence the concept and vision for the location.

Our cases provide illustrative examples. The University of Art and Design in Helsinki decisively shaped Arabianranta's vision, concept and development, mainly at the hands of the dean, who nudged the City to adopt 'art and design' as a transversal concept for the location. Moreover, he was responsible for the introduction of the first 'living lab' experiments in Arabianranta, imported from his personal networks in the USA. Also, in Munich, representatives from the university and the director of a cultural institute joined forces to explore linkages between sciences with culture; further on, they influenced wider reflection on this issue as a potential vision for the future of the Maxvorstadt district as a knowledge location. But the influence of knowledge institutes can even come from abroad – the announcement of the location of a branch of the MIT media lab in Dublin was a key driver in the development of the Digital Hub as a specialized new media location.

Local companies also play an important role in shaping the vision for a knowledge location. For example, lead firms in Helsinki and associations of audiovisual producers in San Sebastian played an active role in the definition of the location's concept. In the case of Songdo – and also coming from overseas – renowned American planners and developers deeply influenced the design and master plan of the entire area; moreover, former returnee US-Korean researchers influenced many of the activities that are currently boosting Songdo and its high-tech vision.

From a policy perspective, it is important to open up the debate on the design of knowledge locations to the real 'knowledge players' like universities and companies (or even museums, in the case of Munich). They often have ideas about what works out and what does not. Moreover, they often have knowledge about concepts from other locations that might fit the new location's context. Our evidence shows that these players are often essential in bringing new insights – and even key investments – from abroad. Their participation in discussion arenas should be fostered and their 'gate keeping' role nurtured.

The regional institutional setting: proactive involvement or vested interests?

Although the participation and proactive involvement of stakeholders like universities, companies and associations may have many positive sides, there is also the risk that actors try to secure their vested interests by orienting and influencing the location's design and supports. This power is in principle proportional to the relevance of the company or sector for the city and region, and may pose threats to a region's adaptability over time. On the other hand, a new knowledge location can be a powerful tool precisely to break vested interests and open new horizons of regional economic diversification. San Sebastian, Munich and Eindhoven strive to use their locations to foster new combinations and support their local established industries towards new stages of development, for example, through linkages with ICT, art and creative industries respectively. Songdo specifically tries to give opportunities to foreign direct investors in new sectors, countering vested interests in construction and logistics in the area.

To avoid lock-in and prevent the protection of vested interests, cities should pay attention to involve 'birds of different feathers' in the discussions and concept definition. They should not only involve established industrialists but also younger international entrepreneurs with new ideas – San Sebastian presents an example of good practice in this sense, giving voice to new and dynamic actors in the development of PI@.

Is it about institutions or about persons?

At this point it is important to stress that our research shows (and confirms) that it is often misleading to speak about local government, universities and even companies as if they were homogeneous entities. To understand the emergence and development of knowledge locations it is essential to take a more fine-grained view and understand that these organizations comprise a number of individuals that simultaneously comply with the routines of their own organization yet bridge knowledge outside its walls and nudge other players towards certain actions – such as the vision for a new knowledge location. Our study clearly spots many professors, directors of planning departments, company managers and so on, that play this role – some locations even become associated with the central role of these persons.

This is far from saying that institutions are irrelevant. On the contrary, they are central in backing the actions of these individuals. However, what is remarkable – and important to grasp from a policy perspective – is the way in which the action of these visionary individuals breaks with old routines and starts to institutionalize new procedures in public administration (such as new departmental routines between planning and economic departments), as well as, for example, new networks between universities and cities. When these procedures do not become institutionalized, relying on key persons may become risky in the medium run, namely when those persons leave their positions (for example, in Helsinki the change of the University's dean threatened the development of Arabianranta to a new stage). Although further research is needed on this issue, a clear challenge for cities is to spot these key visionary and proactive individuals, empower them and institutionalize new behaviours in order to change old, inefficient procedures.

Governance and policy arenas

The physical and organizational shape of a knowledge location is determined and evolves out of a number of negotiation rounds, through the involvement of the previously mentioned actors in governance and policymaking arenas.

Many players are involved, with fundamentally different interests

The governance of a knowledge location is a rather complex process. This complexity starts with the variety of actors involved – each has its own interest: typically, local government wants more jobs and a better image, universities want good premises to attract students and conduct research, developers look for a good return on investment, companies want attractive premises at low cost, and local communities want a diversified area with more jobs and leisure opportunities. Higher government levels – which often financially support the development – want to foster economic diversification and the development of new innovative sectors.

Knowledge locations can thus be seen as 'arenas' in which many conflicting interests meet. For example, the developer's interests may be at odds with the community's and companies' expectations; universities' interests might be to expand facilities in a suburban location while the city planning department might favour an inner-city infilling strategy. But also within one organization interests might differ, such as between urban planning and economic development departments.

Moreover, different actors also have different time horizons – developers' and companies' time frames are usually very different – shorter – from those of universities and cities. Also the apparently convergent objectives of 'more jobs' and 'economic diversification' may have very different policy answers – in the short run the latter is often not convergent with the former.

This clash of interests does not mean that stakeholders cannot find common denominators and converge for a common good: our cases provide several examples of this convergence. However, without guidance and coordination, the development of knowledge locations risks arriving at a standstill. It is a task for urban managers to prevent this situation, organize negotiation platforms, monitor and follow up the many expected rounds of negotiation and decision-making.

Expect plan changes and contingencies

Building a knowledge location is a long and complex process. The planning of Helsinki's Arabianranta started back in the 1990s, and the area is still under development. The same is true for many of the other cases discussed in the essays. Over such long periods, typically, there is no straight line from A to B: over time, economic, social and political conditions change, often with deep implications for the planning process, and random events can have major impacts. Dublin offers a good illustration of this: at its start, Dublin's Digital Hub was built around the multi-million investment of MIT's media lab. Some years later, MIT unexpectedly pulled out, and the Digital Hub had to reinvent itself. It successfully diversified, and attracted smaller new media firms. The financial crisis of 2008 again fully changed the landscape: the urban development planned around the digital hub stalled because of a collapsing property market.

The high level of 'contingency' in long-term projects poses challenges for cities. One implication is that concepts for knowledge locations should be flexible enough to withstand major changes, but at the same time, they need to remain 'recognizable' for the outside world over a longer period of time. Likewise, organizational and management bodies for knowledge locations should reflect this reality, and be sufficiently flexible and 'open' to allow for new entrants and working methods as situations change. It has become a commonplace to state that involving stakeholders is important in the design and conceptualization of urban development projects. The long-term nature of the types of projects under study here asks for structures that are able to respond flexibly to changing circumstances along the way.

The role of 'special purpose vehicles' and dedicated agencies

Cities in our studies deploy different ways to develop and manage their knowledge locations. The choice depends on national planning rules, local planning traditions and cultures, and the specific situation at hand (land ownership conditions, type of development, integrated plan versus single building, type of sector or concept chosen).

Some of our cases (Dublin, Helsinki) have created dedicated organizations (SPVs, special purpose vehicles). Typically, an SPV unites the main actors in the knowledge location, and operates at arm's length from the government. In Helsinki, for example, the ADC – Art and Design City Helsinki – was founded as a public–private company responsible to coordinate the development of Arabianranta involving the relevant stakeholders: landowners, developers, universities and inhabitants, but also other players including the Ministry of Trade and Industry, and companies. Under the umbrella of ADC, different players were involved to share and jointly develop ideas for the area. This was especially important to overcome the rigidity and physically oriented philosophy of the City Planning Department, bringing innovative ideas, communicating openly between partners and overcoming lengthy, closed and bureaucratic decision-making processes. Overcoming bureaucracy, cultural gaps and lengthy processes was also a central reason behind the establishment of Incheon's Free Economic Zone as the managing authority for Songdo.

In Eindhoven, a dedicated management company was created to manage the Strijp-S area with the City of Eindhoven and a real-estate company Volker Wessels as the two shareholders. This organization implements the master plan for the area, in close collaboration with two housing corporations.

Creating an SPV is no guarantee for a smooth decision-making process. In the Eindhoven case, there are frequent discussions and disagreements among the key stakeholders over the strategy to follow. Major disruptive events – like, again, the unexpected economic 2008 financial crisis – can shift the balance of interests and put co-operative institutions under severe pressure.

Other cases in our study do not have this type of partnership. This is the case for example in San Sebastian; the city obtained a soft loan from the national government to create a media and audiovisual centre. From that moment on, the city arranged a series of meetings with many actors in the local media industry, to collect information on the different needs and ambitions. This forms the input for the final layout of the building.

Based on our study, we cannot draw definite conclusions on the 'best model' for developing and running knowledge locations – we can, however, say that the best model is certainly very context-specific. The challenge for cities is to develop a model that allows managing the location: both strategic and operational monitoring bodies will certainly be required.

Financial models and public–private partnerships

Developers (for example, real-estate firms, pension funds) are responsible for the actual development of (parts of) knowledge locations, based on master plans. They will invest in a knowledge location when they expect a healthy internal rate of return, that is, when they expect that the capitalized future yields (rental income) will be higher than the investment, assuming a certain risk premium. On the other hand, the government typically has additional social objectives: urban (re)development, social inclusion and so on. The government is more interested in the external rate of return, that is, returns that cannot be captured directly by the investors but which accrue to society. Figure 12.1 shows the positions of the government and the private developers on the two axes. Public–private partnerships are the logical response when there are relatively low internal rates of return (making private investors hesitant to step in), but high rates of external return.

None of the knowledge locations in our study is developed as a 'normal' commercial real-estate project. The government – local or national – always plays some role in it, assuming that the location generates public benefits like preserving heritage, promoting collective efficiency or contributing to neighbourhood rejuvenation.

In terms of finance and the role division between the public and private sector, the cases in our research are rather different from each other. In some cases, the model is relatively simple. In San Sebastian, for example, the location consists of only two buildings, mainly funded by the City. Most of the other cases are more

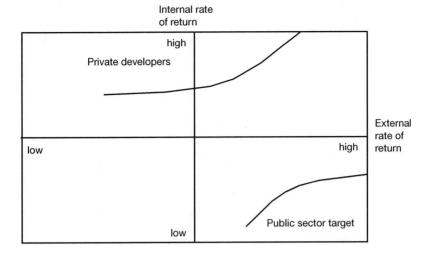

Figure 12.1 Internal and external rates of return

Source: own elaboration

complex in terms of functions and partners involved, and consequently also have more complex financial arrangements. Here, we see all sorts of public–private funding models.

The involvement of higher governments differs per case, from offering a subsidy – as is the case for PI@ – to a strong active role, as we have seen with the support of the Korean Government in Incheon. In the latter case, the Korean state recognizes the importance of Songdo district in the strategy to foster Korea as a North-East Asian Business Hub. Worth mentioning is also Maxvorstadt in Munich, where the City aims to increase state support, as many issues in the development of this inner-city district are the responsibility of the state government (such as the development of universities and certain museums). Without state support, development goes relatively slowly and remains limited to small-scale initiatives.

In a situation of regeneration of industrial or cultural heritage (as in the cases of Helsinki, Dublin and Eindhoven), local governments typically take an active role, making large up-front investments to clean the site and preserve the heritage. Private developers normally have no incentive to do this, so without government intervention, development would take place elsewhere and heritage would be lost. Besides 'cultural' arguments, local governments justify such investments by stating that they yield social returns like neighbourhood regeneration, or preventing urban sprawl.

By funding heritage preservation or restoration – if done properly – governments not only 'save' heritage from a cultural point of view, but also help to increase land and real-estate values in the area. The benefits of this accrue to current landowners. To minimize the 'free-rider' effect, government can acquire the land before restoring the heritage. In the case of industrial heritage, governments may change land use plans – allowing housing or commercial real-estate development – after restorations, and benefit from increased land values. Alternatively, one could think of models in which private landowners are involved in funding the regeneration: it increases the value of their properties, after all. However, we found no cases of the latter in our study.

Not surprisingly, due to its dimensions, the Asian case of Songdo shows the most complex financial engineering in our study, with involvement of multiple private and public players, from many locations in the world. One interesting component of Songdo's model consists in capturing and channelling real-estate profits in the new city towards the revitalization of older neighbourhoods in Incheon which risk detachment from the new developments; this is seen as essential to foster spatial cohesion within the city.

In many of our cases, cities apply methods to 'frame in' private developers, to make sure they contribute to the realization of the desired concept. As is shown in Helsinki, Dublin, Eindhoven and Incheon, cities contract developers to come up with new innovative ideas and to bring variety in the concept. Interesting is the case of Incheon, where the city invited foreign, mainly American, developers to team up with local developers in order to bring new approaches in Songdo's planning system and to increase the external visibility of the project.

In order to safeguard the concept, some cities set concrete goals and boundaries on the freedom of the developers (such as a minimum number of social houses). In addition, governments can take additional measures to cross-subsidize non-commercial goals of projects. For instance, Eindhoven and Helsinki both use a 'cultural budget' to invest in art and culture. The construction of the budget differs; Eindhoven works with a fixed annual fee, while Helsinki asks developers to spend 2.5 per cent of their budget on culture.

The different budget schemes each have advantages as well as disadvantages for the development of knowledge locations and it is up to cities to find the right mix. For instance, the model used in Eindhoven guarantees a constant cash flow in time to spend on culture, but this annual obligation becomes a burden in times of financial downturn as we have seen in the current credit crunch, as both governments and private developers cut cultural budgets.

The voice of the community and the involvement of stakeholders

One key lesson is that stakeholder involvement is essential at the start of the development: that sets the tone for the years to come. The cases of Helsinki and Dublin stand out in the way they involved stakeholders in the design stage. Helsinki's very successful Arabianranta project thrived on a good start, in which many stakeholders reached basic agreement on the path to follow. And in Dublin, a very careful community participation stage helped to ensure support for the development of the Digital Hub. We have also seen that stakeholders can influence major decisions and planning. For instance, in Eindhoven, the management of Strijp-S decided to reconstruct the NatLab – the former physics laboratory of Philips where major inventions where done – after protests of inhabitants and the municipal monument commission against the plan to tear this historical building down. Also, tenants in Strijp-S joined forces to increase their voice in discussions with the SPV.

In this respect, the challenge for cities is twofold. The first is to facilitate stakeholders' participation in the discussion process and in the management structures of the location. It is important to ensure that parties (such as local communities) are not excluded when their 'voice' is difficult to organize collectively. The second is to make sure that the discussion arena is diverse enough to allow for innovative solutions that challenge the status quo of potentially dominant players.

Outcomes

We have stressed that the interplay between a diverse set of actors – taking place in complex governance arenas – shapes the design and organization model of a knowledge location. A central question at this point is to identify what kind of benefits knowledge locations offer in practice, and under what conditions these are more likely to be achieved. In line with our framework, we structured the outcomes in four major types: agglomeration and clustering, image, urban-spatial integration and organizational learning.

Agglomeration and clustering

Locations as catalysts for new combinations and innovation

Knowledge locations are often planned to become prime sites of new innovative combinations between different industries and activities. Innovation is more and more understood as an interactive process, thus requiring proximity and regular contact between knowledge producers and knowledge users. Linear models of innovation (funding → universities → prototypes → industrial applications) are more and more perceived as outdated, while new paradigms of open, user-driven innovation and consumer involvement are being embraced. Therefore, knowledge locations in our study envisage facilitating the 'innovation spark' through the joint location and multidirectional interaction of companies and universities involved in 'new economy' sectors like the creative industries, ICT or biotechnology. Innovations crossing these fields are often the most promising: just think of, for example, smart phones (requiring new materials, design, geo-location technologies, several ICT technologies and applications and so on) or sophisticated medical solutions (requiring bio-engineering solutions, image technology, nanotechnologies, etc).

Our cases provide vivid illustrations of this trend. Arabianranta was conceived as a location to host art and design activities ranging from industrial design to new media; one ambition is to provide conditions for interaction between these sectors, and to continually upgrade traditional industries like furniture or ceramics with symbolic and design inputs. The vision of Strijp-S is somewhat similar: to diversify and upgrade Eindhoven's industrial fabric through creative industries. In Munich, finding new combinations between 'art' and 'science' and fostering interactions between museums and universities is the *raison d'être* behind the Maxvorstadt strategy. Songdo introduces an interesting and flexible concept to foster new combinations in such a diverse knowledge location: the development of 'inner-city factories' where different companies and researchers (national and from abroad) can come together on a temporary basis to work on new product development.

The Digital Hub in Dublin and PI@ in San Sebastian target new combinations within specific sectors. The Digital Hub tries to support the development of new partnerships and co-operation within the new media industry, and its management team organizes meetings between companies to this effect. In San Sebastian, the strategy is to provide a number of shared facilities (plateaus, advanced audio-visual equipment) so that audiovisual companies can evolve towards new stages of advanced production. Moreover, PI@'s infrastructures are also designed to facilitate linkages with other partner companies in the audiovisual and multimedia sectors.

Marshallian heaven and the meeting-in-a-bar: myth or reality?

More than a hundred years ago, Alfred Marshall (1890) introduced what later became one of the most influential ideas in spatial studies of knowledge and inno-vation: the hint that in certain districts (at that time British industrial districts), secrets of trade and technology are 'in the air' and accessible for those who locate within the district. This notion was associated with the advantages of proximity and clustering to support knowledge networks and innovation. It also underlies the vision behind the development of most 'knowledge locations': inspired by narra-tives of places like Silicon Valley and Richard Florida's (for example, 2002) ideals of vibrant and cool districts, fostering agglomeration of companies and 'unex-pected meetings in a bar' became the new must. In line with many recent studies, our research also shows that this notion needs clarification and a more critical look.

In all our case studies we found only slight evidence of dense firm–firm and firm–university relationships within a knowledge location. Most innovation link-ages are with players outside the location, often with well-established partners. This is not to say that important relations do not unfold within the location, its bars, canteens or other informal settings; yet our study pointed to the fact that they often do not relate directly with 'knowledge and innovation' partnerships, but more with access to business information (such as market trends) and policy-related information (such as access to subsidies). As Huber (2010) finds for the case of Cambridge ICT workers, in bars people are often 'too drunk' to say something technically meaningful. Just as in other studies of the geographies of innovation, our research found that for the planning of knowledge locations, the role of proximity has been taken at face value: related with physical or Euclidian proximity and much less with cognitive proximity, which embodies the essential social, cultural and institutional dimensions of the proximity concept (Boschma 2005). Through several talks with companies and universities within knowledge locations, our study indicates that it is when these dimensions come together that the famous 'knowledge-based co-operation' is more likely to emerge, and not when (just any) people are placed together in rooms next to each other.

Physical proximity is thus not a sufficient condition for innovation and knowledge exchange. Cognitive and cultural clashes that reduce 'proximity' (and thus innovation potential) can easily happen within knowledge locations, for example, (i) between different types of organizations (such as firms and universities, but also between universities and museums, as in Maxvorstadt); (ii) between companies with different working practices and cultures (such as Western and Asian players); and (iii) between companies working in different fields and with different modes of innovation (say, biotechnology and creative industries).

Social and cultural – and thus cognitive – proximity between people can be improved over time through fostering encounters and making firms and universities recognize the 'business case' in co-operation, but also here even 'best-practice' knowledge locations seem to face constraints. In Arabianranta, a structural lack of meeting facilities and joint working space for companies is seen as a barrier to nurturing linkages between same-building companies with potential complementarities. In the beginning there were no catering or meeting places at all. To counter this problem, some companies within the location started organizing their own gatherings within the building, designed to meet other tenants ('happy Fridays'); moreover, they lease their own office space to others whose skills and competences are potentially complementary. Similarly, in Eindhoven tenants on Strijp-S organize informal gatherings as the development of bars and restaurant is lagging behind the development of offices.

These recognitions open up an important set of recommendations for planning and designing knowledge locations – especially if the objective of the location is to foster knowledge exchange between tenants and the development of new activities and products.

First, having admission criteria is essential. On the one hand, the broader the concept gets (such as knowledge and creative industries) the less likely it is that the location will generate significant knowledge spill-overs and interactions internally. When the demand for office space in a park is not that high, the tendency is to open the doors to every kind of activity; while in the short run this may make the location financially sustainable, in the medium and long run it downgrades the concept and the value for tenants. On the other hand, setting too narrow a criterion (such as molecular biotechnology, film), may also be unfavourable for innovation and exchange, since the learning potential and the development of new combinations is lower: the tenants are too similar to each other. Hence the challenge, as pointed out by Nooteboom (2000) and Boschma and Frenken (2009) in other contexts, is to find a proper level of cognitive proximity as a basis for an admission criterion: activities that are related to each other but that are not exactly the same. PI@ (audiovisual) and the Digital Hub (new media) are cases where the mixes of activities are the most promising.

Second, a number of knowledge management tools may help to increase 'proximity' and co-operation potential in the knowledge location. Our cases provide a lot of insightful examples, like (i) the planning of joint facilities like canteens, restaurants and other areas in buildings where tenants can be nudged to meet (although, as we saw, this is not a precondition for interaction); (ii) the planning of flexible and ergonomic-friendly working spaces facilitating team work and other temporary arrangements (as in Songdo and in the Strijp-S); (iii) the strategic design of the public space in the location to foster meetings and encounters, such as during walks – new architectural concepts can do a lot in this sense; and (iv) cluster community-building, such as promoting regular meetings, spreading information or developing devoted ICT platforms for the location (like in the Digital Hub).

Third, the design of locations can benefit from more informed distinctions between the types of 'knowledge networking' that the location tries to nurture. In line with Giuliani (2007), our research suggests that knowledge related with market trends is more pervasive than technological-related knowledge (within locations). Further research on the networking within knowledge locations should try to distinguish these two dimensions more clearly.

Different modes of innovation and physical-organizational requirements

Recent research (Asheim *et al.* 2007) demonstrates that different types of activities show rather different sensitivities to proximity for knowledge exchange. For example, in the creative industries, innovation heavily relies on interactions with customers, knowing the right persons, informality and on a number of inspirational ambiences feeding creativity and place-based symbolic content. Freelancing and job rotation are frequent and reputation is a central asset. But in other sectors like biotechnology, innovation processes are highly planned and based on previous formalized knowledge and scientific-deductive methods; know-what and know-why become more relevant and interaction needs are rather selective and not likely to evolve under informal bar settings, but much more in shared laboratorial facilities. Technical co-operation often takes place through international networks of carefully selected partners. But even within certain sectors, modes of innovation differ – industrial design is very different from shooting a film; discovering a new molecule requires other procedures and 'proximity' than developing new human-engineered tissues.

Our examples show that even in locations with a rather selective theme, innovation and organization modes of tenants can be different. In San Sebastian, TV content producers usually rely on the outsourcing policy of a large player (the local broadcaster) and can work in isolated teams of creatives, while other audiovisual multimedia companies rely on close proximity and permanent interaction with a more diverse range of clients (such as for advertising or imaging). Also in Arabianranta and the Digital Hub, design and new media have very different applications, clients and interaction needs. In Munich's Maxvorstadt, fostering innovation links between universities and museums is a justified objective but its accomplishment is far from straightforward. These differences may look marginal at first sight, but entail very important consequences. Beyond the risks of cognitive dissonance for innovation (see above), different types of entrepreneurship policies may be needed. In some cases, start-ups may be effectively encouraged by offering office space and shared labs (as in biotechnology); in other cases, success may be heavily dependent on previous experience and reputation (as in design and audiovisual).

Planners of knowledge locations are wise to adopt this more nuanced view when designing admission criteria, joint facilities and supportive (for example, clustering and entrepreneurship) policies. This becomes more relevant as the more promising innovations and new combinations emerge precisely at the interface of different innovation modes (see, again, the case of San Sebastian and Dublin). Knowledge brokers and 'middlemen' should be identified and empowered for this task; physical locations can also help – the inner factories of Songdo are promising in this respect.

Scales of interaction: the park, the city, the region, the world?

All our cases suggest that co-operation between knowledge institutes and industry mostly takes place at the larger metropolitan and regional level, or even at national and international levels. The knowledge and informational resources that companies and universities benefit from in the location should be seen as complementary to others accessed outside it, and never exclusive alternatives – it is in the interest of the location itself that companies and other organizations are well plugged into regional, national and international networks.

Some knowledge locations have become sites of intense transnational connectivity. Academic researchers and entrepreneurs play a key role linking knowledge locations with the outside world, bringing in new ideas. An important component of Arabianranta's success is related to the development of living lab experiences, a methodology brought from the USA/MIT by a professor at the University of Art and Design – the professor played the role of gatekeeper, accessing external knowledge and diffusing it locally (Giuliani 2005). Other types of important players that fulfil this role are the transnational entrepreneurs: 'individuals that migrate from one country to another, concurrently maintaining business-related linkages with their countries of origin and currently adopted countries and communities' (Drori *et al.* 2009, p. 1001).

For example, in San Sebastian, audiovisual entrepreneurs who studied and/ or worked in hotspots like Hollywood, London, Madrid or Berlin brought fresh ideas, new clients and technology to the local cluster (they also actively participate in the design of PI@ as a knowledge location, countering the vested interests of other established companies). Similarly, Basque knowledge institutes and their most internationalized staff members have cumulated relevant knowledge via their external contacts related to audiovisual technology (such as 3D techniques) through contacts with global firms, students and government agencies. In Songdo, we found evidence that the role of Korean expatriates and highly qualified persons with working experience abroad (new firms' CEOs, research professors and so on) played an important role in attracting new external companies and investments; the same happened in Dublin, through historical links of expatriates and communities in Boston/MIT.

The presence of gatekeepers and transnational entrepreneurs seems to be an important condition for knowledge networking and diffusion, as well as for the challenging of status quo, not only within knowledge locations but also in cities and regions. Through the action of these middlemen and mediators, knowledge locations may eventually become what Hansson *et al.* (2005, p. 1047) called 'social capital catalysts of the knowledge society'. These individuals may be central in fostering new networks and innovative start-up ventures. Further research is needed on how to anchor external knowledge in a location, in particular on how to increase the potential and action of transnational entrepreneurs. Moreover, the other side of the coin requires further analysis: if these individuals are so important in the innovative outcomes of a location, how to reduce the dependency on one or a few key persons?

'Beggaring the neighbour' and displacement effects

New knowledge locations may compete with other business premises in the city region. Developers and city governments are wise to take this into account and seek a distinct identity, avoiding zero and negative sum games and displacements. For example, Songdo was originally planned as a location for international business and new high-tech industries, which would explicitly complement the city centre and other nearby locations. However, displacements are still happening – the relatively low prices and excellent infrastructure in Songdo are attracting companies from the old city centre. Moreover, Songdo also offered irresistible conditions for the relocation of departments of the University of Seoul, generating backlashes from professors, researchers and students. In San Sebastian, PI@ will be a top location for audiovisual companies and will probably generate relocations from other sites in the city where some of these companies are currently based.

From an urban policy perspective, fostering relocations is not bad *per se*, namely when it facilitates the clustering of related activities and facility sharing conducive to innovation. In this sense, the guiding principle when developing locations should be to achieve more coherent and complementary new locations without harming others, or, in other words, foster consistent agglomerations without fragmenting others. To achieve this aim, a central challenge for the location and urban managers in general is to look beyond the location itself, position and integrate it within the spatial-economic context of the city region.

Image: knowledge locations as 'faces' of the knowledge economy

Knowledge locations are strongly linked with urban images: they tend to become leading 'faces' of the knowledge economy in their host cities and regions. In California, the ICT industry is tightly linked with the image of Stanford's research park and Silicon Valley; in London, the Soho district is a central face of the city's creative production. Likewise, all the knowledge locations in our study, directly or indirectly envisage creating a strong brand and image. This not only signals that the city and region are well plugged into the knowledge economy, but also that the location itself is the 'place to be', a unique selling point for certain types of activities and residents.

Specialized, thematic locations usually transmit a stronger image, which may attract new companies and residents. The Digital Hub has developed as a strong brand, and is perceived as the place to be for digital media, both for local and foreign companies. The same goes for Arabianranta, intensively promoted and developed as an art and design district. These are powerful messages for companies. Just imagine the case of a foreign furniture company willing to locate a design 'antenna' in Helsinki, in order to tap into Scandinavian design trends – many good location options are available, but with incomplete information, the image of Arabianranta speaks louder, reducing the uncertainty of selecting a location. The presence of key anchor organizations in the location (such as a large university, a lead firm or a top research institute) also enhances its image further, as companies and tenants perceive it as a locus of information spill-overs, and a place to find qualified staff.

This phenomenon might produce agglomeration effects, even if there is only limited networking and knowledge exchange in the area. In our study, we found evidence that a number of companies relocated to these strong brand locations in order to tap into the promised 'buzz', but got slightly disappointed later on; despite other relevant benefits and quality of the space, it seems that in the end knowledge was not 'in the air'. However, the brand of a specialized and differentiated location increasingly took root as more and more companies agglomerate there.

Songdo, being a rather diverse location ('knowledge and business'), has the most explicit branding and promotion strategies in our study. Songdo can be seen as a marketing tool in itself to signal the change from a culturally closed Korea to an open, vibrant and diverse place, open to foreign investments. An impressive number of amenities reinforce the package, and signal Songdo and Korea as serious competitors in East Asia to attract knowledge and talent. Image building is focused on transmitting the image of a futuristic city to the most diverse targets through promotion centres, events, media and international campaigns.

In sum, it is important to stress that although the image of the planned location is surely a powerful magnet influencing the location's capacity to attract new tenants, jobs and investments (that is, agglomeration), this is not necessarily related to innovation and knowledge networking in the area. Thus, image building policies for planned knowledge locations should be articulated with other knowledge management tools. Images should fit the area's identity, which may evolve over time. However, the starting moment may be crucial: when a location starts out with a poor image (for example, 'a firms' hotel') it may have difficulties in changing the perceptions of investors and other people later on.

Urban-spatial integration

New urbanity and 'phoenix from ashes': regeneration of empty and derelict areas as urban legacy

Knowledge locations do not only play a role as promoters of innovations and 'addresses' of the local knowledge economy, but also as engines for area (re)development. Arabianranta, the Digital Hub and Strijp-S have more than economic development and 'knowledge' objectives: they are also key urban regeneration projects. Even free economic zones are becoming urban – Songdo is a brand new district, built from scratch on sea-reclaimed land, built under a highly integrated city master plan.

This brings new planning challenges. In Helsinki and Dublin, the redevelopment of brownfield areas into knowledge locations was used as tool to regenerate degraded neighbourhoods socially and economically, tackling high unemployment, poverty and environmental problems. In Eindhoven, Strijp-S is also instrumental in filling in an abandoned empty spot after the relocation of Philips facilities (plants, offices, R&D centres and so on). Therefore, a central idea is that behind the development of knowledge locations in urban settings lie key social and physical legacies. Besides the potential to re-fill empty spots, knowledge locations are often a way of preserving the area's identity while giving it a new life, in a 'phoenix from ashes' fashion. The development in Arabianranta evolved around the regeneration of the old Arabia pottery and porcelain factory into showrooms of industrial design, as well as the studios and facilities of the Art and Design University; in Dublin, it evolved around the regeneration of the old Guinness brewery towards a more lively, functionally mixed and diverse location, improving living and housing conditions in the Liberties area. Moreover, these operations contributed to green the area, often heavily polluted due to decades of water and soil pollution.

A new challenge for cities is thus to link these dimensions together towards an integrated and coherent urban area. Another challenge (although not found in our cases) is to regenerate old science locations outside the urban fabric – here the challenge is to bring 'city' and 'integration' into mono-functional science and business areas. Achieving these integration objectives is, however, far from straightforward. Differently from more traditional science park locations, preferences of the users of such locations are likely to be very diverse and heterogeneous. Figure 12.1 provides an 'integration checklist' to bear in mind when designing urban integrated knowledge locations. In the rest of this section, inspired by our examples, we explore some of those challenges.

Unavoidable gentrification and formation of exclusive urban enclaves?

Some of the knowledge locations in our study developed into up-market residential quarters (Maxvorstadt was already an expensive residential and office location). Strijp-S and Songdo envisage becoming a distinctive urban area with a metropolitan and cosmopolitan feeling. Arabianranta, in contrast, complements the city centre by offering a residential environment with an urban feeling and working atmosphere in a waterfront setting, making it attractive for families and wealthy target groups. Also, in Dublin, the planned housing units in the Digital Hub should attract people with higher incomes.

Without policy intervention, land valorization and market forces may drive out former inhabitants and activities, and also some segments of the 'creative class' (like young entrepreneurs and artists) with limited capacity to pay high rents or prices. A gentrification process may endanger the initial diversity and liveliness objectives for the location, and transform it into a social and physical enclave for the well-off.

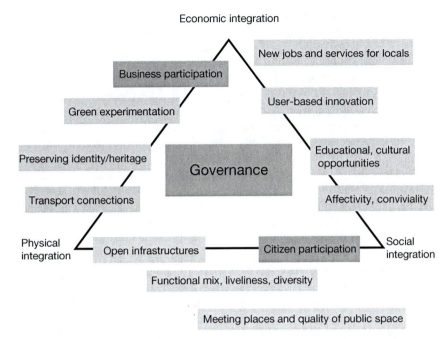

Figure 12.2 Integration challenges: a checklist

Source: own elaboration

Our cases provide good illustrations of policy interventions to avoid the negative effects of gentrification and mono-functionality. This is often achieved through contracts between the city and private developers, binding the latter to the development of more affordable (and typically less profitable) types of housing and office space in return for the rights to develop other areas. In Dublin, the developers pay a lump sum to the city for these rights, which the city uses to develop more socially inclusive facilities and infrastructures. In Arabianranta, in order to preserve the area's diversity, the municipality also developed social renting schemes to keep a mix of incomes and social uses. In Songdo, to make the district more vibrant from the beginning, developers are obliged to build commercial space and at the same time develop residential areas. In a context of financial constraints, economic slowdown and tight municipal budgets, keeping these schemes alive is a true challenge of financial engineering and requires strong political commitment.

Socio-economic integration: community participation, education opportunities and affectivity

The development of knowledge locations is an opportunity to achieve important social remits in old city districts. Dublin is an interesting example. From the start, the city envisaged community involvement to prevent the detachment of the new location from the more deprived populations living in the adjacent area – this has been put in place through programmes of e-literacy and education, supported by the Digital Hub. This helps to integrate the location in the social fabric; moreover, in a time of financial constraints where local policies tend to turn to more short-term job creation investments, measures like this provide places like the Digital Hub with a 'licence to operate'.

In Arabianranta also, community involvement played a key role and was highly innovative. There, a dynamic community association represents the interests of the inhabitants in the management organization ADC. Moreover, a community of e-moderators (managers of each building's intranet and forum platforms) provides the digital backbone of many real-life interactions and civic participation. An example is the organization of car pooling schemes for the elderly to go shopping, but there are many more. These initiatives led some commentators to dub Arabianranta a 'Social Silicon Valley'.

In Songdo, built on virgin land, social integration is at present not an issue but may soon become one – action will be needed to avoid the spatial detachment of this new 'high-tech' and expatriates district and the 'enclave feeling' *vis-à-vis* the old city centre of Incheon. It is therefore also important that the new location can provide jobs and services for the locals – linking the new location with event hosting and eventually with industrial tourism might be good alternatives to foster this interaction.

Other dimensions of 'social embedding' are rather neglected. For instance, more can be done in linking former workers of these locations to its new users. Many former workers of Philips, Arabia and Guinness still live in the city and are emotionally tightly linked with the area. Urban managers and location directors should find new ways to re-connect these people with the location, for example through storytelling or photo expositions – small actions like this might provide a bridge between the past and the future of the area and better integrate it with the social fabric. In such ways, former workers can act as 'ambassadors of knowledge locations'.

Physical integration and smart growth

A central objective of many knowledge locations is to achieve their physical integration in the city. First, these locations are often part of 'compact city' strategies that contribute to counter urban sprawl (and its negative social and environmental consequences). This is true for the cases of Helsinki, Dublin and Eindhoven.

Contrarily to 'gated' locations (such as traditional science parks) all the cases in our research lack walls separating them from the rest of the city. This way, a knowledge location can more easily become part of the city itself, rather than a segregated place where the highly qualified locate and knowledge creation 'happens'. Also in all our cases we can witness a prime preoccupation with the quality of the location's public space, the presence or proximity to advanced amenities (Songdo is extreme in this sense) and excellent transport connections. All these dimensions are central not only for the location's attractiveness, but also for its integration in the larger urban fabric. The accessibility to public transport and open access to the location's public space are also relevant from a social perspective: public transport and the public space are much more democratic than gated locations or areas only accessible by car.

Besides transport connections, the availability of top broadband infrastructure and digital accessibility solutions are also common features of knowledge locations, and may provide their tenants with competitive advantages *vis-à-vis* other locations. Arabianranta was among the first knowledge locations in the world to develop centrally managed broadband infrastructure just like water or electricity – this facilitated the development of e-platforms and e-inclusion experiences in the area. Songdo is also endowed with top broadband infrastructure (Korea is a world leader in this respect); Dublin's high-capacity and cheap broadband access is important for the activities of new media companies, and the infrastructure can also be used by the local community. Moreover, it gives these locations advantages as testbeds of new technologies and innovative concepts.

Locations as testbeds and 'urban laboratories'

Many of the locations under analysis became prime sites of urban experimentation, arenas to test new urban concepts and technologies. The very particular characteristics of some of these places within cities (such as social diversity, superior technological features like broadband or even access to privileged government funding) raised the profiles of some areas as laboratories of 'green experimentation' and user-driven innovation. The cases of Arabianranta, Songdo and Strijp-S are paradigmatic.

Arabianranta was among the first, if not the first, site in Europe to implement living lab innovation concepts – designing and testing new technological concepts based on the user's requirements in their daily city life (such as new technologies for traffic control, geo-location for the elderly). The concept was developed in the MIT, but adapted to the context in Helsinki. Arabianranta was a natural place to implement the concept, with its presence of advanced and centrally managed broadband infrastructure, its diverse social yet culturally homogeneous profile and an existing network of e-moderators trusted by the inhabitants. The first living lab/user-driven experiments were conducted by local government, with the participation of strong local players like the Finnish giant Nokia.

In South Korea, Songdo is a designated arena for the development of ubiquitous computing and augmented reality technologies. Korea has the ambition to develop a network of u-cities, where persons and objects are fully connected in an undistinguishable fashion, any time and everywhere. Korea is a first mover in many of the required technologies (such as advanced sensors and systems), and is strongly betting on innovative and futuristic u-city concepts. Among other things, ubiquitous systems have the potential to contribute to traffic efficiency, health monitor systems, crime prevention or environmental risk reduction. Again, the rather virgin and experimentation-prone character of Songdo makes it the perfect place to test new u-concepts and infrastructures. The wide access to broadband infrastructure and the low 'privacy fear' of Korean society *vis-à-vis* Western cities make it an apt place for these types of experimentation. Songdo also hosts advanced research centres in u-technologies, and national and foreign companies have located in the area to design and test prototypes.

There is more experimentation going on in Songdo: the buildings are also among the first in the world with LEED accreditation – leadership in energy and environmental design – and the entire area strongly invests in climate-proof technologies and clean solutions. A lot of green experimentation is also going on in Eindhoven's Strijp-S, namely of new clean soil technologies for brownfield redevelopment – here groundwater remediation has been combined with groundwater energy. Such tests are generating new knowledge and insights in the form of new localized competences.

The development of this type of experimentation is an arena where economic development and innovation meet sustainability and integrated urban development objectives. Due to the cultural and physical proximity requirements for such experimentation projects, local companies are often involved and develop first-mover advantages when the concept scales up. Bearing in mind technical and socio-cultural specificities of the location, urban managers can do a lot by steering the development of technological niches through experimentation in knowledge locations. Here, existing regional competences can be enlarged through the use of urban experimentation arenas. It is also a way to foster economic diversification.

The new planning orthodoxy of 'mixing'

The development of knowledge locations as mixed areas 'to live, work and play' is increasingly popular (at least in the political discourse). However, it is important to contextualize this trend, and not take the 'urban integration factor' for granted as a necessary success condition for a knowledge location.

In principle, as we described before, urban integration has many advantages and may generate important social, economic and environmental side effects. However, on many indicators (related to innovation, start-up creation, jobs and so on) locations like science and technology parks score pretty well despite their location outside the urban core. It is thus difficult to say *a priori* which type of urban integration a new knowledge location should pursue. It seems to be again very much dependent on the type of activities the location envisages. For example, the working and innovation needs of (most of) the creative industries privilege dense urban environments and vibrant urban atmospheres; moreover, this type of activity is not very space-consuming and living and working premises are often mixed and can be accommodated in a limited number of square meters; cities and the public space are often 'living rooms'.

This may be, however, very different for biotechnology and engineering activities. Biotechnology activities rely on laboratorial facilities and those are more space-consuming; moreover, they are very specialized, expensive and often exist in universities (which are not rarely outside the city core). Innovation does not rely on buzz, but on highly formalized procedures with carefully selected partners. In engineering-related activities, physical proximity to clients for interaction

and development of joint pilots is central; activities are much more space-inten-
sive, can be noisy and have strict safety requirements, making it unfeasible to mix
with, for example, residential and city centre uses.

Beyond the most appropriate urban or suburban setting for a knowledge location, what is always critical is the provision of good internal and external accessibility conditions. This will determine the attractiveness of the location. In the
knowledge economy, easy movement of people and goods remains a prime
requirement for a location's success.

Organizational learning

Our cases show that the development of knowledge locations is a source of
learning for the involved stakeholders, in particular local governments.

One example is Arabianranta. The planning and development of the location
implied the involvement of a number of city departments in multiple platforms.
Moreover, it was one of the first joint development projects between local government and private developers in Helsinki. This experience left roots both within
and outside the municipality. Municipal departments developed new co-operative routines, and social capital between the city and other external stakeholders
increased. Nowadays, regeneration projects in old harbour areas follow a similar
organizational model, highly facilitated by the existence of former co-operation
routines and the organizational model.

The development of PI@ in San Sebastian provides another interesting
example. In order to design PI@, the city's economic development department
organizes meetings and queries among audiovisual companies and stakeholders
in the city, improving the relations between the sector and local government. The
pole is also supposed to be an arena of co-operation in economic affairs between
the city and the famous cinema festival. This will imply new co-operation routines
with the city, for example with departments and structures that organize events.

In order to achieve this outcome, it is essential to have structures and persons
in charge of monitoring the results and evolution of the location. It requires a very
proactive type of urban management and individuals able to spread new routines
within the structures of the local government.

Higher-level institutions and rules of the game

How do higher order institutions that vary across large geographical areas – with
varieties of capitalism and planning systems – influence the process of development of knowledge locations? Our case studies in Central and Southern Europe,
the Nordic countries, Anglo-Saxony and East Asia shed light on this question.

Varieties of capitalism: convergence or divergence?

As hypothesized before, institutional features of each country – which we proxy
as varieties of capitalism – matter in understanding the way knowledge locations unfold in different settings. Understanding these features (for example, the

presence of social institutions that facilitate interactive learning and trust; participation of universities in business affairs; state intervention in the economy and innovation) is important to benchmark policies and best practice and to draw comparisons.

Probably the sharpest contrast can be seen between state intervention levels in Europe and Korea on what is referred to as industrial policy and innovation support. In Europe, competition policy limits the level of state intervention in business affairs, and direct innovation supports 'picking the winners' (companies, industries) are generally not (explicitly) allowed. In Korea, the state traditionally intervenes much more strongly and more directly, providing massive subsidies and R&D incentives for 'new sectors'. Biotechnology, nano-technology and other technologies receive full support in Songdo; moreover, the free economic zone status of Songdo is unmatched in Europe.

There are, however, domains of apparent convergence. One is the involvement of private players in the development of knowledge locations in a risk-taking role. In Southern Europe this is relatively rare: governments simply contract the development to private developers (as in San Sebastian). But more and more, in Europe as a whole, private players have a role not only in taking the risk in the location's premises, but also in influencing its design. In Korea, these developments are traditionally in the hands of the state; and yet Songdo is the first development of its kind in which private developers (a joint venture of a Korean and an American developer) took a central role designing the master plan and building at its own risk. Also in Songdo, the Korean government played a large role attracting foreign universities to the area, something hardly replicable in other European settings.

Throughout the cases, we also observe a significant involvement of universities in development, although the level of involvement varies widely (from being a simple tenant to being an active player in the location's design). Understanding how and why their role varies across varieties of capitalism is an issue for further research.

Planning systems matter

Planning systems across our study zones also explain the different ways locations unfolded. Two central issues are the land ownership and co-operation tradition among stakeholders.

In cases where the land is in the hands of the local government, the development process runs more smoothly and often faster. Moreover, it is easier to define and impose functional mixes in the area. In these cases (traditionally in the Nordic countries and Continental Europe) local governments have more power *vis-à-vis* private developers and can more easily impose rules and control the development. In Southern Europe, private players usually have a lot of power due to land ownership, and expropriations are difficult. In Songdo, the opposite happens: the state has full control of the land, since it was sea-reclaimed and belongs to the state; besides, its virgin character makes it fully flexible for new developments.

In Arabianranta, most of the land was in the hands of the city of Helsinki, making it easier to set the rules. However, not all of it was – there were some private owners that could endanger the consistency of the entire concept. When this is the situation, the planning and co-operation culture plays a decisive role. The Finns have a long tradition of co-operation, and their culture favours consensus. The alignment of different parties involved could be smoothly achieved around the 'art and design' concept. In other cultures, achieving consensus often takes a long time and may endanger the momentum of the development.

13 Assessing the added value of knowledge locations

We found out in our study that cities have difficulties assessing the degree of 'success' of their knowledge locations. Usually, the most common success indicators focus on issues like the rise in property value, number of new jobs in the location, number of start-ups, number of students and new inhabitants and so on. These are surely important indicators; moreover, they are susceptible to comparisons across locations and data can easily be collected. These quantifications and estimations are often essential in order to feed in cost–benefit analysis to judge the (social) return on investment.

However, on the flip side, these data have substantial limitations. First, they conflate knowledge and innovation outcomes with urban and spatial development outcomes. For example, the number of students can mean a lot for the vibrancy of the location but might mean nothing for innovation and knowledge networking outcomes. Second, indicators like 'number of firms' fail to account for displacements from other locations; third, they provide a very limited capture of the potential benefits, limitations and problems (for example, social polarization and gentrification) associated with knowledge locations, and hence, how to plan and achieve 'success'. In this view, the usual set of indicators is no more than the tip of a much larger iceberg (see Figure 13.1).

In our study, we suggested that the success of knowledge locations needs to be seen from two angles, which are related, but should not be conflated: (i) economic development, clustering and innovation, plus image outcomes, and (ii) urban-spatial integration (which includes sustainability dimensions) plus organizational learning outcomes. We thus argue that a challenge for cities and knowledge locations is to develop better tools and indicators to qualify and assess (and not necessarily 'measure') the success of knowledge locations. The design of these assessment tools requires further efforts. In Figure 13.1 we provide some first inputs for this task.

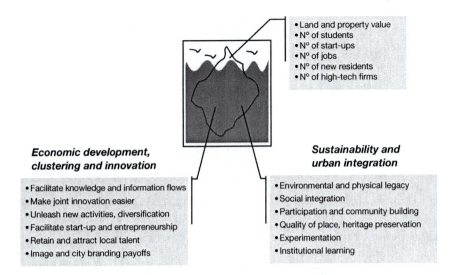

- Land and property value
- N° of students
- N° of start-ups
- N° of jobs
- N° of new residents
- N° of high-tech firms

Economic development, clustering and innovation

- Facilitate knowledge and information flows
- Make joint innovation easier
- Unleash new activities, diversification
- Facilitate start-up and entrepreneurship
- Retain and attract local talent
- Image and city branding payoffs

Sustainability and urban integration

- Environmental and physical legacy
- Social integration
- Participation and community building
- Quality of place, heritage preservation
- Experimentation
- Institutional learning

Figure 13.1 Assessing the success of a knowledge location

Source: own elaboration

14 Theoretical framework and propositions

In Chapter 4 we presented a theoretical framework (Figure 4.1) to guide us through the case studies. A central question was, and still is, 'how does a knowledge location emerge and evolve over time in its spatial-economic context?'. We linked a number of constructs from economic geography, urban studies, political science and public management studies, and conceptualized cities and regions as ensembles of political, economic and spatial systems that shape (and are also dynamically shaped by) the development of knowledge locations.

During our study, and informed by the cases' evidence, we felt the need to fine-tune the initial theoretical framework towards a more fine-grained view on the relationships and mechanisms that tie the building blocks together. As mentioned in Chapter 5, we made use of inductive, theory building methodologies, crossing differences and similarities among the cases and main variables under analysis in an interactive fashion. In order to increase the consistency of the framework and its relationships, we also tested it against evidence from extant literature and our own previous research (see Chapter 4).

The reworked framework is depicted in Figure 14.1. The key building blocks remained in place, but there are two important add-ins: (i) the conceptualization of feedback loops between the location's outcomes and its spatial-economic context, namely the systems of production and innovation, and policy and local planning; and (ii) the introduction of moderator effects between the location's design and its outcomes. The remainder of this section presents a group of propositions (P1 to P16) underlying our framework.

Emergence and development of knowledge locations

Knowledge locations do not emerge and develop in virgin socio-economic landscapes. On the one hand, the city's economic system and involved actors will strongly influence its emergence and shape (for example, through the alignment of agents, institutions and their vested interests; through the action of emerging, 'out-of-the system' agents; or combinations of both). On the other hand, also central is the character of the political and planning system: the emergence and design of a knowledge location is tightly linked with the policymaking process, the will and legitimacy of political representatives, the knowledge of their advisors, and deeply rooted co-operation and planning traditions.

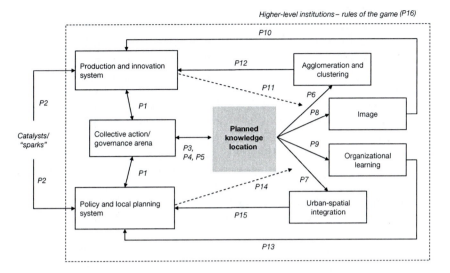

Figure 14.1 How does a knowledge location emerge and evolve over time?

Source: own elaboration

The interests and power of the actors from these two systems will determine the 'design' of the location. On the one hand, actors from the production and innovation system will tend to privilege designs that favour clustering, innovation and knowledge transfer. Moreover, certain activities are likely to be privileged over others. On the other hand, actors from the policy and planning system are in principle more prone to favour job creation, increases in land value and spatial integration objectives such as reconverting unused areas to new functions. The latter might cohere with the visions of leaders in the production and innovation system, or propose and adopt different solutions. The power distribution among the actors (or simply the participation or non-participation in the governance arena) will determine the speed of the negotiation process and the degree of integrality and balance of the concept.

Out of a number of negotiation rounds a first design for the location emerges. But this design is not static or once-and-for-all. New external developments and catalysts may imply further changes. Moreover, the design may evolve as the location's dynamics unfold – the location (as a group of actors and as a new institution in its own right) becomes itself part of the socio-economic landscape and can influence further developments. In these next rounds, previous influential actors from both systems may leave and others may enter, making the location's design evolve in a dynamic fashion.

To sum up, we put forward the following propositions.

P1   The emergence of a knowledge location results from a dynamic governance process in which actors from two distinct and localized systems strategically engage: systems of production and innovation, and political and local planning systems.

P2   Governance dynamics are triggered by the need to anticipate or respond to challenges that can be both external and internal to the localized systems.

P3   The design of a knowledge location depends on the power exerted by the actors of each system in governance arenas.

P3a   In governance arenas with more uneven power distributions and/or less wide participation, the location's concept design will emerge faster, but is likely to be more volatile.

P3b   In governance arenas with more uneven power distributions and/or less generalized participation, the location's concept design will be more unbalanced.

P4   Governance arenas co-evolve with the knowledge location, as the location (as an agent and as an institution) becomes part of both localized systems over time.

P5   The vision for a knowledge location evolves over time, over multiple rounds of decision-making.

Outcomes of a knowledge location

We posited that the design of a knowledge location depends on the interplay of different actors, whose interests are coupled in governance arenas. However, some issues remain unanswered, namely what impacts can we expect from a certain location's design, and what they depend on. It is now evident that the resulting design of a knowledge location influences its outcomes. For example, while some designs may result in a very holistic type of location serving several objectives at once, some locations will be more prone to excel in fostering innovation in certain sectors; others still will put a strong focus on, for instance, urban regeneration or property development. As we had the chance to analyse, despite being related, these outcomes do not always go hand in hand, although they always emerge to a greater or lesser degree.

There are thus four types of outcome associated with a knowledge location: 'clustering and agglomeration', 'image', 'urban-spatial integration' and 'organizational learning'. So, for the sake of completion we make the following propositions.

P6   The development of a knowledge location provokes new spatial agglomeration and clustering effects.

P7   There is a degree of urban-spatial integration associated with the development of a knowledge location.

P8   There is a degree of image effects associated with the development of a knowledge location.

P9   There is a degree of organizational learning associated with the development of a knowledge location.

Locations tend to become associated with images, and those images play a role in attracting more companies, investments and talent to the location. Although the presence of agglomeration and innovation dynamics at the location may influence this image effect further (for example, the presence of knowledge circulation and innovation networks), they do not directly determine, at least exclusively, the perceived image of the location (which may be, for example, more directly linked with the premises or the region's characteristics). Thus, image itself has an impact on the attraction of new companies and tenants to the location, which over time becomes part of the local production and innovation system itself. Thus our tenth proposition is:

P10 Over time, the image of a location affects the local production and innovation system.

It is expected that a knowledge location contributes to agglomerate 'knowledge-based activity' in a certain area (Chapter 1 and P6). However, new knowledge locations do not emerge and develop in a virgin productive and economic landscape: its antecedents and history ('what a region is good – and weak – at') will always influence the capacity of a location to attract and nurture certain types of economic activity. For example, when a region is traditionally strong in industrial design, with systems of aligned actors and institutions, a new location with the aim of steering new art and design activities further is very likely to succeed. On the contrary, promoting knowledge locations for biotechnology or laser technology in regions with no knowledge production in the field or related entrepreneurial tradition is likely to be like 'throwing seeds in the desert'. This is not to say that new locations with visionary objectives cannot attract tenants and generate innovation and new knowledge networks: these efforts may effectively challenge the status quo, avoiding regional lock-in and regenerating production and innovation systems. However, the productive and innovation history of the region will still moderate and condition the agglomeration and clustering potential of the location at a certain moment in time. Hence, we propose that:

P11 The history of the localized system of production and innovation moderates the agglomeration and clustering potential of knowledge locations.
P12 Over time, the capacity of a knowledge location to attract new tenants and steer clustering effects feeds back into the localized system of production and innovation.

Knowledge locations also provoke impacts in the urban fabric. For example, it may affect traffic movements, gentrification patterns, district revitalization, liveliness, urban experimentation or social integration. However, the degree of these effects – and namely the achievement of 'sustainable' results from a broader societal perspective – depends on the character and history of the policy and local planning system, namely planning and organizing capacity, tradition of co-operation within the city administration and between different stakeholders (developers, community associations and so on). This capacity and tradition will moderate what is expected to be achieved with the location in terms of urban-spatial integration. Over time, the new knowledge resulting from the location's experience will feed back into the policy and local planning system (such as in new planning traditions, organizing capacities and political discourses). Thus we propose:

P13   The history of the localized system of policy and local planning moderates the urban-spatial integration potential of knowledge locations.

P14   Over time, the capacity of a knowledge location to steer urban-spatial integration dynamics feeds back into the local system of policy and local planning.

Independently of the spatial integration outcomes of a location, the process of planning and development will be associated with organizational learning from the city and in its relation to other stakeholders (whether in the case of the location's success or failure). Just like above, new knowledge will feed back into the system of policy and local planning. Hence we propose:

P15   Over time, organizational learning effects of a location affect the local system of policy and local planning.

Finally, as depicted above, the functioning of this whole system, its institutions and actors' behaviour, is likely to vary considerably in space, namely across varieties of capitalism and higher order planning traditions specific to different world regions – these are the 'rules of the game' under which knowledge locations emerge and unfold. As mentioned, this is essential to compare best practices and benchmark other experiences. To conclude, we put forward that:

P16   The whole process underlying the emergence and development of knowledge locations is influenced by higher-level political economy institutions and planning systems.

15 Final remarks

In the last decade, the planning of specific locations where the knowledge economy can unfold – for example, science parks, knowledge hubs or creative districts – has become one of the most visible initiatives of local governments worldwide. These types of areas are central ingredients in what has been called a knowledge turn in urban policy (van Winden 2010).

Local governments, alone or in co-operation with other stakeholders, are investing large sums of money in the development of knowledge locations. The complexity of these investments and their insertion in urban areas require an integrative planning approach – however, not many studies analyse knowledge locations from this perspective. In this study we paid close attention to the functioning of a number of these locations within their spatial-economic contexts, and, when possible, how they evolved over time. We focused our research on a number of European cases: the Digital Hub in Dublin, Strijp-S in Eindhoven, Arabianranta in Helsinki, Maxvorstadt in Munich and PI@ in San Sebastian; moreover, we extended our research to North-East Asia in order to learn from the process of development of an entirely new 'knowledge district': Songdo, in Incheon (South Korea).

In this study, we reviewed existing literature on planned locations, and developed a conceptual framework to understand the development of knowledge locations within their spatial-economic contexts. This framework – refined during our fieldwork – combines otherwise disperse constructs from economic geography, urban studies, political science and public management studies, conceptualizing cities and regions as ensembles of political, economic and spatial systems that shape (and are also shaped by) the development of knowledge locations. Each of the cases in this study was analysed in depth; subsequently, we made an international comparison, and developed a checklist of integration challenges and criteria to better assess the 'success' of a knowledge location.

The contributions of this study hopefully can guide further theoretical advances in the study of knowledge locations; moreover, we expect that these contributions can support the design of better-informed policies, more contextualized benchmarking and possibilities to learn from real-world practices. An important concern in our study is to provide insights on the social added value of knowledge locations.

Our study shows that the challenges cities face in developing knowledge locations are growing. Beyond the more 'conventional' clustering, networking and innovation concerns, the increasing urbanity of these locations raises integration challenges – economic, social and environmental – but also plenty of opportunities to regenerate derelict areas, preserve identity, create urban liveliness and control urban sprawl.

This implies that multiple policies and tools need to be deployed simultaneously, involving multiple departments in the city administration and other stakeholders, including private companies. In the context of tight municipal budgets and credit constraints, but also in the face of increasing societal demands, the design of innovative and committed multi-stakeholder partnerships will be a determinant condition for the success of planned knowledge locations. This is certainly a key challenge for the future.

Notes

4 Building blocks of an integrative framework

1 Three combined sets of mechanisms are often designated: (i) labour mobility, for example by the tacit knowledge embodied in employees that change jobs in the region in the same or related industries (Almeida and Kogut 1999; Boschma *et al.* 2009); (ii) knowledge spill-overs, for example through localized social networks (Breschi and Lissoni 2001) and casual interaction and exchange between firms and other organizations just by 'being there' (Gertler 2003; Maskell and Malmberg 1999); and (iii) spin-offs (for example, Wenting 2008), such as when new firms inherit the competences, knowledge and routines of rooted 'parent' organizations, like older established firms or research institutes.

2 For the sake of simplification, we did not specifically frame important players like real-estate developers and community associations, though we deal with them throughout the essays in this book.

3 Also 'quadruple helix' variations have been used nowadays, adding the civil society and community as the fourth actor.

6 Dublin: Digital Hub

1 http://news.bbc.co.uk/2/hi/business/7965664.stm (accessed 21 April 2009).
2 http://www.decentralisation.gov.ie/News/GD_GovtDecision%20011203.html (accessed 28 March 2009).
3 http://medialabeurope.org/about (accessed 22 April 2009).
4 http://www. thedigitalhub.com/digital_hub/cppp_process.php (accessed 23 March 2009).
5 Dublin Institute of Technology (DIT) will consolidate all of its activities throughout the city on one campus in the Grangegorman area.
6 Based on interviews with CEOs of Digital Hub companies.
7 Based on interviews with CEOs of Digital Hub companies.
8 http://www.ndrc.ie/about-ndrc/ (accessed 24 March 2009).

7 Eindhoven: Strijp-S

1 For instance, Eindhoven ranks fourth on the European scoreboard for innovation power, after Stockholm, Helsinki and Munich. It even leads the ranking in terms of patent density per worker. In 2001, it had nearly 550 patents per 10,000 active workers, which is more than three times as high as the second, Oberbayern, which had about 150 patents per 100,000 workers (Commissie Sistermans 2006).

2 The triple-helix co-operation started in the 1990s during a deep crisis which forced actors to join forces and to develop a joint vision and strategy in order to receive financial support from the EU. Nowadays, there is still successful co-operation and many actors often jointly lobby for national funding.

3 To name a few: ASML, Philips, DAF and VDL Group.
4 http://strijpbinnen.dse.nl/06021701.htm (accessed 10 November 2010).
5 The term key project (in Dutch *sleutelproject*) is used in the Dutch planning system for large projects which also include financial support and involvement of the national government.
6 Inter-city trains connect major cities and do not stop at small places.
7 SRE was a regional development partnership between municipalities. Recently it merged with another regional development organization (Stichting Brainport) and continues with the name Brainport Development.
8 It is difficult to make a clear distinction between creative and cultural industries, as there are several definitions and categorizations in theory as well in formal statistics, often overlapping and contrasting each other with many grey areas (for example, see Hesmondhalgh and Pratt 2005; Sunley *et al.* 2007). Creative industries often refer to commercial industries whereas cultural industries refer to non- or low-profit industries which are often subsidized by governments (Cooke and Lazzeretti 2008). Even with this distinction there are many grey areas; for example, many museums are heavily subsidized, whereas others are highly profitable. Being aware of the limitations, we use this categorization. The category 'creative industries' consists of multimedia; graphic design; fashion design; architecture; product design; interior design; web design and various design. 'Art and culture' includes theatre; video; photography; music; sports; art and antiques; galleries; cultural platforms; and others. As formal statistics were not available, we categorized the firms ourselves, based on website descriptions.
9 Unfortunately these data were not available.
10 http://www.klokgebouw.nl/default.aspx?pid=8&itemid=12471 (accessed 13 July 2010).
11 Also the possible extension of Eindhoven Airport is beneficial for Bosch. Currently, Bosch mainly uses the airports of Amsterdam (Schiphol) and Dusseldorf as these airports have better connections. Dusseldorf is especially important due to its strong position in the German flight network.
12 For instance, in one project, the company tries to integrate audio systems with stadium speakers. This is developed jointly with a Bosch subsidiary in the USA.

8 Helsinki: Arabianranta

1 The crisis in the first half of the 1990s was characterized by a banking crisis, a fivefold increase in unemployment and government debt approaching international lending limits, representing 15 per cent of Finnish trade and deregulation of financial markets (World Bank 2005).
2 For instance, over 40 per cent of Helsinki's population has third level of education. This is much higher than other knowledge-intensive cities according to a study by van den Berg *et al.* (2005), such as Munich (about 25 per cent), Amsterdam (31 per cent) or Eindhoven (23 per cent).
3 For instance, the Helsinki region has nearly a quarter of the country's population and has a share of 30 per cent of the total Finnish GDP (Susiluoto 2003).
4 There is a formal competitiveness strategy for the Helsinki Metropolitan Area, set up by Culminatum, the major regional development organization that consists of representatives of governments, firms and knowledge institutes.
5 For instance, in the Cushman and Wakefield European Cities Monitor (2008), Helsinki takes a 28th place in terms of quality of life for employees. This is much lower than other cities in Northern Europe, like Stockholm (3rd place), Copenhagen (9th) and Oslo (12th).
6 During the 1960s and 1970s, the need to accommodate fast population growth led to the development of suburban areas, focused on traditional and mono-functional zones, mainly based on undifferentiated housing.
7 For instance, Kone, one of the largest firms that produces elevators, has its headquarters in the Helsinki region. Besides industrial design, the company increasingly uses

aesthetical design to improve its products. Therefore, the company works with special-ized design companies, such as Marimekko, to decorate elevators.

8 For example, Nokia has 300 in-house designers, and sources design from specialized companies (interview).

9 One product designed and developed in the Design Factory Finland is the 'Power Kiss', a charging system for mobile phones that is wireless and integrated in furniture.

10 See the *Electronic Journal for Virtual Organizations and Networks*, Vol. 10, August 2008, for a special issue on Living Labs.

11 Source: citation from Website Helsinki Virtual Village: http://www.helsinkivirtual village.fi/Resource.phx/adc/opiskelu/livinglab/livinglabinenglish.htx (accessed 23 September 2009).

12 It should be mentioned that it is possible to make a vision for the area which includes various scenarios (such as development with and without TaiK). This prevents the development from coming to a standstill.

9 Incheon: Songdo International City

1 Value that the bank and/or evaluator thinks the developed assets are worth.

2 For example, Ter Wal (2008) demonstrates that in the case of the large French Science Park Sophia-Antipolis, even after 20 years of co-location, collaboration between multi-national and local firms was almost non-existent in biotechnology and only slightly higher in the realms of ICT, the latter largely due to firm spin-offs.

10 Munich: Maxvorstadt

1 Overview p. 14, http://www.dfg.de/download/pdf/dfg_im_profil/geschaeftsstelle/ (accessed 19 December 2009).

2 www.mstatistik-muenchen.de (accessed 19 December 2009).

3 For instance, Munich has, with 5 per cent, one of the lowest unemployment rates of the German large cities. It is followed by Stuttgart (5.7 per cent), while Berlin has the highest unemployment rate of 14.1 per cent. Source: City of Munich (2010); data 2009. Source: Landeshauptstadt München, Referat für Arbeit und Wirtschaft, Munich the Business Location. Facts and Figures, 2010.

4 The GDP per capita in the Munich metropolitan region is €72,163 and has grown by 34.6 per cent since 1997. This exceeds the German average (€59,410 / +21.2 per cent) and competitors Hamburg (€68,957/ +21.9 per cent) and Berlin-Brandenburg (€50,605 /+10.1 per cent). Data stem from the economic crisis that started in 2009. Source: http://www.metropolregion-muenchen.eu/ueber-die-region/hintergrundinformationen/ wussten-sie-schon-dass.html (accessed December 2009).

5 Some data to illustrate Munich's strong knowledge base are: (i) 18.2 of every 1,000 employees in Munich are working in the field of R&D, which is roughly 2.5 times the German average; (ii) the private sector spends 3.8 per cent of the GDP on R&D, which is roughly double the German average; (iii) Oberbayern – one of the administrative districts in the Free State Bayern of which Munich is the core city – ranks third, after Stockholm and the Helsinki region, on the European Innovation Scoreboard (2003) and with over 150 patents per 100,000 workers it takes a second position in patent density after the Eindhoven region. Data from City of Munich (2005); Commissie Sistermans (2006).

6 For instance, Munich received 4.7 million visitors (arrivals) and registered 9.5 million bed nights in 2007. Source: City of Munich (2008).

7 For instance, in the Cushman & Wakefield European Cities Monitor (2008), Munich ranks second after the city of Barcelona in terms of quality of life for employees.

8 http://www.wirtschaft-muenchen.de/publikationen/pdfs/Stadt_des_Wissens_2005. pdf, p. 13 (accessed 19 December 2009).

9 Overview p. 14, http://www.dfg.de/download/pdf/dfg_im_profil/geschaeftsstelle/ publikationen/exin_broschuere_0809_en.pdf (accessed 19 December 2009).

10 http://www.mstatistik-muenchen.de/themen/bevoelkerung/berichte/berichte_2008/
mb080104.pdf (accessed 19 December 2009).
11 http://www.muenchen.de/verticals/Stadtteile/Maxvorstadt/114185/index.html
(accessed 19 December 2009).
12 This part is based largely on http://www.mvhs.de/3.1/mvhs.de/index.php?StoryID=
5978 (accessed 22 August 2010).
13 The Oskar von Miller Forum is an independent educational initiative supported by
the Bayerische Bauwirtschaft (association of construction workers' union and of the
Bavarian construction industry) and dedicated to enhancing the image of construction
engineering in wider society. See: http://www.oskarvonmillerforum.de/ (accessed 22
August 2010).
14 http://webcache.googleusercontent.com/search?q=cache:GcKVIUzihPkJ:www.bsb-
muenchen.de/Archiv-inzeldarstellung.395%2BM5658c5b0a04.0.html+%22Grund
+f%C3%BCr+die+rasante+Steigerung+der+Besucherzahlen%22&cd=1&hl=de&ct=
clnk&gl=de&client=firefox-a (accessed 22 August 2010).
15 The location is too expensive, for example, for starting artists and for artists who are
focusing on the aesthetical value of art and have little interest in making money.
16 http://www.siemens-stiftung.org/en/siemens-stiftung.html   Satzung: http://www.
siemens-stiftung.org/media/uploads/projekt/siemensstiftung/Satzung.pdf (accessed
22 August 2010).
17 http://www.stadt-muenchen.net/literatur/kulturgeschichtspfad.php (accessed 22 August
2010).
18 For instance, TUM, LMU and the the University of Applied Sciences co-operate
with various city departments. City department heads give lectures at universities
and university professors provide new ideas for city management and co-operate in
thinking about solutions to city problems. Specific programmes have been developed
where architects and city planners that graduate follow an internship with the City of
Munich. The best students are then retained and offered a job. This co-operation is
for the long term. On a yearly basis the city gives a prize to the University of Applied
Sciences for the best plan to improve the city of Munich. It should be noted that
according to our discussion partners the contact between the City of Munich and LMU
seems to be weaker than with TUM and HM. An explanation might be that LMU's
priorities lie elsewhere, for example at academic performance. This is key for LMU,
and TUM as well, as both are in the top Germany university rankings. This allows them
to use the label 'university of excellence' which is rewarded by substantial funding.

11 San Sebastian: PI@

1 The film commission is a networked structure within city government coordinating
efforts related to the shooting of films in the city (for example, closing streets,
collecting taxes, dealing with the production teams, getting local service providers for
the directors) and it involves many city departments like transport, planning, finance,
public infrastructure, beach management, hotels, horeca, etc.). It targets the creation of
a unique selling point between a film producer and the city where shooting activities
take place. It links departments of the Municipality to provide permits, for example,
but also hotels, discounts and so on.
2 However, as interview partners pointed out, these markets are highly specialized and
technologies are often not compatible.

References

Almeida, P. and Kogut, B. (1999) 'Localization of knowledge and the mobility of engineers in regional networks', *Management Science*, 45(7): 905–17.

Almirall, E. (2008) 'Living labs and open innovation: roles and applicability', *Electronic Journal for Virtual Organizations and Networks*, 10: 22–46.

Amin, A. (2001) 'Moving on: institutionalism in economic geography', *Environment and Planning*, A, 33(7): 1237–42.

Amsden, A. (1989) *Asia's Next Giant: South Korea and Late Industrialization*, New York: Oxford University Press.

Arbonies, A. L. and Moso, M. (2002) 'Basque Country: the knowledge cluster', *Journal of Knowledge Management*, 6(4): 347–55.

Asheim, B. (2009) 'Guest editorial: introduction to the creative class in European city regions', *Economic Geography*, 85(4): 355–62.

Asheim, B. and Hansen, H. K. (2009) 'Knowledge bases, talents, and contexts: on the usefulness of the creative class approach in Sweden', *Economic Geography*, 85(4): 425–42.

Asheim, B., Coenen, L. and Vang, J. (2007) 'Face-to-face, buzz, and knowledge bases: sociospatial implications for learning, innovation, and innovation policy', *Environment and Planning*, C: Government and Policy, 25: 655–70.

Astor, M., Klose, G., Steden, P., Zelmann, S., Berewinkel, J., Salameh, N. and Müller, F. (2010) *Impact-Analyse des Wissenschaftsstandortes Europäische Metropolregion München (EMM)*, Prognos, Basel.

Audretsch, D. B. and Feldman, M. P. (1996) 'R&D spillovers and the geography of innovation and production', *American Economic Review*, 86(3): 630–40.

Bakouros, Y. L., Mardas, D. C. and Varsakelis, N. C. (2002) 'Science park, a high tech fantasy?: an analysis of the science parks of Greece', *Technovation*, 22(2): 123–8.

Bang, H.-S. and Park, K.-S. (2005) *Factors to be Considered for Improving Free Economic Zone in Korea*, Working paper, University of Washington, Seattle.

Bathelt, H. (2002) 'The re-emergence of a media industry cluster in Leipzig', *European Planning Studies*, 10(5): 583–611.

Bathelt, H. (2005) 'Cluster relations in the media industry: exploring the "distanced neighbour" paradox in Leipzig', *Regional Studies*, 39(1): 105–27.

Bathelt, H. and Gräf, A. (2008) 'Internal and external dynamics of the Munich film and TV industry cluster, and limitations to future growth', *Environment and Planning*, A, 40(8): 1944–65.

Bayliss, D. (2007) 'Dublin's digital hubris: lessons from an attempt to develop a creative industrial cluster', *European Planning Studies*, 15(9): 1261–71.

Benneworth, P. and Hospers, G. J. (2007) 'The new economic geography of old industrial regions: universities as global–local pipelines', *Environment and Planning*, C: Government and Policy 25: 779–802.

Bigliardi, B., Dormio, A. I., Nosella, A. and Petroni, G. (2006) 'Assessing science parks' performances: directions from selected Italian case studies', *Technovation*, 26(4): 489–505.

Boschma, R. (2004) 'Competitiveness of regions from an evolutionary perspective', *Regional Studies*, 38(9): 1001–14.

Boschma, R. (2005) 'Proximity and innovation: a critical assessment', *Regional Studies*, 39: 61–74.

Boschma, R. and Frenken, K. (2009) 'Technological relatedness and regional branching', *Papers in Evolutionary Economic Geography* (PEEG), Utrecht.

Boschma, R. A. and Iammarino, S. (2009) 'Related variety, trade linkages and regional growth in Italy', *Economic Geography*, 85(3): 289–311.

Boschma, R. A. and Lambooy, J. G. (1999) 'Evolutionary economics and economic geography', *Journal of Evolutionary Economics*, 9(4): 411–29.

Boschma, R. A. and Sotarauta, M. (2007) 'Economic policy from an evolutionary perspective: the case of Finland', *International Journal of Entrepreneurship and Innovation Management*, 7: 156–73.

Boschma, R., Eriksson, R. and Lindgren, U. (2009) 'How does labour mobility affect the performance of plants? The importance of relatedness and geographical proximity', *Journal of Economic Geography*, 9(2): 169.

Brainport (2010) *Extra vluchten Eindhoven Airport ondersteunen Brainport*, newsletter no. 6, July 2010.

Braunerhjelm, P. and Feldman, M. P. (2006) *Cluster Genesis: Technology-based Industrial Development*, Oxford University Press, New York.

Breschi, S. and Lissoni, F. (2001) 'Localised knowledge spillovers vs. innovative milieux: knowledge "tacitness" reconsidered', *Papers in Regional Science*, 80(3): 255–73.

Brown, A., O'Connor, J. and Cohen, S. (2000) 'Local music policies within a global music industry: cultural quarters in Manchester and Sheffield', *Geoforum*, 31(4): 437–51.

Camagni, R. (1991) *Innovation Networks: Spatial Perspectives*, Belhaven Press, London and New York.

Capello, R. (2009) 'Indivisibilities, synergy and proximity: the need for an integrated approach to agglomeration economies', *Journal of Economic and Social Geography*, 100(2): 145–59.

Carayannis, E. G. and Campbell, D. F. J. (2009) '"Mode 3" and "Quadruple Helix": toward a 21st century fractal innovation ecosystem', *International Journal of Technology Management*, 46: 201–34.

Carlsson, B. (2006) 'The role of public policy in emerging clusters', in P. Braunerhjelm and M. P. Feldman (eds), *Cluster Genesis: Technology-based Industrial Development*, Oxford University Press, New York.

Carlsson, L. (2000) 'Policy networks as collective action', *Policy Studies Journal*, 28(3): 502–20.

Carvalho, L. (2009) 'Four challenges of a new science and technology park – AvePark in Guimarães, Portugal', *Urban Research and Practice*, 2(1): 103–8.

Carvalho, L., Mingardo, G. and van Haaren, J. (2012) 'Green urban transport policies and clean tech innovation: evidence from Curitiba, Goteborg and Hamburg', *European Planning Studies*, forthcoming.

Castells, M. and Hall, P. (1994) *Technopoles of the World: The Making of 21st Century Industrial Complexes*, Routledge, London.

Chan, K. F. and Lau, T. (2005) 'Assessing technology incubator programs in the science park: the good, the bad and the ugly', *Technovation*, 25(10): 1215–28.

Chesbrough, H. W. (2003) 'The era of open innovation', *MIT Sloan Management Review*, 44: 35–41.

City of Eindhoven (2002a) 'Nieuwe toekomst Strijp S een stap dichterbij', Press release, 26 February 2002, available online at: http://www.eindhoven.nl/artikelen/Persbericht-Park-Strijp-26022002.htm (accessed 10 November 2010).

City of Eindhoven (2002b) 'Visie Centrumgebied Eindhoven – concept, Dienst Stedelijke Ontwikkeling en Beheer, Secor Stratgie', available online at: http://www.bergenbinnen. info/documenten/centrumvisie_concept.pdf (accessed 10 November 2010).

City of Helsinki (2007) *Arabianranta: Rethinking Urban Living*, Helsinki, City of Helsinki Urban Facts.

City of Helsinki (2008) *Statistical Yearbook of the City of Helsinki 2008*, City of Helsinki, Department of Urban Facts.

City of Munich (2010) *München – Stadt des Wissens*, München: Landeshauptstadt Muenchen, Referat fuer Arbeit und Wirtschaft.

City of Munich (2008) *München, Stadtteil Maxvorstadt*, München.

Clarysse, B., Wright, M., Lockett, A., Van de Velde, E. and Vohora, A. (2005) 'Spinning out new ventures: a typology of incubation strategies from European research institutions', *Journal of Business Venturing*, 20(2): 183–216.

Coenen, L. (2007) 'The role of universities in the regional innovation systems of the North East of England and Scania, Sweden: providing missing links?', *Environment and Planning*, C: Government and Policy, 25(6): 803–21.

Comissie Sistermans (2006) *Brainport Eindhoven – Brainport navigator 2013, Lissabon voorbij!*, Drukkerij Jémé, Eindhoven.

Cooke, P. (2001) 'Regional innovation systems, clusters and the knowledge economy', *Industrial and Corporate Change*, 10(4): 945–74.

Cooke, P. and Lazzeretti, L. (2008) *Creative Cities, Cultural Clusters and Local Economic Development*, Edward Elgar, Cheltenham.

Cortese, A. (2007) 'An Asian hub in the making', *New York Times*, 30 December.

Corvers, F. (2001) 'European policies for European border regions', in Geenhuizen, M. Van and Ratti, R. (eds), *Gaining Advantage from Open Borders: An Active Space Approach*, Ashgate, Avebury.

Cumbers, A., MacKinnon, D. and McMaster, R. (2003) 'Institutions, power and space: assessing the limits to institutionalism in economic geography', *European Urban and Regional Studies*, 10(4): 325–42.

Currid, E. (2009) 'Bohemia as subculture; "Bohemia" as industry: art, culture, and economic development', *Journal of Planning Literature*, 23(4): 368–82.

Curulli, I. (2007) *Industrial Wastelands: Intepreting the Urban Heritage. History and Memory, Urban Heritage: Research, Interpretation, Education*, Vilnius Gediminas Technical University Publishing House 'Technika', available online at: http://www. vgtu.lt/leidiniai/vgtu_leidiniai/lt/urban_heritage_research_interpretation_education/ 21586.15982 (accessed 23 September 2010).

Cushman and Wakefield (2008) *European Cities Monitor 2008*, Cushman and Wakefield, London.

Da Cunha, I. V. and Selada, C. (2009) 'Creative urban regeneration: the case of innovation hubs', *International Journal of Innovation and Regional Development*, 1: 371–86.

Davenport, S. (2005) 'Exploring the role of proximity in SME knowledge-acquisition', *Research Policy*, 34(5): 683–701.

DCC (2005) *Dublin City Development Plan 2005–2011*, Dublin City Council, Dublin.

DCC (2008a) *The Liberties DRAFT Local Area Plan*, Dublin City Council, Dublin.

DCC (2008b) *Well-being Survey*, Dublin City Council, Dublin.

DCENR (2008) *Administrative Budget, Composite Brief, Part 5*, DCENR, Dublin.

Deloitte (2008) *Alleen ga je sneller, samen kom je verder: de toekomst van publiek-private samenwerking bij gebiedsontwikkeling*, Deloitte Real Estate Advisory: Amsterdam.

De Pablo, S. (1999) 'Defenicion nacional e identidad nacionalista a traves del cine: dos coproduciones vascas de los anos ochtenta', *Sancho el Sabio, Estudios Vascos*, 10: 97–106.

De Propris, L. and Wei, P. (2007) 'Governance and competitiveness in the Birmingham jewellery district', *Urban Studies*, 44(12): 2465–86.

Design Forum Finland (2004) 'Finnish Design – 125: Classic and Contemporary Design from Finland', presented by Design Forum Finland, Hong Kong Design Centre, 5–21 March, 2004.

Dettwiler, P., Lindelöf, P. and Löfsten, H. (2006) 'Utility of location: a comparative survey between small new technology-based firms located on and off science parks – implications for facilities management', *Technovation*, 26(4): 506–17.

DHDA (2003) *Annual Report 2003*, Digital Hub Development Agency, Dublin.

DHDA (2004) *Annual Report 2004*, Digital Hub Development Agency, Dublin.

DHDA (2005) *Annual Report 2005*, Digital Hub Development Agency, Dublin.

DHDA (2006) *Annual Report 2006*, Digital Hub Development Agency, Dublin.

DHDA (2007a) *Digital Hub Development Plan*, Digital Hub Development Agency, Dublin.

DHDA (2007b) *Enterprise Survey 2007*, Digital Hub Development Agency, Dublin.

Dingli, S. (2010) 'Four steps to prosperity', in McKinsey and Company (ed.), *South Korea: Finding its Place on the World Stage: Five Essays from Leading Thinkers Explore the Country's Present and Future*, McKinsey Quarterly.

Dobbs, R. and Villinger, R. (2010) 'Beyond manufacturing', in McKinsey and Company (ed.), *South Korea: Finding its Place on the World Stage: Five Essays from Leading Thinkers Explore the Country's Present and Future*, McKinsey Quarterly.

Dosi, G. (1997) 'Opportunities, incentives and the collective patterns of technological change', *Economic Journal*, 107(444): 1530–47.

Douglass, M. (2000) 'Mega-urban regions and world city formation: globalisation, the economic crisis and urban policy issues in Pacific Asia', *Urban Studies*, 37(12): 2315.

Drejer, I. and Vinding, A. L. (2007) 'Searching near and far: determinants of innovative firms' propensity to collaborate across geographical distance', *Industry and Innovation*, 14(3): 259–75.

Drori, I., Honig, B. and Wright, M. (2009) 'Transnational entrepreneurship: an emergent field of study', *Entrepreneurship Theory and Practice*, 33(5): 1001–22.

Ducruet, C. (2007) 'Incheon, Port City of South Korea', *The Oxford Encyclopedia of Maritime History*, Vol. 2, pp. 186–7, Oxford University Press, Oxford.

ED (2009) 'Veemgebouw wordt grote design-attractie', 28 February 2008, available online at: http://www.ed.nl/regio/eindhovenstad/2738361/Veemgebouw-wordt-grote-designattractie.ece (accessed 10 November 2010).

ED (2010a) 'Huurders slaan alarm over veiligheid Strijp S', 30 July 2010, available online at: http://www.ed.nl/regio/eindhovenstad/7058925/Huurders-slaan-alarm-over-veiligheid-Strijp-S.ece (accessed 10 November 2010).

ED (2010b) 'Recepties op Strijp S wellicht bemand', 3 August 2010, available online at: http://www.ed.nl/regio/eindhovenstad/7075187/Recepties-op-Strijp-S-wellicht-bemand.ece (accessed 10 November 2010).

Eindhoven Airport (2009) *Jaarverslag 2009*, Eindhoven Airport, Eindhoven.

Eisenhardt, K. M. (1989) 'Building theories from case study research', *Academy of Management Review*: 532–50.

Ekblaw, J., Johnson, E. and Malyak, K. (2009) *Idealistic or Realistic?: A Comparison of Eco-city Typologies*, Working paper, Cornell University, Ithaca, NY.

Eriksson, M., Niitamo, V. P. and Kulkki, S. (2005) *State-of-the-art in Utilizing Living Labs Approach to User-centric ICT Innovation – a European Approach*, CDT, Luleå University of Technology, Sweden.

Etzkowitz, H. (2006) 'The new visible hand: an assisted linear model of science and innovation policy', *Science and Public Policy*, 33(5): 310–20.

Etzkowitz, H. and Leydesdorff, L. (2000) 'The dynamics of innovation: from National Systems and "Mode 2" to a Triple Helix of university–industry–government relations', *Research Policy*, 29(2): 109–23.

Evans, G. (2000) 'Hard-branding the cultural city – from Prado to Prada', *International Journal of Urban and Regional Research*, 27(2): 417–40.

Evans, G. (2009) 'Creative cities, creative spaces and urban policy', *Urban Studies*, 46(5–6): 1003.

FDI (2010) 'European cities and regions of the future 2010/2011', *FDI Magazine*, February/March 2010.

Feldman, M. P. (1994) *The Geography of Innovation*, Kluwer Academic Publishers, Dordrecht.

Florida, R. (2002) *The Rise of the Creative Class: and How it's Transforming Work, Leisure, Community and Everyday Life*, Basic Civitas Books, New York.

Florida, R. (2005) *The Flight of the Creative Class: The New Global Competition for Talent*, HarperBusiness, New York.

Florida, R. (2008) *Who's Your City?,* Basic Books, New York.

Florida, R. (2010) 'South Korea: moving into the Creative Age', *JoonAng Daily*, 19 May, Seoul.

Florida, R., Gulden, T. and Mellander, C. (2008) 'The rise of the mega-region', *Cambridge Journal of Regions, Economy and Society*, 1: 459–76.

Franzen, A. and De Zeeuw, F. (2009) *De engel uit graniet: perspectief voor gebiedsontwikkeling in tijden van crisis*, Stichting Kennis Gebiedsontwikkeling, Delft.

French, J. and Raven, B. (1959) 'The bases of social power', in D. Cartwright (ed.), *Studies of Social Power*, Institute of Social Research, Ann Arbor, MI.

Fukugawa, N. (2006) 'Science parks in Japan and their value-added contributions to new technology-based firms', *International Journal of Industrial Organization*, 24(2), 381–400.

Gale (2009) *Songdo International Business District*, Gale, New York.

Gannon, A. (2008) *Knowing Dublin: Know Your City Council*, Dublin City Public Libraries, Dublin.

Garnsey, E. and Heffernan, P. (2005) 'High-technology clustering through spin-out and attraction: the Cambridge case', *Regional Studies*, 39(8), 1127–44.

Garreau, J. (1991) *Edge City: Life on the New Frontier*, Doubleday, New York.

Garud, R., Hardy, C. and Maguire, S. (2007) 'Institutional entrepreneurship as embedded agency: an introduction to the special issue', *Organization Studies*, 28(7): 957.

Geels, F. W. (2005) *Technological Transitions and System Innovation*, Edward Elgar, Cheltenham.

George, A. L. and Bennett, A. (2005) *Case Studies and Theory Development in the Social Sciences*, MIT Press, Cambridge, MA.

Gertler, M. S. (2003) 'Tacit knowledge and the economic geography of context, or the undefinable tacitness of being (there)', *Journal of Economic Geography*, 3(1): 75.

Gertler, M. S. (2008) 'Buzz without being there? Communities of practice in context', in A. Amin and J. Roberts (eds), *Community, Economic Creativity and Organization*, Oxford University Press, Oxford.

Gertler, M. S. (2010) 'Rules of the game: the place of institutions in regional economic change', *Regional Studies*, 44(1): 1–15.

Getz, D. (2008) 'Event tourism: definition, evolution, and research', *Progress in Tourism Management*, 29: 403–28.

Gibson, C., Waitt, G., Walmsley, J. and Connell, J. (2010) 'Cultural festivals and economic development in nonmetropolitan Australia', *Journal of Planning Education and Research*, 29(3): 208–93.

Giuliani, E. (2005) 'Cluster absorptive capacity', *European Urban and Regional Studies*, 12(3): 269–88.

Giuliani, E. (2007) 'The selective nature of knowledge networks in clusters: evidence from the wine industry', *Journal of Economic Geography*, 7(2): 139.

Glaeser, E., Kolko, J. and Saiz, A. (2001) 'Consumer city', *Journal of Economic Geography*, 1(1): 27–50.

Glaser, B. G. and Strauss, A. L. (1967) *The Discovery of Grounded Theory: Strategies for Qualitative Research*, Weidenfeld and Nicolson, London.

Grabher, G. (1993) 'The weakness of strong ties: the lock-in of regional development in the Ruhr area', in G. Grabher (ed.), *The Embedded Firm: On the Socioeconomics of Industrial Networks*, Routledge, London.

Grabher, G. (2002a) 'Cool projects, boring institutions: temporary collaboration in social context', *Regional Studies*, 36(3): 205–14.

Grabher, G. (2002b) 'Fragile sector, robust practice: project ecologies in new media', *Environment and Planning*, A, 34(11): 1911–26.

Graves, C. (2010) 'Designing a distinctive national brand', in McKinsey and Company (ed.), *South Korea: Finding its Place on the World Stage: Five Essays from Leading Thinkers Explore the Country's Present and Future*, McKinsey Quarterly.

Guston, D. (2000) *Between Politics and Science – Assuring the Integrity and Productivity of Research*, Cambridge University Press, Cambridge.

Hafner, S., Miosga, M. Sickermann, K. and Von Streit, A. (2007) *Knowledge and Creativity at Work in the Munich Region, Pathways to Creative and Knowledge-based Regions*, Acre Report 2.7, Amsterdam.

Hall, P. A. (1997) 'The university and the city', *GeoJournal*, 41(4): 301–9.

Hall, P. A. and Soskice, D. W. (2001) *Varieties of Capitalism: The Institutional Foundations of Comparative Advantage*, Oxford University Press, Oxford.

Hansen, H. K. and Niedomysl, T. (2009) 'Migration of the creative class: evidence from Sweden', *Journal of Economic Geography*, 9(2): 191.

Hansson, F., Husted, K. and Vestergaard, J. (2005) 'Second generation science parks: from structural holes jockeys to social capital catalysts of the knowledge society', *Technovation*, 25(9): 1039–49.

Harms, E. (2007) 'Transformatie Strijp-S, Eindhoven', *Real Estate Magazine*, 52: 40–5.

HEBI (2004) *Higher Education–Business Interaction Survey 2001–2*, Department for Employment and Learning, Higher Education Funding Council for England, Higher Education Funding Council for Wales, Scottish Higher Education Funding Council, Office of Science and Technology, London.

Hesmondhalgh, D. and Pratt, A. C. (2005) 'Cultural industries and cultural policy', *International Journal of Cultural Policy*, 11(1): 1–13.

Hill, R. C. and Kim, J. W. (2000) 'Global cities and developmental states: New York, Tokyo and Seoul', *Urban Studies*, 37(12): 2167–95.

Hitters, H. and Richards, G. (2002) 'The creation and management of cultural clusters', *Creativity and Innovation Management*, 11(4): 234–47.

Hommen, L., Doloreux, D. and Larsson, E. (2006) 'Emergence and growth of Mjärdevi Science Park in Linköping, Sweden', *European Planning Studies*, 14(10): 1331–61.

Huber, F. (2010) 'Do clusters really matter for innovation practices in information technology? Questioning the significance of technological knowledge spillovers', DRUID 2010 Conference, Copenhagen, CBS, Denmark.

Huggins, R., Johnston, A. and Steffenson, R. (2008) 'Universities, knowledge networks and regional policy', *Cambridge Journal of Regions, Economy and Society*, 1(2): 321.

Hutton, T. A. (2004) 'The new economy of the inner city', *Cities*, 21(2): 89–108.

IDI (2010) *Urban Plans of Incheon Metropolitan City*, Incheon Development Institute, Incheon.

IFEZ (2009) *Welcome. Incheon Free Economic Zone. Institutional Presentation*, IFEZ Public Relations Office, Incheon.

IFEZ (2010) *Business Hub of Asia – Incheon Free Economic Zone*, IFEZ Public Relations Office, Incheon.

IIEA (2008) *The Next Leap: Competitive Ireland in the Digital Era*, IIEA, Dublin.

Ilmonen, M. and Kunzmann, K. (2007) 'Culture, creativity and urban regeneration', in C.o.H.U. Facts (ed.), *Arabianranta: Rethinking Urban Living*, City of Helsinki, Helsinki.

IMF (2009) *World Economic Outlook, Gross Domestic Product, Constant Prices*, IMF, Washington, DC.

Incheon Metropolitan City (2009) *Compact-Smart City*, Incheon Facilities Management Corporation, Incheon.

Jacobs, J. (1961) *The Death and Life of Great American Cites*, Random House, New York.

Jacobs, J. (1969) *The Economy of Cities*, Vintage Books, New York.

Jones, B. W., Spigel, B. and Malecki, E. J. (2010) 'Blog links as pipelines to buzz elsewhere: the case of New York theater blogs', *Environment and Planning, B: Planning and Design*, 37(1): 99–111.

Judd, D. and Fainstein, S. (1999) *The Tourist City*, Yale University Press, New Haven, CT.

Kang, J. (2004) *Valuing Flexibilities in Large Scale Real Estate Development Projects*, Massachusetts Institute of Technology, Boston.

Kangasoja, J. and Schulman, H. (2007) 'Introduction', in City of Helsinki Urban Facts (ed.), *Arabianranta: Rethinking Urban Living*, City of Helsinki, Helsinki.

Katzy, B. and Klein, S. (2008) 'Editorial introduction: special issue on Living Labs', *Electronic Journal for Virtual Organizations and Networks*, 10: 1–21

Keane, M. (2009) 'Great adaptations: China's creative clusters and the new social contract', *Continuum*, 23(2): 221–30.

Kelly, R. M. and Palumbo, D. (1992) *Theories of Policy Making: Encyclopedia of Government and Politics*, Routledge, London.

Kelly, T., Gray, V. and Minges, M. (2003) *Broadband Korea: Internet Case Study*, International Telecommunication Union, Seoul.

Kenney, M. and Patton, D. (2006) 'The co-evolution of technologies and institutions: Silicon Valley as the iconic high-technology cluster', in P. Braunerhjelm and M. P. Feldman (eds), *Cluster Genesis: Technology-based Industrial Development*, Oxford University Press, New York.

Kim, C. (2007) *A Study on the Development Plan of Incheon Free Economic Zone, Korea: Based on a Comparison to a Free Economic Zone in Pudong, China*, University of Oregon, Oregon.

Kim, C. (2010) 'Place promotion and symbolic characterization of New Songdo City, South Korea', *Cities*, 27(1): 13–19.

Kim, W. S. and Lee, Y. I. (2007) 'Challenges of Korea's Foreign Direct Investment-led globalization: multinational corporations' perceptions', *Asia Pacific Business Review*, 13(2): 163–81.

Kim, W. S. and Lee, Y. I. (2008) 'Korea's FDI-led economic liberalism: a critical view', *Asian Perspective*, 32(1): 165–92.

Kincaid, H. V. and Bright, M. (1957) 'Interviewing the business elite', *American Journal of Sociology*, 63(3): 304–11.

Kloosterman, R. C. (2010) 'Building a career: labour practices and cluster reproduction in a Dutch architectural firm', *Regional Studies*, 44(7): 859–71.

Knight, R. V. (1995) 'Knowledge-based development: policy and planning implications for cities', *Urban Studies*, 32(2): 225–60.

Koh, F. C., Koh, W. T. and Tschang, F. T. (2005) 'An analytical framework for science parks and technology districts with an application to Singapore', *Journal of Business Venturing*, 20(2): 217–39.

Korea Ministry of Finance and Economy (2002a) *The Axis of Asia: Transforming Korea into Northeast Asia's Business Hub*, Seoul, Korea.

Korea Ministry of Finance and Economy (2002b) *Today's Potential, Tomorrow's Promise*, Seoul, Korea.

Korea Ministry of Finance and Economy (2004) *Korea Free Economic Zones Update*, Seoul, Korea.

KuiperCompagnons (2007) *Bestemmingsplan Strijp-S*, KuiperCompagnons: Rotterdam.

Kuznetsov, Y. and Sabel, C. (2008) 'Global mobility of talent from a perspective of new industrial policy: open migration chains and diaspora networks', in A. Solimano (ed.), *The International Mobility of Talent: Types, Causes and Development Impact*, Oxford University Press, New York.

Laffitte, P. (1991) *Birth of a city? Sophia-Antipolis. Foundation Sophia-Antipolis*, available online at: http://www.sophia-antipolis.org/GB/sophia-antipolis/sophia-antipolis/naissance-ville/naissance-ville.htm (accessed 6 September 2010).

Lagendijk, A. and Boekema, F. (2008) 'Global circulation and territorial development: Southeast Brabant from a relational perspective', *European Planning Studies*, 16(7): 925–39.

Landabaso, M. and Mouton, B. (2005) 'Towards a different regional innovation policy: eight years of European experience through the European Regional Development Fund Innovative Actions', in Geenhuizen, M. Van, Gibson, D.V. and Heitor, M.V. (eds), *Regional Development and Conditions for Innovation in the Network Society*, Purdue University Press, West Lafayette.

Landeshauptstadt München (2008) *City Council Decision – Draft on Strategic Guideline Stadt des Wissens*, Referat für Arbeit und Wirtschaft, Munich.

Landeshauptstadt München (2009) *Wohnungsmarktbarometer*, Referat für Stadtplanung und Bauordnung, Munich.

Landeshauptstadt München (2010) *Münchner Jahreswirtschaftsbericht*, Referat für Arbeit und Wirtschaft, Munich.

Landry, C. (2000) *The Creative City: a Toolkit for Urban Innovators*, Earthscan, London.

Landry, C. (2006) 'Lineages of the creative city'. Comedia. Originally published in *Creativity and the City*, Netherlands Architecture Institute, 2005, available online at: http://irogaland.no/ir/file_public/download/Noku/Lineages%20of%20the%20Creative%20City.pdf (accessed 14 October 2009).

Lavanga, M., Stegmeijer, E. and Haijen, J. (2008) *Incubating Creativity; Unpacking Locational and Institutional Conditions that can make Cultural Spaces and Creative Areas Work*, Working paper presented during the ICCPR Conference, 20–4 August 2008, Istanbul, Turkey.

Lawton Smith, H. (2007) 'Universities, innovation and territorial development: a review of evidence', *Environment and Planning*, C, 25: 98–114.

Le Blanc, H. (2010) 'Strijp S heeft "hangout" nodig om ambitie waar te maken', *Eindhovens Dagblad*, 14 August.

Lee, S. H., Yigitcanlar, T., Han, J. H. and Leem, Y. T. (2008) 'Ubiquitous urban infrastructure: infrastructure planning and development in Korea, innovation: management', *Policy and Practice*, 10(2–3): 282–92.

Lee, Y. I. (2004) 'MNCS' perception on the feasibility of South Korea as a business hub of Northeast Asia', *Asian Academy of Management Journal*, 9(2), 97–112.

Lee, Y. I. and Hobday, M. (2003) 'Korea's new globalization strategy: can Korea become a business hub in Northeast Asia?', *Management Decision*, 41(5): 498–510.

Lindelöf, P. and Löfsten, H. (2003) 'Science park location and new technology-based firms in Sweden – implications for strategy and performance', *Small Business Economics*, 20(3), 245–58.

Link, A. N. and Scott, J. T. (2003) 'US science parks: the diffusion of an innovation and its effects on the academic missions of universities', *International Journal of Industrial Organization*, 21(9), 1323–56.

Löfsten, H. and Lindelöf, P. (2001) 'Science parks in Sweden – industrial renewal and development?', *R&D Management*, 31(3): 309–22.

Löfsten, H. and Lindelöf, P. (2002) 'Science parks and the growth of new technology-based firms – academic–industry links, innovation and markets', *Research Policy*, 31(6): 859–76.

Luger, M. and Goldstein, H. (1991) *Technology in the Garden: Research Parks and Regional Economic Development*, University of North Carolina Press, Chapel Hill.

McAdam, M. and McAdam, R. (2008) 'High tech start-ups in university science park incubators: the relationship between the start-up's lifecycle progression and use of the incubator's resources', *Technovation*, 28(5): 277–90.

McKinsey and Company (2010) *South Korea: Finding its Place on the World Stage. Five Essays from Leading Thinkers Explore the Country's Present and Future*, McKinsey Quarterly, April.

McNeill, D. (2009) 'South Korea builds a global university, with help from the U.S.', *Chronicle of Higher Education*, 19 June.

Maggioni, M. (2006) 'Mors tua, vita mea? The rise and fall of innovative industrial clusters', in P. Braunerhjelm and M. P. Feldman (eds), *Cluster Genesis: Technology-based Industrial Development*, Oxford University Press, New York.

Maillat, D. (1995) 'Territorial dynamic, innovative milieus and regional policy', *Entrepreneurship and Regional Development*, 7(2): 157–65.

Maldonado, A. M. F. and Romein, A. (2009) 'The reinvention of Eindhoven: from industrial town in decline to capital city of a technology and design region', paper presented at the City Futures congress, Madrid, 4–6 June 2009.

Malecki, E. J. (2002) 'Hard and soft networks for urban competitiveness', *Urban Studies*, 39: 929–45.

Malecki, E. J. (2007) 'Cities and regions competing in the global economy: knowledge and local development policies', *Environment and Planning*, C: Government and Policy, 25: 638–54.

Malerba, F. (2002) 'Sectoral systems of innovation and production', *Research Policy*, 31(2): 247–64.

Malmberg, A. and Maskell, P. (2006) 'Localized learning revisited', *Growth and Change*, 37(1): 1–18.

Marshall, A. (1890) *Principles of Economics*, Macmillan, London.

Martin, R. (2010) 'Roepke Lecture in Economic Geography – rethinking regional path dependence: beyond lock-in to evolution', *Economic Geography*, 86(1): 1–27.

Martin, R. and Moodysson, J. (2010) 'Innovation in symbolic industries: the geography and organisation of knowledge sourcing', DRUID 2010 Conference, CBS, Copenhagen, Denmark.

Martin, R. and Sunley, P. (2003) 'Deconstructing clusters: chaotic concept or policy panacea?', *Journal of Economic Geography*, 3(1): 5–35.

Martin, R. and Sunley, P. (2006) 'Path dependence and regional economic evolution', *Journal of Economic Geography*, 6(4): 395–437.

Maskell, P. and Malmberg, A. (1999) 'Localised learning and industrial competitiveness', *Cambridge Journal of Economics,* 23(2): 167–85.

Maskell, P. and Malmberg, A. (2007) 'Myopia, knowledge development and cluster evolution', *Journal of Economic Geography*, 7: 603–18.

Maskell, P., Bathelt, H. and Malmberg, A. (2006) 'Building global knowledge pipelines: the role of temporary clusters', *European Planning Studies*, 14(8): 997–1013.

Massey, D., Quintas, P. and Wield, D. (1992) *High-tech Fantasies. Science Parks in Society, Science and Space*, Routledge, London.

Merton, R. K. and Kendall, P. L. (1946) 'The focused interview', *American Journal of Sociology*, 51(6): 541–57.

Miles, S. and Paddison, R. (2005) 'Introduction: the rise and rise of culture-led urban regeneration', *Urban Studies*, 42(5): 833–9.

Mingardo, G., van den Berg, L. and van Haaren, J. (2009) *Transport, Environment and Economy at Urban Level: the Need for Decoupling*, Euricur, Erasmus University, Rotterdam.

Ministry of the Knowledge Economy (2009) *RFID/USN, Incheon*, Korean Ministry of Knowledge Economy.

Mommaas, H. (2004) 'Cultural clusters and the post-industrial city: towards the remapping of urban cultural policy', *Urban Studies*, 41(3): 507–32.

Monck, C. and Peters, K. (2009) 'Science parks as an instrument of regional competitiveness: measuring success and impact', IASP 2009 Conference.

Monck, C., Porter, B., Quintas, P., Storey, D. and Wynarczyk, P. (1988) *Science Parks and the Growth of High-technology Firms*, Croom Helm, London.

Moodysson, J. (2008) 'Principles and practices of knowledge creation: on the organization of "buzz" and "pipelines" in life science communities', *Economic Geography*, 84(4): 449–69.

Mortice, Z. (2008) 'New Songdo City looks back at the New World for older urban models', *The News of the American Community of Architects*, 28 July.

Murray, A. J. and Greenes, K. A. (2007) 'From the knowledge worker to the knowledge economy', *VINE – The Journal of Information and Knowledge Management Systems*, 37(1): 7–13.

NDP (2007) *National Development Plan 2007–2013, Transforming Ireland, A Better Quality of Life for All*, Stationery Office, Dublin.

Neff, G. and Stark, D. (2003) 'Permanently beta: responsive organization in the internet era', in E. Howard and S. Jones (eds), *The Internet and American Life*, Sage, Thousand Oaks, CA.

Newman, P. and Thornley, A. (1996) *Urban Planning in Europe*, IONON/Routledge, London.

Nooteboom, B. (2000) *Learning and Innovation in Organizations and Economies*, Oxford University Press, Oxford.

North, D. (1990) *Institutions, Institutional Change, and Economic Performance*, Cambridge University Press, Cambridge.

NSF (2006b) *Science and Technology Indicators*, National Science Foundation. Arlington, VA.

OECD (1996) *The Knowledge Based Economy*, OECD, Paris.

OECD (2005) *Territorial Reviews: Seoul, Korea*, OECD, Paris.

OECD (2006) *Competitive Cities in the Global Economy*, OECD, Paris.

OECD (2007) *Policy Considerations for Audiovisual Content Distribution in a Multiplatform Environment*, OECD, Paris.

OECD (2010) *OECD Economic Surveys: Korea, June 2010 – Overview*, OECD, Paris.

OpenDoors (n.d.) 'Foreign students enrolled in the US', Institute for International Education, Washington DC available online at: http://www.opendoors.iienetwork. org/ (accessed 20 June 2010).

Orsenigo, L. (2006) 'Clusters and clustering: stylized facts, issues and theories', in P. Braunerhjelm and M. P. Feldman (eds), *Cluster Genesis: Technology-based Industrial Development*, Oxford University Press, New York.

Paiola, M. (2008) 'Cultural events as potential drivers of urban regeneration', *Industry and Innovation*, 15(5): 513–29.

Peck, J. (2005) 'Struggling with the creative class', *International Journal of Urban and Regional Research*, 29(4): 740–70.

Peck, J. and Theodore, N. (2007) 'Variegated capitalism', *Progress in Human Geography*, 31(6): 731–72.

Phan, P. H., Siegel, D. S. and Wright, M. (2005) 'Science parks and incubators: observations, synthesis and future research', *Journal of Business Venturing*, 20(2): 165–82.

Phelps, R. P. (1998) 'The effect of university host community size on state growth', *Economics of Education Review*, 17(2): 149–58.

Philips (2009) 'Revolutionary public lighting', June 2009, available online at: http://www. design.philips.com/sites/philipsdesign/about/design/designnews/newvaluebydesign/ june2009/revolutionary_public_lighting.page (accessed 19 July 2010).

Phillimore, J. (1999) 'Beyond the linear view of innovation in science park evaluation: an analysis of Western Australian Technology Park', *Technovation*, 19(11): 673–80.

Pinakothek der Moderne (2009) *Kunstareal München*, Stiftung Pinakothek der Moderne, Munich.

Pinkowski, J. (2009) 'Consultation to enhance Dublin, Ireland as a global competitive city with diversity of opportunity, tolerance, and cultivating the talent of immigrant entrepreneurs', Dublin City Council, Dublin.

Polèse, M. (2005) 'Cities and national economic growth: a reappraisal', *Urban Studies*, 42(8): 1429.

Ponzini, D. and Rossi, U. (2010) 'Becoming a creative city: the entrepreneurial mayor, network politics and the promise of an urban renaissance', *Urban Studies*, 47(5): 1037.

Porter, L. and Barber, A. (2007) 'Planning the cultural quarter in Birmingham's Eastside', *European Planning Studies*, 15(10): 1327–48.

Porter, M. (1990) *The Comparative Advantage of Nations*, Free Press, New York.

Porter, M. (1998) *On Competition*, Harvard Business School Press, Cambridge, MA.

Porter, M. E. (2000) 'Location, competition, and economic development: local clusters in a global economy', *Economic Development Quarterly*, 14(1): 15–34.

Powell, W. W. and Snellman, K. (2004) 'The knowledge economy', *Annual Review of Sociology*, 30: 199–220.

Prahalad, C. K. and Ramaswamy, V. (2004) 'The future of competition: co-creating unique value with customers', *Strategy and Leadership*, 32(3): 4–9.

Pratt, A. C. (2000) 'New media, the new economy and new spaces', *Geoforum*, 31(4): 425–36.

Queré, M. (2007) 'Sophia-Antipolis as a reverse science park: from exogenous to endogenous development', in K. Frenken (ed.), *Applied Evolutionary Economics and Economic Geography*, Edward Elgar, Cheltenham.

Quintas, P. and Massey, D. (1992) 'Academic-industry links and innovation: questioning the science park model', *Technovation*, 12(3): 161–75.

Randeraat, van, G. (2006) *Sturen in complexiteit van binnenstedelijke gebiedsontwikkeling*, Erasmus University, Rotterdam.

Reichert, S. (2006) *The Rise of Knowledge Regions: Emerging Opportunities and Challenges for Universities*, European University Association, Brussels.

Roach, S. and Lam, S. (2010) 'The resilient economy', in McKinsey and Company (ed.), *South Korea: Finding its Place on the World Stage: Five Essays from Leading Thinkers Explore the Country's Present and Future*, McKinsey Quarterly.

Rodriguez, P., Cristóbal, M. and de Ron, F. (2009) *Nuevas oportunidades de negocio para la industria audiovisual de San Sebastián*, Fomento San Sebastian, San Sebastián.

Romer, P. M. (1986) 'Increasing returns and long-run growth', *Journal of Political Economy*, 94(5): 1002–37.

Roper, S. and Grimes, S. (2005) 'Wireless valley, silicon wadi and digital island – Helsinki, Tel Aviv and Dublin and the ICT global production network', *Geoforum*, 36: 297–313.

Rosenthal, S. and Strange, W. (2004) 'Evidence on the nature and sources of agglomeration economies', in V. Henderson and J. F. Thisse, *Handbook of Regional and Urban Economics*, volume 4, Elsevier, Amsterdam.

Rossiter, N. (2008) 'Creative industries in Beijing (Introduction)', *Urban China*, 33, December.

Rothaermel, F. T. and Thursby, M. (2005) 'Incubator firm failure or graduation? The role of university linkages', *Research Policy*, 34(7): 1076–90.

Rotmans, J. (2005) *Societal Innovation: Between Dream and Reality Lies Complexity*, Erasmus University, Rotterdam.

Saxenian, A. L. (2007) *The New Argonauts: Regional Advantage in a Global Economy*, Harvard University Press, Cambridge, MA.

Scott, A. J. (1996) 'The craft, fashion and cultural-products industries of Los Angeles: competitive dynamics and policy dilemmas in a multisectoral image-producing complex', *Annals of the Association of American Geographers*, 86(2): 306–23.

Scott, A. J. (2000) *The Cultural Economy of Cities*, Sage, London.

Scott, A. J. (2006) 'Creative cities: conceptual issues and policy questions', *Journal of Urban Affairs*, 28: 1–17.

Segel, A. I. (2005) *New Songdo City, Harvard Business School Case No 9-206-019*, Harvard Business School Publishing, Boston, MA.

Seitinger, S. (2004) 'Spaces of innovation: 21st century technopoles', Master's thesis, Massachusetts Institute of Technology, Department of Urban Studies and Planning, available online at: http://hdl.handle.net/1721.1721/17707 (accessed 6 September 2010).

Shin, D. H. (2009) 'Ubiquitous city: urban technologies, urban infrastructure and urban informatics', *Journal of Information Science*, 35(5): 515.

Siegel, D. S., Westhead, P. and Wright, M. (2003) 'Assessing the impact of university science parks on research productivity: exploratory firm-level evidence from the United Kingdom', *International Journal of Industrial Organization*, 21(9): 1357–69.

Slenders, H. L. A., Dols, P., Verburg, R and de Vriesm A. J. (2010) 'Sustainable remediation panel: sustainable synergies for the subsurface: combining groundwater energy with remediation', *Remediation*, 20(2): 1–153.

Smeaton, A. F., McConnell, G. and Parkes, K. (2009) *The Needs of the Business Community and Other Actors in the New Media Sector: a Report on the Dublin Region, EU 7th Framework Programme*, REDICT project 206480, Dublin Region REDICT Partners, Dublin.

SongdoTechnopark (2010) *All About Technology!* Songdo Technopark, Incheon.

Sotarauta, M. (2009) 'Power and influence tactics in the promotion of regional development: an empirical analysis of the work of Finnish regional development officers', *Geoforum*, 40(5): 895–905.

Sotarauta, M. and Kautonen, M. (2007) 'Co-evolution of the Finnish national and local innovation and science arenas: towards a dynamic understanding of multi-level governance', *Regional Studies*, 41: 1085–98.

Spradley, J. (1979) *The Ethnographic Interview*, Holt, Rinehart and Winston, New York.

Stegen, R. and Streit, A. (2003) 'Die Maxvorstadt – Leben zwischen Wissenschaft, Kunst und Kommerz', in G. Heinritz, C.-C. Wiegandt and D. Wiktorin (eds), *Der München Atlas. Die Metropole im Spiegel faszinierender Karten*, Köln.

Sternberg, R. (1999) 'Innovative linkages and proximity: empirical results from recent surveys of small and medium sized firms in German regions', *Regional Studies*, 33(6): 529–40.

Stiftung Pinakothek der Moderne (2009) *Kunstareal*, Munich.

Storper, M. and Manville, M. (2006) 'Behaviour, preferences and cities: urban theory and urban resurgence', *Urban Studies*, 43(8): 1247.

Storper, M. and Scott, A. J. (2009) 'Rethinking human capital, creativity and urban growth', *Journal of Economic Geography*, 9(2): 147.

Storper, M. and Venables, A. J. (2004) 'Buzz: face-to-face contact and the urban economy', *Journal of Economic Geography*, 4(4): 351–70.

Stubbs, R. (2009) 'What ever happened to the East Asian Developmental State? The unfolding debate', *Pacific Review*, 22(1): 1–22.

Süddeutsche Zeitung (2009) 'Wo die Szene hinzieht', 14 July.

Süddeutsche Zeitung (2010) 'Und alle sind glücklich; Warum die Hype um die Maxvorstadt berechtigt ist', 23 June.

Sunley, P., Pinch, S., Reimer, S. and Macmillan, J. (2007) 'Innovation in a creative production system: the case of design', Draft manuscript available from authors at School of Geography, University of Southampton, Southampton.

Susiluoto, I. (2003) 'Portrait of the Helsinki Region, City of Helsinki Urban Facts', web publications, 2003, available online at: http://www.hel2.fi/Tietokeskus/julkaisut/pdf/03_12_30_susiluoto_vj1.pdf (accessed 23 September 2009).

Sydow, J., Lindkvist, L. and DeFillippi, R. (2004) 'Project-based organizations, embeddedness and repositories of knowledge: editorial', *Organization Studies*, 25(9): 1475–89.

Sydow, J. and Staber, U. (2002) 'The institutional embeddedness of project networks: the case of content production in German television', *Regional Studies*, 36(3): 215–27.

Tamasy, C. (2007) 'Rethinking technology-oriented business incubators: developing a robust policy instrument for entrepreneurship, innovation, and regional development?', *Growth and Change*, 38(3): 460.

Taylor, P. J. (2000) 'World cities and territorial states under conditions of contemporary globalization', *Political Geography*, 19(1): 5–32.

Teisman, G. R. and Klijn, E. H. (2002) 'Partnership arrangements: governmental rhetoric or governance scheme?', *Public Administration Review*, 62(2): 197–205.

Teisman, G. and Klijn, E. H. (2008) 'Complexity theory and public management', *Public Management Review*, 10(3): 287–97.

Ter Wal, A. L. J. (2008) 'Cluster emergence and network evolution: a longitudinal analysis of the inventor network in Sophia-Antipolis', DRUID – 25th Celebration Conference, Copenhagen, CBS, Denmark.

Tijssen, R., van Leeuwen, T. and van Wijk, E. (2009) 'Benchmarking university–industry research co-operation worldwide: performance measurements and indicators based on co-authorship data for the world's largest universities', *Research Evaluation*, 18(1): 13–24.

Urlings, D. (2007) *Community Planning, Draagvlak, participatie en sturing in de Nederlandse stedelijke gebiedsontwikkeling*, Erasmus University, Rotterdam.

Vale, M. and Carvalho, L. (2009) 'Territorial knowledge dynamics in health-oriented biotechnology: cases from the Centro Region', Eurodite paper – Regional Trajectories to the Knowledge Economy, WP5, University of Lisbon.

Vale, M. and Carvalho, L. (2012) 'Knowledge networks and processes of anchoring in Portuguese biotechnology', *Regional Studies*, forthcoming.

van den Berg, L. and Braun, E. (1999) 'Urban competitiveness, marketing and the need for organising capacity', *Urban Studies*, 36(5–6): 987–99.

van den Berg, L., Braun, E. and van der Meer, J. (1997a) *Metropolitan Organising Capacity – Experiences with Organising Major Projects in European Cities*, Ashgate, Aldershot.

van den Berg, L., Braun, E. and van der Meer, J. (1997b) 'The organising capacity of metropolitan region', *Environment and Planning*, C: Government and Policy, 15(3): 253–72.

van den Berg, L., Braun, E. and van Winden, W. (2001a) 'Growth clusters in European cities: an integral approach', *Urban Studies*, 38(1): 185.

van den Berg, L., Braun, E. and van Winden, W. (2001b) *Growth Clusters in European Metropolitan Cities: a Comparative Analysis of Cluster Dynamics in the Cities of Amsterdam, Eindhoven, Helsinki, Leipzig, Lyons, Manchester, Munich, Rotterdam and Vienna*, Ashgate, Aldershot.

van den Berg, L., Pol, P., van Winden, W. and Woets, P. (2005) *European Cities in the Knowledge Economy: the Cases of Amsterdam, Dortmund, Eindhoven, Helsinki, Manchester, Munich, Münster, Rotterdam and Zaragoza*, Ashgate, Aldershot.

van den Berg, L. and Russo, A. P. (2004) *The Student City; Strategic Planning for Student Communities in EU Cities*, Ashgate, Aldershot.

Van der Borg, J. and van Tuijl, E. (2008) *The Role of Design in the Urban Knowledge Economy – Case Study Helsinki*, Euricur, Erasmus University, Rotterdam.

Van der Borg, J. and van Tuijl, E. (2010) *Design Cities: Design as a Fundamental Input for the Urban Knowledge Economy*, Euricur, Erasmus University, Rotterdam.

Van der Klundert, M. and van Winden, W. (2008) 'Creating environments for working in the knowledge-based economy: experiences from the Netherlands', paper presented at the Colloquium Corporations and Cities, Brussels, 26–28 May 2008.

Van Geenhuizen, M. and Altamirano, M. (2004) *How Science-based Regional Development is Perceived: Consensus and Ambiguity in a Multi-actor Setting*, Delft University of Technology, Faculty of Technology, Policy and Management, Delft.

Van Geenhuizen, M. and Soetanto, D. (2008) 'Science parks: what they are and how they need to be evaluated', *International Journal of Foresight and Innovation Policy*, 4: 1–2.

Van Gool, T. (2008) *Strijp-S als Creative Stad*, Number 1, October 2008.

Van Gool, T. (2010) *Strijp-S als Creative Stad*, Number 2, March 2010.

van Tuijl, E. and Van der Borg, J (2011) 'Designing the dragon or does the dragon design? Analysis of the impact of the creative industry on the process of urban development of Beijing, China', forthcoming in *Journal of Chinese Culture and Management*, 3.

Van 't Verlaat, J. (2002) *Stedelijke gebiedsontwikkeling in hoofdlijnen*, Erasmus University, Rotterdam.

van Winden, W. (2010) 'Knowledge and the European city', *Tijdschrift voor Economische en Sociale Geografie*, 101(1): 100–6.

van Winden, W. and van den Berg, L. (2004) 'Cities in the knowledge economy: new governance challenges', research paper for the Urbact project STRIKE (Strategies of Regions in the Knowledge Economy), Euricur, Erasmus University, Rotterdam.

van Winden, W., van den Berg, L. and Pol, P. (2007) 'European cities in the knowledge economy: towards a typology', *Urban Studies*, 44: 525–49.

van Winden, W., van den Berg, L., Carvalho, L. and van Tuijl, E. (2010) *The Role of Manufacturing in the New Urban Economy*, Routledge, Abingdon, Oxford.

Vedovello, C. (1997) 'Science parks and university–industry interaction: geographical proximity between the agents as a driving force', *Technovation*, 17(9): 491–531.

Vicari Haddock, S. (2010) *Brand-building: the Creative City. A Critical Look at Current Concepts and Practices*, Firenze University Press, Florence.

Von Hippel, E. (2005) *Democratizing Innovation*, MIT Press, Cambridge, MA.

Wade, R. (1990) *Governing the Market: Economic Theory and the Role of Government in East Asian Industrialization*, Princeton University Press, New Jersey.

Waitt, G. (2008) 'Urban festivals: geographies of hype, helplessness and hope', *Geography Compass*, 2(2): 513–37.

Wall, R. (2009) *NETSCAPE: Cities and Global Corporate Networks*, Erasmus University, Rotterdam.

Wang, J. H. (2007) 'From technological catch-up to innovation-based economic growth: South Korea and Taiwan compared', *Journal of Development Studies*, 43(6): 1084–104.

Wenting, R. (2008) 'Spinoff dynamics and the spatial formation of the fashion design industry, 1858–2005', *Journal of Economic Geography*, 8(5): 593–614.

Westhead, P. and Storey, D. (1994) *An Assessment of Firms Located on and off Science Parks in the UK*, HMSO, London.

Whitman, C. T., Reid, C., von Klemperer, J., Radoff, J. and Roy, A. (2008) 'New Songdo City: the making of a new green city', paper presented at the Conference on Tall Buildings and Urban Habitat (CTBUH) 8th World Congress 2008, March, Dubai, United Arab Emirates.

Wolfe, D. and Gertler, M. S. (2006) 'Local antecedents and trigger events: policy implications of path dependence for cluster formation', in P. Braunerhjelm and M. P. Feldman (eds), *Cluster Genesis: Technology-based Industrial Development*, Oxford University Press, New York.

Wong, K. W. and Bunnell, T. (2006) 'New economy discourse and spaces in Singapore: a case study of one-north', *Environment and Planning*, A, 38(1): 69–83.

World Bank (2005) *Finland as a Knowledge Economy, Elements of Success and Lessons Learned*, World Bank, Washington.

Wright, M., Liu, X., Buck, T. and Filatotchev, I. (2008) 'Returnee entrepreneurs, science park location choice and performance: an analysis of high technology SMEs in China', *Entrepreneurship Theory and Practice*, 32(1): 131–55.

Yeung, H. W. (2009) 'Drivers of globalization: an evolutionary perspective on firm–state relations in the Asian newly industrialized economies', unpublished manuscript, Department of Geosciences, University of Utrecht.

Yin, R. (1984) *Case Study Research: Design and Methods*, Sage, Beverly Hills.

Zhang, Y. (2005) 'The science park phenomenon: development, evolution and typology', *International Journal of Entrepreneurship and Innovation Management*, 5(1): 138–54.

Zhou, Y. and Xin, T. (2003) 'An innovative region in China: interaction between multinational corporations and local firms in a high-tech cluster in Beijing', *Economic Geography*, 79(2): 129–52.

Zhou, Y., Sun, Y., Wie, Y. and Lin, C. (2009) 'De-centering "spatial fix"-patterns of terri-torization and regional technological dynamism of ICT hubs in China', *Journal of Economic Geography*, 1–32.

Zukin, S. (1989) *Loft Living: Culture and Capital in Urban Change*, Rutgers University Press, Piscataway, NJ.

Index

Note: page references with 't' refer to tables, with 'f' refer to figures and with 'b' refer to boxes.

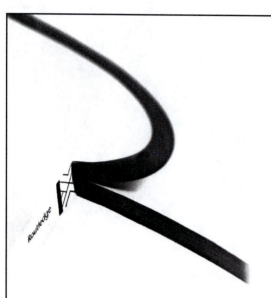